The Women of
Troy Hill

The Women

The
Back-Fence Virtues
of Faith
and Friendship

CLARE ANSBERRY

of Troy Hill

A HARVEST BOOK
HARCOURT, INC.
San Diego   New York   London

www.HarcourtBooks.com

Photos on pages x and 8 copyright, Martha Rial/Pittsburgh Post-Gazette/2000,
all rights reserved. Reprinted with permission.

Photo on pages ii–iii copyright, Mark Murphy/Pittsburgh Post-Gazette/2000,
all rights reserved. Reprinted with permission.

Library of Congress Cataloging-in-Publication Data
Ansberry, Clare.
The women of Troy Hill: the back-fence virtues of faith and friendship/Clare Ansberry.
p.   cm.
ISBN 0-15-100400-5
ISBN 0-15-601342-8 (pbk.)
1. Troy Hill (East Pittsburgh, Pa.)—Biography. 2. East Pittsburgh (Pa.)—Biography.
3. Women—Pennsylvania—East Pittsburgh—Biography. 4. Women—
Pennsylvania—East Pittsburgh—Social life and customs. 5. Women—
Pennsylvania—East Pittsburgh—Conduct of life.   I. Title.
F159.E125 A57 2000
974.8'86—dc21
[B]   99-047131

Text set in Fournier
Designed by Linda Lockowitz

Printed in the United States of America

First Harvest edition 2002

A C E G I K J H F D B

Praise for
The Women of Troy Hill

"Nobody builds monuments for women who stay with their families despite hardships and raise their kids to be good people. Clare Ansberry, however, has honored them with a book. . . . In a warm, casual and understated style, Ansberry connects the high points of long lives . . . The story of a crucial American generation through the lives of a few 'amazing' Pittsburghers."
—*The Plain Dealer* (Cleveland)

"With all the detail of a *New Yorker* profile, Ansberry has turned the lives of these women into gorgeous domestic history, where china figurines and rosette pillows carry as much meaning, and more, as state documents and legal briefs. Tremendous . . . certainly it will make a great choice for women's reading groups."
—*Booklist*

"A remarkable book about six women in their late 70s and early 80s and their remarkable lives."
—*Pittsburgh Tribune-Review*

"An affecting narrative that loops back and forth, intertwining the community's history and the women's friendships and acts of neighborliness."
—*Catholic Life*

"[Ansberry] skillfully evokes a microcosm of urban life. . . . Those interested in women's history and close-up shots of life in the U.S. will enjoy this anecdotal study of an insular community."

—*Publishers Weekly*

"An admirably nuanced group portrait of six elderly women whose wise reflections on life, friendship, and faith quietly affirm the enduring values of close-knit communities. . . . Without being sentimental or condescending, Ansberry perceptively celebrates women who still honor and nurture friends and neighbors as a way of life. A rich read."

—*Kirkus Reviews*

"Eloquent. Ansberry captures the joy and tragedy of ordinary lives, the heroism of a woman who loses her husband and three sons, the beauty of a long-term loving marriage, and the pleasures of a good woman friend."

—Mary Pipher

To my parents, Jay and Coletta
To my husband, Matthew Smith, and our children,
Jessie and Peter

CONTENTS

Troy Hill.

Introduction

AT THE DAWN OF this new century, many tributes have been paid to the great scientists, artists, and leaders of the last hundred years.

Another group of people, far less praised, made a significant mark on the lives they touched in the course of the last century. They are ordinary women, who spent much of their existence as Mrs. Ray This or Mrs. Lou That, as a child's mother or as an aunt. The roles they played were little acknowledged or honored. They lived simply, but to dismiss them would be an act of hubris and simplemindedness.

I was looking for a community, a city block or set of streets with a large population of older people. I was curious about their lives, how they were growing older, whether they were happy and at peace, what filled their days, what sort of relationships they had with one another and their families. Someone suggested I visit Troy Hill.

Less than two miles from downtown Pittsburgh, Troy Hill is more urban than suburban, although not urban in a trendy sense. Inside well-ordered homes, thirty-year-old wallpaper with cumin and parsley in shades of avocado and pumpkin looks fresh. When a Hollywood filmmaker came here to shoot a movie set in the 1930s, about the only thing the crew had to do was move the stone monument sitting in the middle of Lowrie Street because it interfered with the scene of a car crashing into the side of a building.

Getting to this isolated plateau is a deliberate act. Likewise, leaving this neighborhood takes will, or at least a reason, and for generations there didn't seem to be a good one. Thus, by design and default, people stayed and became part of the landscape. Most are now older women who have split their seven-plus decades between two houses, the one they grew up in and the one they are growing older in. Often, the two homes are down the street or around the corner from each other.

For the most part, these women know one another by face, name, and by the colors of their winter coats, their paths crossing less from formal introduction than from spending a lifetime in such a little place. At roughly three hundred acres, Troy Hill is no larger than a midsize farm, though much less tidy. Its tangled streets turn abruptly and collide at forty-five degree angles. Cobblestone walks ripple like tossed throw rugs someone forgot to straighten. Up here, neighbor doesn't mean the person next door or down the street. It means the entire hill. All are neighbors.

Like the streets, people's relationships don't follow neat lines or, for that matter, even have a clear beginning. Ties among these women were established before they were born. Their grandfathers may have stood next to one another digging a school foundation, or their mothers and aunts played cards together as young women. They grew up hearing one another's family names, their lives so intertwined that few could say quite how they met. A woman tries to explain how she knows the sisters down the street. Finally, she gives up. "They were *always* there. We just know each other."

The women of Troy Hill have much more continuity in their relationships than we can ever hope to have; they grew up sharing the same classrooms from kindergarten through eighth grade and have had children and grandchildren together. They attended funerals for one another's loved ones. Chances are that somewhere in a scrapbook or tucked in a cedar chest is a photo of each of them as a baby or young child sitting on a brown-and-white pony, snapped by a sidewalk photographer named Buster.

Edna McKinney on a horse.

If you gathered these women in a big room, they might blend into one sweet but indistinguishable mass of gray hair and squarish eyeglasses, although a few stand straighter and are brunet. Other than that, they look and seem the same, all of them grandmothers or great-aunts.

Such ordinariness belies the richness of their past and present. Their compelling stories of love and courage begin as asides, little strings that, once pulled, spin sometimes beautiful, sometimes sad, scenes. Again and again, I was struck by, how in the course of their years in which nothing seemed to happen, everything did happen. They know all about loss and disappointment and much about human nature. They have learned what ultimately succeeds and what fails, that everyone is imperfect, themselves included, and their hard-won wisdom gives them a generous nature and less proclivity to judge others.

Troy Hill may be isolated and distinctive, but there are still neighborhoods, streets, and city blocks all over filled with women—mothers and grandmothers—whose lives were grounded by similar forces. In the women of Troy Hill are bits and pieces of my own mother, her sisters, and my grandmother. Their struggles may not have been the same, but what saw them through those struggles is. And in letting us see what gave meaning to their lives, they help us better appreciate those closest to us.

In a way, too, they also offer us a path to follow as we grow older. Living on this sliver of land and left largely on their own, they have been remarkably self-sustaining. Over the years, through small daily deeds, passing flowers over a fence, bringing Communion to shut-ins, sharing books, and comforting one another in grief, they formed and maintained a simple back-fence symbiosis. Their constancy to one another and themselves in a world of change, where people are as rooted as dandelion puffs, makes their ordinary lives extraordinary.

When places like Troy Hill are gone, we will miss them, look back nostalgically and wonder just when they disappeared, sensing that it wasn't a moment or even a year. It was a slow fading, not quite glacial. Sometime between one sunrise and another dusk. A mound of snow there in the morning but gone by

late afternoon, having melted into the ground leaving the outline of where it was.

And yet, the women of Troy Hill cannot and won't fade
completely because what gave meaning to their lives continues
to do so. Greatness always has been how people relate to one
another from one day to the next. So their stories are far more
instructive than nostalgic. We can choose to ignore this remnant, these women and what they represent. Or we can sit and
listen for a spell in their living rooms with tea and pumpkin
rolls, and bring into this new century the riches offered by these
women.

CHAPTER ONE

Mary, the Free Spirit of Troy Hill

MARY WOHLEBER, an eighty-one-year-old grandmother, is about to give, if not her most, certainly one of her most notable performances.

A local film producer approached Mary, asking her to appear in his documentary on Pittsburgh's North Side, specifically the segment on Troy Hill. The choice was natural. By sheer force of energy and knowledge, not to mention being a fourth-generation Troy Hiller—which is impressive but not as impressive as the six-generation Kunzmann family—Mary has become the public face, the persona, of this tiny hilltop neighborhood of three thousand. Flip on the evening news; there's Mary fighting to save the hill's fire station. Pick up the morning newspaper; Mary is winging a hockey puck toward a goal, representing the hill in Senior Olympics. Without her—earnest one moment, animated the next—Troy Hill might be just another collection of narrow streets, of which there are many ringing the city of Pittsburgh below.

The documentary is called "North Side Story." The portion on Troy Hill is sandwiched between segments on local stock-yards and making ketchup, using a secret ingredient called Essential Oil No. 30, at the H. J. Heinz plant at the base of Troy Hill Road. Mary appears for only a few minutes. But they are memorable minutes.

The scene opens as Mary walks briskly in her blue canvas shoes, white cotton hat in hand, and stops in the middle of the bridge, the green paint flecking from its railing. Below is Rialto Street, better known here as Ravine Street and better still as Pig Hill.

As a child she could come and watch hundreds of pigs squeal and grunt up the street, prodded by men with sticks taking them up the steep hill and over to a stretch of buildings on the other side of the hill, fittingly called Butcher's Run, where sausage and ham were made. The pig era followed an earlier and more notorious cow era, when fattened wayward cows wedged themselves between houses, their forlorn moos waking households nearby. Women came out in housecoats, fit to be tied and waving brooms.

"Right here," says Mary. She points down below to a narrow blacktopped road rising, like the first hill on a roller coaster, from the banks of the Allegheny River below. "Did you know that Ravine Street is one of the steepest hills in the city of Pittsburgh?" she asks the camera. Mary taught kindergarten for twenty-four years on Troy Hill. Instructing and informing come naturally to her.

The sky is blue. Mary is in white—a white-and-blue cotton smock with a full skirt that floats around her when she walks. Mary prefers funky, decidedly ungrandmotherly clothes, like

Mary Wohleber in the Catholic diocese archives.

long dangling earrings and the flowered skirts she picked up from bins at a secondhand store in France.

She is short, perky, and looks at least ten years younger than her eighty-one years. Her straight, fawn-colored hair is cut in bangs across her forehead. She is not a bouffant, or even a soft-curl, person. She has neither the time nor the inclination to fuss with beauty parlors. Give her something blunt, right below her ears, so she can just run out of the house. Her face always looks tan.

Gazing through the chain fence above the bridge railing, she sees an older man climb the steps that serve as a terraced sidewalk. He pulls himself along by the handrail. At the turn of the century, an enclosed cable car carried people up and down the hill. Since then, people have walked. Mary nods at the man, somewhat proud of his model fortitude.

"Try it sometime. Do come up and down. Find out how good your wind is," she says.

With that, Mary pulls on her white hat and sets off in a brisk march, the camera following, as she delivers some basic facts. Troy Hill itself is very narrow. "Only about six hundred yards wide and little more than a mile long," she notes.

The camera cuts, then pans Lowrie, the hill's main street. Mary spent her entire life in two houses on Lowrie Street. Her best friend lived across the street when they were children, and three doors down after each married.

One side of the street echoes the other. Domino-shaped houses rise abruptly from the sidewalk. Metal awnings hang above white screen doors. Windows, narrow and rectangular like the homes themselves, stand side by side. Two on the first floor. Ditto for the second.

Homes were built with economy, allowing just enough room for the wind to pass between, though some blocks are entirely seamless. Families sit down to eat on either side of a so-called party wall. It sounds benign enough, almost jovial, but the builder was simply trying to save money. The way to tell one household from another is when the aluminum siding changes color. Lime green. Light tan. Dark tan. Robin's egg blue. One block looks like a square rainbow sliced in chunks.

Front doors open to the sidewalk. Ninety years ago, when horses and wagons sloshed through the muddy streets, vigilant housewives ended the day with a bucket and brush, scrubbing their splattered steps and door. If anyone has a yard, it's generally in the back. Those who lack any green space and truly love flowers improvise. A thick wall of roses climbs the trellis along a front porch of one house creating a private and scented sanctuary. Buckets of tiny red cherry tomatoes sit on the porch, and a basket of strawberries hangs from an awning.

In the warm evenings, after the dinner dishes are washed, screen doors open. Men, women, and children gather on the front steps. Few people have air-conditioning. Years ago when the meat-processing plant turned carcasses into glue and fertilizer, the stench was so bad people had to stay inside, close doors and windows and even the little transoms over the doors. Fresh air is a joy.

An American flag juts out from one house. A boy rides his bike down the middle of the street. Lopsided cars and vans park half on the street, half on the curb. Garages and driveways were an afterthought. No one drove when the homes were built. The hill had stores, dentists, and doctors. People could walk everywhere or take a streetcar that ran witlessly up and down Troy Hill all day long.

The sign CHILDREN CRY FOR FLETCHER'S CASTORIA, painted in fancy script letters two-feet tall, covers the entire side of a redbrick house. Though fading, the ad has outlasted the long-gone castoria. A striped barber pole hangs outside the front door of the home of a barber who died a decade ago.

The hill was originally, and remains heavily, Germanic, with streets named Liedertafel and Lager. Sparrows are called Sputzies, and stockings dangle from the mantel, hung on December 6—Saint Nicholas Day, not Christmas Eve. German Catholics do that. Along with being predominantly German, Troy Hill was, and is, predominantly Catholic. A small Lutheran church and an even smaller Presbyterian church draw loyal but dwindling congregations. On Sundays, women rose early to get supper in the oven, and the ecumenical smell of sauerkraut followed them into the pews of all the churches.

"This side of the street," says Mary to the camera, and pointing to her left, "is almost all old-timers." She knows them and they know her. Pretense is futile. Everyone knows everyone else's age simply by thinking back to grade school and remembering how many years ahead or behind he or she was. She walks past Cecilia Uhlig's house. Mary was a few grades ahead of Cecilia at Most Holy Name of Jesus grade school but a year behind Cecilia's older sister, Margaret Fichter, who now lives two blocks off Lowrie. Mary breezes by Helen Steinmetz's house. Helen has lived eighty-three years in the same house. She is Margaret Fichter's best friend and has been for more than seventy years. All of these women are members of the church's Christian Mothers' and Women's Guild. They see one another once, twice, or several times a week—walking to the mailbox, going to church, playing cards, or attending meetings.

Across the street, a house is for sale, which is noteworthy. Homes on Troy Hill have always stayed within families. At one time vacancies were so precious that before the casket was closed, deals were made to rent or buy the dearly beloved's momentarily empty home. Next door a young woman had just moved into the tiny cottage set back from the road. "She thinks she is in heaven," Mary says.

The camera cuts to Fire Station No. 39. More than one hundred years old, it is the oldest fire station in Pittsburgh. It has a brass pole and a huge bell named Sarah. A ghost supposedly lives there and pulls blankets off sleeping firefighters and snaps the window shades up and down. A visiting psychic confirmed the ghost's presence but determined it was friendly.

Wedged on a bench out front of the fire station are three women and one man. The seat is more than a resting place on the way from here to there. It is a destination. During the school year, the crossing guard stands out front. Firefighters lean against the wall. Those who went to the latest Troy Hill Citizens meeting update those who didn't about the upcoming community picnic. A rough wood carving of a fireman holding a child silently mans the corner. A wooden dalmatian sits at his side.

"If you want to know what is happening, go to the firehouse. Most towns have lost that central meeting place," Mary says.

Years ago, the firemen roped off a four-block area. As many as fifty kids grabbed their roller skates after dinner and skated until 10 P.M., sailing over the smooth streets and jumping over manhole covers. Every New Year's Eve, firefighters throw a big party. The whole hill is invited for pork and kielbasy. A television set is raffled off. At midnight five pounds of confetti fill the air and merrymakers are invited to ring Sarah.

Just after the fire-station scene, Mary is informed that the crew is running out of time so she speeds up her tour. She scurries, then breaks into a run, her white dress flitting about. The camera crew, still filming, chases her.

She wants them to see her favorite view of Pittsburgh from Troy Hill, which is from behind the Texaco station. She turns to the camera and mentions that her mother, an enigmatic businesswoman, obtained the franchise for the gas station. "This building over here," she says, pointing ahead, "used to be the Deutscher Unterstützenbund." She continues her charge, while the narrator, Rick Sebak, who is also the producer, is left to elaborate, explaining that Mary was referring to a benevolent society that provided social services to its German members, had a bar in the basement and picnics out back. German music plays softly in the background as he speaks.

Mary is twenty feet ahead of the camera, hustling uphill through the center of a narrow blacktopped street that is cracked in the middle and bends like an elbow. Still running, her arms opened wide like Julie Andrews in *The Sound of Music,* Mary finally reaches a grassy edge of a cliff. The city of Pittsburgh and the Allegheny River, whose name means "fair water," spread out below. She turns around with a huge smile of satisfaction.

"There you are! Was I right? Isn't this beautiful? Now you know why I want to live up here...Now, that's a view you're not going to get anywhere else. God, I love it."

Troy Hill used to be a river bottom, but the glaciers arrived, then departed, and changed that. The land, relieved of the tremendous weight of the masses of ice, rebounded. The rivers cut deeper into the earth, and the former river bottoms rose into terraces along the river, Troy Hill being one of them.

Several epochs later a surveyor came, took one look at the hills around Pittsburgh, including this one, and essentially declared them useless. An unreachable mass of tangled trees. One might as well live on the moon as there.

"I cannot think that ten-acre lots on such pits and hills will profitably meet with purchasers, unless, like a pig in a poke, it be kept out of view," he wrote in 1788.

Germans and Czechs—apparently too determined, desperate, or both to heed the surveyor's advice—settled here about one hundred and fifty years ago, coming up a long dirt road that later became Troy Hill Road. They had little choice. They needed to be close to work. Tanneries, breweries, steel plants, and Heinz consumed the flatland along the Allegheny River, leaving little but the land above on which to build their homes.

The hill, and just about everything north of Pittsburgh, belonged to Allegheny City until 1907. In those early industrial days the sun seemed little more than a round blur suspended above a canopy of dirt and soot.

A local councilman suggested passing legislation barring the sale of rope on particularly gloomy days so people wouldn't hang themselves. His more levelheaded counterparts refused, fearing the move would make Allegheny the laughingstock of the country. One local newspaper played up the story and published a morbid poem titled "In Allegheny" that began:

> *Short is the span of human life,*
> *In Allegheny.*
> *Brightly gleams the butcher knife,*
> *In Allegheny.*
> *Filled with remorse and beer,*
> *Another citizen dear-dear*
> *Has slit himself from ear to ear,*
> *In Allegheny.*

Troy Hill rose physically and metaphorically above that gloom and thrived. Houses up on the hill were safe from swollen rivers, which spilled their banks with such regularity that at the first sound of ice cracking, those below began rolling up rugs and carting furniture to the second floor. Moving up Troy Hill Road from the flatlands was a sign of prosperity and advancement.

The hill had everything. The umbrella man wheeled his cart along the cobblestones, stopping to sharpen scissors and umbrella tips. Mary, the gypsy lady, told fortunes. The ragman, his face, hands, and clothes crusted with dirt, blew his fife and yelled, "Rags, rags, rags." If anyone dared mix rags with new scraps from sewing, he thrashed his arms about and scolded them in broken English. Small children, seeing his thin, wild form coming around the corner, hid in cupboards until his shouts melted away. He didn't do much business on Troy Hill, anyway. People didn't throw things away.

A half dozen butchers and bakers sold fresh bread and meat. One bountiful department store carried dresses, hats, underwear, and Clark's cotton thread no. 50. All the ladies used this light cotton thread. Never synthetic. The Guehl and the Oscar Miller funeral homes sat a few blocks away from each other on Lowrie Street, and farther down the street was the cemetery. The other end of the hill had Lovers' Lane, which was the houseless dark stretch of Goettmann Street. Cronenweth Dairy delivered fresh milk. Minor league baseball teams, the Troy Hill Triangles and the Troy Hill Millers, competed in the twilight—until a line drive hit an infant, in its mother's arms, a street away and killed the baby on the spot. The incident marked the end of the local minor league on the hill and the beginning of a legend.

The children of Troy Hill went to one of two schools, depending on faith. Anyone who wasn't Catholic went to the Troy Hill Elementary School and likely had Miss Bowen in the fifth grade. Miss Bowen, now ninety-three, outlasted the school, which closed in 1960. Though she moved, Miss Bowen returned for the fiftieth reunion of the class of 1940, extended her hand to her former students, and with a gracious, gentle smile, called them each by name.

Catholics went to Most Holy Name of Jesus School, and still do, though only to fourth grade.

After school the children waged their own little unholy wars, deliberately trying to step on each other's toes while standing at the candy counter and fighting over who was going to heaven and who wasn't. Some Catholics taunted the public school kids on various feast days when Most Holy Name was closed, such as the Feast of the Immaculate Conception. "Ha-ha, the publics have school." That was the ultimate in one-upmanship. Not only would your soul be saved if you were Catholic, they seemed to say, but you wouldn't be in school, either.

Troy Hill even had its own orphanage and a home for way-ward girls, just down the street from each other. Every Labor Day the entire hill gathered at Saint Joseph Orphanage for a big picnic. The lucky ones won a red wagon to take home. On that day, orphans could leave the iron gates and skip rope in the streets. As eagerly as the orphans left, mystified children from the hill ran in, poking their heads into dormitory rooms. Rows and rows of clean white beds with a ball on every pillow lined the walls. Those orphans, they thought, were lucky. A slide and swing set sat in the yard.

The wayward girls in the Good Shepherd Home didn't seem half as fortunate. They never had picnics or jumped rope in the street. They were stuck behind that mysterious five-foot brick wall and watched over by white-robed cloistered nuns, who didn't show their faces and answered the door through a screen with a deep: "State your name and purpose." The mission of the Good Shepherd nuns was to "bring back the tainted ones who have fallen by the way, bring them back in all kindness and mercy and forgiveness, and give them home and hope." Some of the girls weren't tainted at all but had simply outgrown the orphanage down the street and had nowhere else to go.

Nearly every parent on the hill took advantage of those very real and imposing institutions to threaten their children into good behavior. *Watch your step or you'll be off to St. Joseph's.*

"We had an orphan home and a home for bad girls," says one woman. "We had everything, when you think of it. I mean we were a total community."

Neighborhood taverns flourished. Horses halted in front of them without prodding, nosing up to the metal ring embedded in the curb to hold their reins. Two men who lived on Troy Hill, John Ober and William Eberhardt, ran a German brewery at the bottom of the hill, employing many of their neighbors. The name Eberhardt and Ober Brewery was a little cumbersome, and it was called the E&O for short. Its slogan for beer was Early and Often. Stopping for a cold draft was a coda to a workday in the hot factory, as it is in many industrial towns. Culture made it even more so here. The Italians had wine, the Irish whiskey, the Germans beer. Saturdays were devoted to bottling homemade brew.

Being isolated up on the hill, such traditions and norms

lingered longer than they might down below, where people and cultures migrate across flat city blocks like fog before disappearing completely in a gust. On the hill, everyone knew they were to make doughnuts for Fastnacht and keep emotions in check. Stoic, they didn't laugh too hard or cry too hard. A simple "Come in, sit down, make yourself at home" is preferable to hugging and kissing at the front door. They guarded, respected, and protected one another's privacy. Don't talk bad about anyone, they warn visitors, because chances are someone within earshot is related. One front door is only twenty feet away from the next. Someone sneezes and the whole block says, "Bless you," so they say.

The hill was white and European, although over the years there were a few exceptions, like the Chinese laundry on Lowrie Street. When anyone entered, a bowed man came from behind a huge curtain and shuffled out. If he or the laundry had a name, no one seemed to use it. It was just "that Chinese laundry." The building is now gone. Then, there was Barney Michael and his family. They were Jewish and owned the Troy Hill Department Store, now the site of Billy's Troy Hill Bistro, which serves microbrews and fish with capers.

Otherwise, the closest hint of diversity consists of the two blocks on the far western portion of the hill called Bohemian Hill. A water basin, which is now a ball field, physically separated it from Troy Hill proper. What further and more deeply distinguishes the little enclave is that Czechs, not Germans, and Presbyterians, not Catholics, settled it. Bohemian Hill, to those born and raised there, seemed like an amendment to Troy Hill, a tail that never wagged anything. The four roads here were the last to be paved and are the last to be plowed after it snows. Even the sun gets here last, waking the rest of the hill first.

The hilltop world was neatly ordered. Girls learned from a young age that every day had a chore. Monday, clothes were boiled, scrubbed, wrung, and put out to dry. Hanging laundry was an exercise in efficiency and modesty. The socks on one line, the shirts on another. Underwear dangled discreetly between the rows of sheets. Tuesday, they ironed, and Wednesday, washed windows. Thursday was general cleaning. Friday belonged to floors and Saturday to baking.

Depending on the size of their family or their family's fortunes, girls quit school after eighth grade, or went to a two-year commercial school or high school, mainly to learn typing and shorthand. Louise Lacher had a scholarship to pay half the cost of art school but couldn't come up with the rest. Her father was a basket weaver. One year for Christmas, he crafted a willow baby buggy. The following Christmas, he painted it blue. The next year, it was pink, and then dark brown. After that she was too big for baby buggies. Instead of going to art school, Louise began selling floor wax door-to-door.

Once married, the young women quit working. It was time to start a family and be a full-time wife and mother. They easily immersed themselves in the routines that gave structure and order to the week and the house, finding comfort in knowing and doing what was expected of them.

With that, whatever aspirations they may have had to teach, style hair, or nurse were put aside as they went about making two rented rooms into a home. Beds and cribs lined the walls of one room. The stove, icebox, and table filled the other. If their homes were cramped and hectic, they had no idea.

Keeping house was their main role. But they had other work, not directly stated or assigned. It was more intuitive, something they saw their mothers doing.

"Women neighbored," eighty-one-year-old Mildred Mares explains. Then, by way of contrast and amplification, she adds, "Men worked. *Women neighbored.*" Their whole world rested on those four words. There was nothing more to say, as if the sentence ended with an understood "and that's that." It is declared in passing, so understated yet clearly comprehended by everyone who grew up here.

Mildred lived eighty-one years in one home, on the Bohemian side of Troy Hill. She went to college, taught school until she married, and, by law, had to quit. She and her husband visited every U.S. state except Texas, Louisiana, and Mississippi. They went to the West Coast three times and in Europe sailed up the Rhine River. She drove a car, when few others did, including the men, which made her all the more beloved by women up here. She uplifted them all. Well, you know, Mildred went to college, they would note, not with jealousy but with pride and some ownership. As Mildred's friends and neighbors, they could share in her accomplishments, which made darning socks more tolerable. No one dared admit smoking to Mildred, although if they did, she would have told them that she did, too, until her husband developed lung problems. Other women came to her for advice and she offered it generously, not in a preachy, superior way.

Mildred is wise. An entire way of life is wrapped up in that

one word *neighbored*. These women kept this community together. Out sweeping the sidewalks, they exchanged local news.
They ran across the street to borrow a cake pan and spent the
next half hour inside updating each other on who was sick,
born, or married, who was in need of prayers or a ride to the
bank. Men have destinations. They go to work. They come
home and close the door behind them. They're not used to
pausing on the front stoop, Mildred explains.

The women took turns staying with the sick. One neighbor
cooked. Another washed and curled the hair of a bedridden
friend, lifting her spirits. If a mother had another baby, the lady
next door visited and took home the family's laundry and ironing. Are you done with your homework? Mary Wohleber
would ask her children. If you are, go next door and scrub Aunt
Ida's windows. Aunt Ida was an older woman with no children.
Children often called older neighbor-women Aunt, reinforcing
the sense of familiarity with, and concern for, the people up and
down the street.

For them, neighboring was an extension of their faith, regardless of religion. Essentially, they lived the message: You are
your brothers' and your sisters' keepers.

Now in their seventies and eighties, the women of Troy Hill
continue to neighbor.

Every week, as she has done for seven years, Florence
Klingman takes a bus to visit a woman from Troy Hill who now
lives in a nursing home a few miles away. They weren't lifelong
friends or distant relations. They simply met on the street. The
woman was cutting her hedges, and Florence said, "Good
morning." "Good morning," the woman replied.

"I got to be friends, well, not *friends* but friends. I start looking out for her," Florence says. The woman, a widow, had no children. Only a cousin, in Colorado.

She seemed odd, but Florence always checked in on her. During one visit, Florence noticed that the woman was sick and could barely stand. Florence insisted on calling the doctor. Later the doctor told Florence that the woman would have died if she had not made that call. Many people would have left it at that: I've done my good deed. But Florence became her guardian, overseeing the woman's moves, from the hospital to a personal care home, and finally to a nursing home. She handled hundreds of medical and insurance bills, forms, and letters that she keeps in cardboard shoe boxes. She consulted with the doctors. When it became clear the woman could not come home, Florence, with help from the attorney on the hill, sold the house. The attorney urged Florence to take some money for herself as payment for all her work. Florence refused. Florence spends every Christmas, Easter, and Thanksgiving with the woman, too.

Asked why she would become so vested in someone she met on her way to the store, Florence explains that the woman had no one, and they were neighbors. Both were from the hill. They had that common bond. Their husbands are buried in the cemetery on Lowrie Street. As children they went to the Labor Day picnics at the orphanage.

These women help each other in smaller ways, too. After making two stuffed peppers, a woman who loves to cook brings one of the peppers down to her close friend two houses away who doesn't. If one goes to the doctor, another accompanies her on the bus and sits in the waiting room. Having sewn their children's clothes, they now hem the pants of grandchildren or the curtains of a friend. When a neighbor dies, the women cook, comfort, and retreat when it is time to retreat. In the early spring, they share sprigs of pussy willows, in the summer, tomatoes, and in the winter, holly, all bounty from their tiny yards.

As the years pass, those who can no longer freely leave their homes, adjust. Ruth Leder hasn't been to her tiny Troy Hill Presbyterian Church for years because it doesn't have a wheelchair ramp. But she still makes the Christmas and Easter decorations, insisting on new ones each year to surprise and delight the others. Sitting at a card table, with a magnifying glass and small reading lamp, she sews hundreds of beads, sequins, and tiny pieces of felt—some the size of a pencil eraser—to make a nativity scene to lay beneath the church's Christmas tree. The last one took her 127 hours.

Such vitality and resilience can't easily be explained by genetics, education, or wealth, which are the often-cited determinants of longevity. The women of Troy Hill don't match this profile. Some of their parents died young. Mildred went to college, but few others did. None are rich. Rather, this vitality seems to rest in an age-old, benevolent paradox: in giving, they receive. As long as they are nurturing something, be it each other, a church, or even a garden, they are needed.

Most of their children or nieces and nephews have married and moved, which they understand more or less. They have plenty of solitude, but they aren't alone. They know their neighbors and friends—the one across the street or in the next pew—care deeply about them, and will note if they are not outside one sunny afternoon.

In the morning these women raise their blinds, letting their neighbors know all is well. And with that silent small action, neighbors have conveyed much. Good morning, thank you for checking up on me, and have a good day.

Mary Wohleber lives next door to the Voegtly Cemetery. Outside her window, a flowering crabtree is in pink bloom. A pair of ducks nest in the tall grass between two stone monuments. The male watches over his partner while she sleeps. When the male leaves, Mary looks up from her book, the biography of the first woman to obtain a Ph.D., and takes over, assuming the guard from her window. She is so careful and attentive that she notices the female duck is a half-inch taller. When the male returns, Mary resumes reading but only for a moment.

Across the street a woman leaves her house with a plate of strawberry shortcake, locks her door, and begins walking down the sidewalk. Mary can't see her face but recognizes the green coat. She knows where the woman is going and why, that she is bringing the dessert to a former classmate of Mary's, who is confined to her bed. They will visit for a while, giving the sister of the sick woman a chance to go out. The woman pulls the front gate. It's stuck. Mary quietly cheers her on, "C'mon, you can do it," and is relieved when the gate finally opens.

Mary's dark brown home looks like the others up and down Lowrie Street. Tall and lean, it sits at the edge of a cobblestone sidewalk. Her front steps are painted a cheery red. Out back is a small yard, which she leaves to the wildflowers. One year she found horseradish growing by her back door.

Inside, though, Mary's home is like no other. A large Maxfield Parrish print called *Stars* hangs in her living room, between her two front windows. Her mother loved blue and bought it because Parrish imbued his works with that color. It's risqué, a young nude perched on a rock, gazing up to the heavens. Few women during the first half of this century would buy such a print, and not many of Mary's contemporaries would hang it so prominently in their living room. The Russian samovar that Mary carried strapped to her back while trekking in the mountains sits by her mantel. Masks from Egypt gaze wide-eyed from the shelves in the library. Little wooden Russian dolls stand dutifully in a row.

Century-old walnut bookcases are packed with travel and local-history books. Her husband, Alan, would die all over again if he saw paperbacks there. He thought dust jackets crude. He never let her put books on the shelves, when he was alive. Only his classics, Plato and Aristotle. He was a brilliant man, as were his brothers, and spent his wages and time, before he married, in bookstores. On the streetcar, other people would flip through the morning newspaper, while a Wohleber would be engrossed in a book written in Greek.

Mary's kitchen is simple. No electric coffeepots or can openers. She boils water for tea. The blue flames dance freely. The faint little hiss from the burner blends into the background like wallpaper. A slab of dark brown wood hangs above the doorway bearing a short poem.

> *Here's health to enjoy the blessing sent*
> *From heaven, a mind unclouded strong,*
> *A cheerful heart, a wise content,*
> *An honored age and song.*

It was a wedding gift to her parents. Most things in her home are old and have a history. She collects, but not in the traditional sense of accumulating goods for their monetary value. Rather, she salvages with intensity what has been abandoned and rescues what is about to be destroyed. She knows how quickly pictures, buildings, or letters can disappear and with them the memory of the people they belonged to. Five sites on Troy Hill have been designated historic landmarks, only because of Mary's dedicated research. Her children bought a tile at the new Senator John Heinz Pittsburgh Regional History Center and had her name etched in it. MARY WOHLEBER, TROY HILL HISTORIAN, it reads.

This afternoon, a few shiny new medallions dangle over a stand in her library, providing a sharp contrast with the surrounding heirlooms. For a lark, she entered the Senior Olympics this year, fell flat on her back when she lifted the javelin, but came home with three gold and five silver medals.

"I have a wonderful life. I've always been different. People here know this about me. I could drop dead on the sidewalk and they would walk around me and say, 'Oh, there's Mary. She's just tired.' They know I do off things. It's not out of character."

As rooted and tied to the hill as she is, Mary has always been a little distant by virtue of being her mother's daughter.

Her mother, Loretta Brueckner, was a successful and powerful real estate agent and an insurance broker, which in the 1920s was exceptional, not just on Troy Hill but everywhere. Women at that time were expected to keep house and keep quiet. For the most part they did.

But Loretta Brueckner, as all who knew her would say, was a woman ahead of her time. Powerful city councilmen and county politicians sat around the Brueckner dining-room table, seeking her advice and input. German-speaking neighbors respected and trusted Loretta to write their wills and deeds but kept her at a distance, as they would a priest, because she knew so much. Mary learned to be discreet. Never repeat other people's business. Do that and you lose trust. That same lesson was preached in homes across the hill. People lived too close to one another to tolerate whispers.

Along with a cook and a cleaning lady, Loretta had a chauffeur. Eventually, she learned to drive herself. Her furs had to be let out so she could reach the clutch. She outearned Mary's father, a gang foreman in the electric department of a local railroad company. If her husband weren't the man he was, she once joked, one of them would have been in jail and the other dead. They were partners. He understood her energy. When she retired in 1946, so did he. They traveled to Bali, summered in Canada, and wintered in Florida.

"We were a little separate on account of Mother. She was looked at with some envy because she was so free," says Mary.

Mary went to grade school at Most Holy Name of Jesus with the Fichter, the Steinmetz, and the Guehl children. After they graduated, they joined Sodality, the club for unmarried Catholic girls that marked the passage from being a young girl to being a young woman, with the Blessed Virgin Mary as their inspiration. Lest they forget, each member received a solid metal statue of Mary. They danced in a clubroom of the convent and played Ping-Pong. On Mother's Day, the girls staged a skit and served their mothers lunch. When the nuns moved into a new convent, Sodality threw a linen shower.

But then Mary was sent to boarding school a few miles away, leaving her contemporaries and, in a way, breaking a bond with them. For Thanksgiving breaks, her mother had tickets for Mary to travel to New York or Niagara Falls by herself. She was only a teenager. Other mothers wouldn't think of such a thing. They were protective, accompanying their daughters to job interviews and sitting on the benches outside the offices. One mother in Bohemian Hill climbed out the window and onto her little roof, watching until her daughter made it safely inside Troy Hill Elementary School. Mary was unfazed. "I never even thought about it. I just did it. I've never been afraid."

At boarding school, away from the hill and home, Mary further distinguished herself as a free spirit. Every Monday, anyone who misbehaved the week before was summarily sent to the chaplain with a note written by Sister Annunciata detailing the offense. Mary made the trip weekly. "I was in trouble all the time. It was a challenge to try to do something you weren't supposed to do. And I love challenges. Nothing drastic, just little thorny things."

At the end of each school year, the girls lined up outside Sister's office. One by one, they went in, and closed the door. Sister then proceeded to interview them to see if they were potential nuns.

Mary walked in. Sister was writing something at her desk. "Sister looked up. I didn't open my mouth. I didn't say anything. She just looked. 'Brueckner, we don't want you.' She didn't even give me a chance to say good morning."

At her twenty-fifth reunion, Mary dressed elegantly in a yellow silk dress, a fox fur collar, and a big horsehair hat, thinking there was no way Sister would recognize the former troublemaker now polished and sophisticated. But she did. Sister

Annunciata walked right up to her and said, "Mary Brueckner, don't think you can fool me."

Mary and her husband, Alan, married at Most Holy Name. The priest granted the young couple special permission for an evening ceremony so she could walk down the candlelit aisle as the 6 P.M. Angelus bells rang.

The whole traditional homemaker role, which came so instinctively to other young wives, was foreign to her. When Mary was a child, the cook cooked, the cleaning lady cleaned. Mary wasn't at her mother's side learning how to make German Bundt cake with hallmark red-and-green candied cherries. She tried it after she married, forgot the cherries, whipped it out of the oven, and swirled them in by hand. The cake stuck to the pan, broke in two, and had to be iced together. She was masterful at mashed potatoes, though. Every night Alan would tell her, "My god, you make the best mashed potatoes."

Much as her father understood her mother, so did Alan understand Mary. While he was content to sit quietly and read, he knew Mary had to have some challenge, or some pursuit or activity outside the home. She went to night school, took up the accordion, was a volunteer librarian, and taught kindergarten for twenty-four years. The school burned down in the late 1970s. Instead of allowing the kindergarten children to be bused off the hill while a new school was being built, Mary offered to teach for free in the basement of Grace Lutheran Church. That act alone endeared her to parents, who bought her chicken à la king dinners and a new outfit for Christmas as some small payment.

At home she ran back and forth through the library, past Alan, fetching papers or the typewriter. Gently, he scolded her. "For god's sake, don't move so fast. You're making too much wind." One minute she would be clanging pans and the next, clicking at her typewriter.

At an open house for Mary and Alan's twenty-fifth wedding anniversary, a friend approached Alan. "Well, Al, how was it?" the friend asked.

"I'll tell you one thing. By god, it was never dull," Alan responded.

"It was the greatest compliment anyone paid me," Mary says.

After thirty-six years working as a civil engineer for the Fort Pitt Bridge Works, Alan lost his job, his insurance, and his pension when his company was taken over by a bigger one.

He seemed to die inside, Mary says. A man's life was his work, or so it seemed then. "After men retire, they have no sense of what to do. Their work was their life. For women, there is always a need to be filled," she says. "That's why women live longer."

Alan was considerate, she says. He died on Thanksgiving. She buried him on Saturday and was back to work on Monday. She insists she had to. Her forty kindergarten children were waiting. "I was needed. I never even thought about it as hard. I don't indulge in self-pity. It's the worst thing you can do. It's demeaning to yourself."

Sarah Wohleber Lucas, Mary's daughter, says her mother puts her heart into everything she does. "When Mom was a mother, she was totally committed to being a mother. And when she was a wife, she was totally committed to being a wife. Once my dad died, then it was her turn. And that's the way it should be," says Sarah. "She's gotten involved in a million things, gone a million places, and just had herself a grand time."

Mary has received more local civic awards and done more traveling in the twenty years since Alan died than in her first sixty years. She's been to Sri Lanka and Tibet. She went to France simply to rest her hand on the tomb of Eleanor of Aquitaine. Savannah, Georgia, and Charleston, South Carolina, were nice but left her glutted, as if she'd eaten too many sweets. "If I see any more pink or white," she told a friend, "I think I'm going to throw up."

She chose Syria because she hadn't seen it. She and her roommate each grabbed a piece of sausage, bread, and a bottle of beer, and sat on the curbside watching whatever protests came by. Several people in the travel group ate in restaurants and ended up sick in their hotel rooms. Mary, who was several years older than any of them, ran out and gathered their prescriptions.

Usually before Mary takes off on one of her trips, she stops in to let her good friends Cecilia and Loretta Guehl know where she is going and when she will be back. The sisters, who never married, are both in their eighties and live on the top two floors of the funeral home. Their father ran the funeral home business, but it was sold when John Guehl Sr. died.

Mary had been a year ahead of Cecilia at Most Holy Name of Jesus School and a couple years behind Loretta. Mary and their sister, Dorothy, who died a few years ago, helped start Troy Hill Citizens in the early 1970s to fight the construction of a high-rise apartment building on the hill. The citizen's group won. A Uni-Mart and laundry were built instead.

Now Mary wants to ask the funeral director about rules and laws regarding burials overseas in case she dies on the trip. She is going someplace with a high altitude. She had been to mountainous Tibet, but that was five years ago. She was only in her mid-seventies then. Her lungs are a little older now.

After she talks to him, she goes upstairs to see Cecilia and Loretta. Thelma Wurdock is visiting, too. Thelma and Cecilia have been best friends for seventy-five years.

"I don't really want to be brought back," Mary tells them. "That's what I told my kids. Wherever I am, leave me there. Have a memorial service. Put a tombstone up. No one will ever know if I'm there or not. You know how people forget."

But the funeral director told Mary it wouldn't work. "Some countries don't want to keep the body. They want to get rid of you," Mary informs her friends.

"But what if you're on one of those boat trips going somewhere like the Amazon?" Thelma asks.

"On those kinds of boats, they just let you sink and the piranhas eat you," Mary says.

"Oh," says Thelma.

On warm summer days it can take Mary a half hour to walk a few blocks, because people on the hill stop to talk. They don't just pass the time, they engage each other in conversations, inquiring about family and well-being with interest and specificity, "Did your granddaughter get that job?" Even the shyest, most backward person can't help but develop relationships or be known here.

"You don't *meet* people on Troy Hill," Mary explains. "They're there. You pass them every day. You see them.

They're a part of life, and when you don't see them, you miss them. You inquire. Dr. Heck's father was our doctor. His grandparents and his parents were very good friends with my parents. Dr. Rechtenwald, whose grandfather delivered me, is here. He's a podiatrist. I had the dentist in kindergarten. Our lawyer—I let him have it once when he was a little kid. We don't have to question here. There's an inherent trust. Their people—their forefathers—earned it." Mary's mother sold her real estate business decades ago to a local man. His daughter runs it now. She was in one of Mary's kindergarten classes.

Mary refers to women by their maiden names, though they haven't signed that name to letters since the 1930s. Deliberate or not, it preserves them forever as a young girl and honors their individuality, who they were before they became Mrs. Someone. Norma Weir wouldn't declare herself a great seamstress but Mary does and then marches a visitor right into Norma's living room to present Norma's formal drapes hanging in perfect folds.

That familiarity engenders a certain loyalty, bordering on responsibility and duty. Three of Mary's Troy Hill friends are in three different nursing homes. Mary visits them regularly. Another woman broke her hip and was in rehabilitation for months. Every week, Mary sent her a card. "Mary, I was the queen of the mailroom," the woman said when she finally came back home. Mary clips a column written by a local priest and sends it to a friend who admires the priest. It only takes a minute and thirty-three cents. And it means so much, she knows.

Such concern distinguishes this community, says Mary's daughter Sarah. Sarah lived on Troy Hill a short time after she married but has since moved.

One afternoon Sarah took her own daughter to voice lessons at a home in a beautiful Pittsburgh suburb. Everyone had large grassy lots. It was a glorious sunny day. The teacher invited Sarah inside. Sarah thanked the woman but said she would rather sit on the porch and enjoy the weather. An hour passed. She saw no one. She almost thought she had missed some momentous occasion, a lunar landing or great speech. Everyone must be inside watching it on TV, she thought. Then she realized all the homes were air-conditioned. People were sealed inside, their doors and windows firmly closed.

The homes are so far apart that even when neighbors are outside, they are distant. They can't carry on conversations with each other from their porches or front steps. When they leave, they climb into their cars, roll up the window, crank up the air-conditioning and radio. If they pass a neighbor or friend, they wave.

Of course, many people covet and sow that privacy. Good riddance to being able to hear dishes clattering in the middle of the night as a wife prepares supper for a husband who worked the late shift. A lot of people want to walk down the sidewalk uninterrupted and unnoticed.

Not Mary. Who would notice or really care if you were gone?

In 1996 Mary's closest friend, Annette Kellerman Stephens, nicknamed Snook, died. As children they lived across the street from each other. Mary sneaked food out of her kitchen, behind the cook's back, and carried the bounty to Snook's cellar, where they would feast. They had their first cigarette and their first drink together. Snook went to Grace Lutheran Church as a child, and Mary joined her for Easter sunrise services, defying the nuns' warnings never to step inside a church that wasn't Catholic. They had babies within years of each other and were godparents for each other's children.

After they both married, Snook moved into a house three doors away from Mary's. They barged into each other's kitchens. "'You're not going to believe what this kid did!' I knew I could tell her and it would never be brought up again. And she did the same thing to me. You can't say those things to your own children. They think you're being critical and you're not. You're just getting it out.

"We could talk to each other about anything—parents, schools, grandparents—because we knew everything about each other. There were things neither of us would talk to anyone else about. I still miss her. She was not a passage in my life; she was there my whole life."

When Snook was sick, Mary visited her. During one visit, Mary told her, "I don't know what I'm going to do without you." And what has she done? "Felt very lonely. We all need to belong to someone."

At times Mary says she forgets that Snook is even gone. "I think, Oh, wait till I tell Snook. And then I remember. See, I'm so busy it's easy to forget what I don't want to remember. Then I'm brought up short when it comes to mind."

Mary has loads of friends here and all over the world. One night she was up until 2 A.M., writing twenty-two letters. This fall, she and a group of younger friends drove in a van out to Utah to kayak. Every New Year's Eve, Mary joins another group that is involved in preserving city landmarks for a 10 P.M. buffet at a splendid restored train station in downtown

Pittsburgh. At midnight, balloons fall from a net, drifting lazily down to the revelers.

But none shared as much with her as Snook. "When you live this long, you lose almost all contact with your past. You treasure what you have."

That, in part, explains the salvation of Saint Anthony Chapel.

Saint Anthony is a quiet little chapel that sits on a backstreet of Troy Hill, an area once graced by a grove of hemlock trees. It is beautiful but unassuming from the outside. Twin spires topped with crosses flank the statue of Saint Anthony, the wonder-worker, holding the infant Jesus in his arms. The street out front is quiet. Few cars drive by.

Across the street in the parking lot, schoolgirls in blue-and-white uniforms from Most Holy Name of Jesus skip rope. Boys bounce basketballs. A long white bus pulls up to the front door of the chapel. The door of the bus opens. A Golden Agers group from Ohio files out and climbs the four steps to the two heavy wood doors leading into the chapel.

Inside, a few women are sitting quietly in the pews. They have volunteered to spend a few hours in the chapel in case any visitors have questions. Thelma Wurdock sits on Tuesday afternoons. Cecilia Uhlig has Thursday, and if Cecilia isn't feeling well, her sister Margaret Fichter fills in. It is quiet and somewhat dark. The chandeliers suspended in a single row seem to accent rather than illuminate. The low lights are solemn, more fitting.

One of the ladies in the tour group stops as soon as she passes through the front door. "Oh my," she says. The attendants turn around to see. Thelma says you can always tell a first-time visitor. Their eyes widen and they don't know where to look first.

A central arch divides the chapel into front and back, each with its own distinct and separate marvels. Inscribed on the arch is the Latin phrase: CORPORA SANCTORUM IN PACE SEPULTA SUNT. It means "Here lie the saints in peace."

Below the arch, filling the three walls in the front from floor to ceiling, are hundreds of gold monstrances, lockets, and miniature cathedrals holding nearly five thousand relics belonging to saints and martyrs. The tiny pieces of cloth and fragments of bone are said to be the largest collection of relics in the world, outside of the Vatican. A skull, so old it looks gauzy, sits in a velvet-lined box. Plaster statues of two martyred soldiers, their throats slit for vowing allegiance to a holy king, rest in separate glass cases. The entire skeleton of Saint Demetrius, each bone wrapped in silk, lies below the altar. There is something both haunting and holy about it.

Most of the relics are no larger than a peppercorn. But they have been painstakingly cataloged, and each identified on a strip of paper the size of a single match. Up on the ceiling, inside a large triangle, is a huge eye. The eye of God looking down.

The back half of the chapel belongs to fourteen life-size statues, seven along each wall, depicting the stations of the cross. Though carved in wood, Christ's face seems to grow more pale and gaunt as he journeys from Pilate's court to his death. Huge stained-glass windows bear images of the eleven disciples and three saints. The craftsmanship of the gold reliquaries, as well as the artistry of the century-old windows and statues, is something to admire even for the agnostic with no interest in seeing the tiny tooth of Saint Anthony, worn away by time and age.

More than anything else, the little chapel has given Troy Hill stature and enriched its lore. A hundred years ago, thousands of blind and lame came from all over the world, hoping for miracles. "I came here a week ago. I was unable to walk and could scarcely move my body. Now I can run and jump and kick as high as the next man." And suiting the action to the word, the healed man vaulted over the porch railing to the street below, a distance of nearly eight feet, one newspaper reported.

Conductors dubbed the Troy Hill streetcar line "the ambulance" because it carried so many of the hopeful infirm up the hill. Residents rented stairwells as sleeping space and put signs in their front windows. HOT MEALS. ALL DAY.

People were drawn not simply by the chapel and its collections but by word of the miraculous healing power of Father Suitbert Mollinger, who studied medicine in Europe and dispensed prescriptions as well as blessings. Father Mollinger was the first pastor of Most Holy Name of Jesus and the son of a wealthy Belgian statesman. He amassed the collection of relics and the stations with his own personal fortune and built the private chapel in the late 1800s to house them, completing the project in 1883.

A portrait of him—his long white beard falling to his chest making him appear holy, wise, and imposing—hung in nearly every living room on the hill. When he died in 1883, just days after the chapel was completed, a crowd of six thousand people, including three hundred schoolchildren, attended his funeral.

He left no will, and his heirs seized what they could, including the black marble altar, crystal chandeliers, and candelabras.

The chapel itself, the relics, and stations were sold to the parishioners of Most Holy Name for thirty thousand dollars. Though the sum was a fraction of the cost, this working-class parish had to borrow money from the diocese.

Every week, Mary's grandmother would put a few coins aside to pay off the debt. "This is for Anthony," she would say. Ultimately, the parishioners owned the chapel.

Over the years, though much beloved, the chapel fell into disrepair. Their church—Most Holy Name, down the street from the chapel—was the parishioner's primary focus, where they went to mass on Sundays, and where their children went to school.

The chapel grew dark. The skylight leaked and was tarred over. Smoke from votive candles and factories had turned the walls gray, inside and out. The doors weren't locked. Older children, feeling daring and defiant, stole into the cool chapel to escape the hot summer sun. Lightning toppled Saint Anthony, who fell from the peak of the roof. People rushed to the streets, scrambling to take pieces of the saint home, hoping even a small presence of the wonder-worker would provide added protection and blessings. Rust ate at the tall crosses on the spires. Slates fell from the roof and crashed into pieces on the sidewalk below. Termites consumed a square foot from a station of the cross. Tips from the crown of thorns and fingers, were broken off.

Though dark and dirty, it remained no less holy to the people of Troy Hill and no less a part of their life. Every Tuesday, mass was said at the chapel. The faithful knelt in the near dark on slanted wooden kneelers that gave women and girls splinters in their knees. After mass the priest led the congregation in special prayers to the saint known for restoring what has been lost. Children asked Anthony to find their misplaced treasures. Adults sought lost health, hope, or love.

The dinginess never bothered people up here. They assumed it could and would be that way forever. Diocesan officials, though, began rumbling about closing the chapel and moving the relics before someone got hurt by a chunk of falling plaster.

Mary wasn't about to lose the chapel without a fight.

Her dear father had been baptized and named Anthony by Father Mollinger. Father Mollinger did his best to encourage every family to name one son Anthony. "You may not have gone in Anthony, but you came out Anthony," Mary says. Father Mollinger was a shrewd man, well aware that doing this would inspire devotion.

One afternoon in the early 1970s, after hearing talk that the chapel might be closed, Mary was visiting with her friends Cecilia and Loretta Guehl and Thelma Wurdock. The ladies were sitting around the Guehl kitchen table, discussing the sad physical shape of the chapel and their fears of it being destroyed. It seemed impossible that anything could be done to reverse eighty years of neglect.

But Mary wanted to try.

"If we could get one hundred dollars from so many people, that would do it," she told her friends.

"I can remember her saying that so well," says Thelma.

Mary says she didn't know enough to be intimidated by the enormity of the task.

The bishop gave his blessing to the idea but said no church money could be used. Few believed it would work. Mary

Wohleber and a handful of older ladies trying to raise a couple hundred thousand dollars?

But Mary was just what the chapel needed. She can bring people together. She knew just about everyone on the hill through her mother or from her teaching, and she set about recruiting the community's most respected names. Cecilia Guehl, who was secretary to the chief executive officer of the giant Heinz Company and daughter of funeral director John Guehl, had arguably the best typing skills on the hill. She became the group's secretary.

They got their hands on every mailing list they could. Cecilia typed a draft letter, submitted it to the committee for approval, made copies, and mailed them. Letters were sent to all 1,800 parishioners, 315 Christian women's clubs all over the country, and former parishioners.

The committee sent pleas to 45 Pittsburgh corporations and 62 foundations. Cecilia wrote a personal letter to Rose Kennedy. "I thought, Rose is a good Catholic. She ought to get into this thing," says Cecilia. She paged through the Bible and found the quote about how those with much are expected to give much, and included it in the letter. She never heard anything from Mrs. Kennedy. All but one of the big businesses and foundations replied with best wishes for success, but no money.

The first big break came when Mary was invited to lunch at the home of Catherine Arnold, a local arts patron. Several of Mrs. Arnold's friends were there. As they sat around the table, Mrs. Arnold asked Mary to explain her plan. First, the chapel needed a new roof to prevent further damage, Mary explained. That job alone would cost seventy thousand dollars, which to the committee was a nearly inconceivable sum.

"The only terms I can think in are one thousand dollars. All I need are seventy people with one thousand dollars," Mary told them.

Mrs. Arnold laughed. "Mary, look under your plate," she told her. Mary lifted her plate. Underneath was a check for one thousand dollars. Mrs. Arnold explained that someone had done the same for her when she was president of a large nonprofit group and facing daunting fund-raising challenges. The donation had given her heart. She wanted to do the same for Mary. When Mrs. Arnold was later bedridden, a grateful Mary brought slides to her bedside so she could see the chapel's progress.

The next and only other big contribution, twenty-five hundred dollars, came from Heinz. Cecilia's boss directed his staff to make a donation. The company and its foundation don't normally contribute to religious causes, but the chapel was a historic landmark. Mary had wisely seen to that a few years earlier.

Most other donations were for one hundred, twenty-five, or five dollars. Children held little yard sales and proudly handed Mary rolls of pennies. Adults hosted wine-tasting parties. One day Thelma Wurdock, who lives a few doors down from the chapel, looked out her window and saw Mary up on a ladder pulling old slates from the roof. "I couldn't believe it. I looked out, and there was Mary up there," says Thelma. The slates were silk-screened with pictures of the chapel and SAINT ANTHONY CHAPEL, TROY HILL, 1883, and they were sold for five dollars apiece.

It took three years to raise $175,000 to repair the outside. At that point the chapel was closed, a new roof laid, and the limestone exterior sandblasted.

Once the outside was finished, the committee set about raising the second $175,000, to fix the interior. The walls had to be washed five times to get to the original surface. A craftsman rebuilt the portions of the wooden carvings eaten away by termites. A new crystal chandelier was hung. Three closed-circuit television cameras now scan the interior, and signs warn visitors not to reach across a brass railing or an alarm will sound.

The completely restored chapel was dedicated on Sunday, November 27, 1977, with a joyous mass, celebrated by the bishop. It was a proud and glorious moment for the hill and its people.

Residents of all faiths bring visitors up to see Saint Anthony's. "You heard about our chapel didn't you?" they ask.

At the hundredth anniversary of the chapel, in 1983, the parish decided to throw a party. Margaret Fichter and her sister Cecilia and other members of the Christian Mothers spent days in the Most Holy Name school kitchen making a German supper of white all-veal sausage, sauerkraut, German potato salad, pumpernickel bread, strudel, and beaten-egg soup. The local newspaper carried a photo, story, and some of the recipes. After cooking in the school, Margaret went home and baked eighteen apple cakes to be served as dessert.

The festival was such a success, the church decided to do it every year on the weekend closest to June 13, the Feast of Saint Anthony.

It had been raining all week but stopped Friday morning, hours before the start of the festival. The otherwise quiet backstreet is packed with cars. Booths, covered with blue plastic sheets in case showers return, offer prizes of stuffed animals and framed photos of the Pittsburgh Penguins hockey team.

A little train runs in ovals. Three children have the train to themselves. Their parents wave to them at every pass. Adults stand three-deep at the blackjack booth. Two women hold Styrofoam plates filled with pineapple upside-down cake purchased at the bake sale. The Christian Mothers' and Women's Guild is serving ham dinner in the school cafeteria of Most Holy Name. Tomorrow night they'll serve lasagna. A notice in the Sunday church bulletin asked for lasagna donations.

Cecilia and Loretta Guehl walk quietly together, looking at each booth. They don't need or want anything. They are there to support the church and chapel. Cecilia remains secretary for the chapel committee and is one of two original committee members. The other is Bill Fichter, Margaret's brother-in-law, who is now president.

Cecilia's job remains the same as it has been for the past three decades, typing minutes of monthly meetings and annual letters to about five hundred past and loyal donors, seeking contributions to help with ongoing maintenance and improvements.

She drums up whatever publicity she can. She called the *Pittsburgh Post-Gazette* about a forty-one-minute video on the chapel called "The Saints' Keeper," filmed by a local man and aired on Eternal Word Network. A woman from Texas, who had seen the video on that station while flipping through the channels late one night, recently took a tour, as did a man from New York. The paper wrote a nice feature.

Cecilia stops by the Ladies of Charity booth. Margaret Fichter is working tonight. They talk. Cecilia puts a quarter down and wins a stuffed elephant. That is the first of the sisters' winnings. By the end of the weekend, she and Loretta have also claimed three T-shirts and a small toaster oven that grills. They have a toaster oven. It doesn't grill, but neither do they. Cecilia sends the winnings home with her grandniece and two great-grandnephews.

At nightfall, when the streetlights come on, teenagers clump together in front of the disc jockey, a thin, short, and balding man. They move in waves, migrating between the DJ and the concession stand, buying cans of Coke and round crunchy nacho chips covered with an orange cheese slick. They poke each other with long skinny balloons, inflated and twisted into bloated swords.

Margaret leans against the metal pole at the front of her booth, taking advantage of a lull in the crowd. Margaret is the granddaughter of Nickolas Kunzmann, making her the fourth generation of a family now in its sixth still living on the hill. Her grandfather and Mary's grandfather helped build the church and school. Margaret and her husband, Joe, rented an apartment through Mary's mother shortly after they were married.

Margaret lives one block away from the chapel, and to help raise money for it, she organized card parties in her home, pushing chairs and furniture back along the walls to make room for tables. Anytime sugar or Kleenex went on sale, she drove to the store and bought it in bulk to give away as prizes. The parties didn't bring in much, Margaret said, but Mary always told her every little bit helps. Once tour buses started coming through, Margaret would get a group of women together to make and serve lunches to the visitors. Cecilia Guehl pitched in.

A sign on Margaret's booth reads BIRTHDAYS 25 CENTS. Two small children come up. Their mother stands a few steps behind them.

Margaret becomes animated. "Put your twenty-five cents on the month you were born, or any month," she directs them.

The girl picks November. Her little brother, July. Margaret spins a wooden wheel, which is divided evenly into twelve pie-shaped pieces, one for each month. The months whirl into a blur. As the wheel slows, the children try to locate their month and quietly cheer it on. "C'mon, November." "C'mon, July." Margaret, grinning, watches them. The wheel slows. *Marchh, Aprilll, Mayyyy, Juuunnnne.* The final flick. July. The boy jumps up and down. The girl scowls at her little brother. He's already won a basketball. Margaret reaches for a foot-tall gray stuffed elephant dressed in a blue sailor suit and hands it to the boy. She waves good-bye.

This year the parish raised more than thirty-three thousand dollars from the festival and a booklet filled with ads from local businesses and church groups, wishing the parish a successful festival. The Guehls bought a two-inch square ad. Mary Wohleber is listed with other 1998 boosters. The Most Holy Name class of 1935 placed a half-page ad: "In Memory of the Superb teachers guiding us, the School Sisters of Notre Dame." In memory because there are no more nuns teaching there.

Mary doesn't take full credit for the chapel's salvation. "No one," she says, "does anything alone." But if it weren't for her, say friends and just about everyone on Troy Hill, the chapel wouldn't be standing. Driving by and seeing its tall twin spires standing above all else on Troy Hill gives her great joy. Her children have left the hill. But the chapel remains.

"If I didn't live for anything besides my children and that chapel, my life is worthwhile," she says. "Every time I pass it, I look at it and say, 'By god, the chapel is still here.'"

CHAPTER TWO

Margaret Fichter,
a Lady of Charity

MARGARET FICHTER leaves her narrow two-story brown brick house—one of the few with a tree out front—comes down her walk, and passes a sundial resting in the earth among a small patch of flowers. It is inscribed: IN LOVING MEMORY OF JOSEPH FICHTER, 1912 TO 1994. FROM HIS CHILDREN. Her kids gave it to Margaret the first Father's Day after Joe died. It is simple and classic looking. They bought it from the Smithsonian. Joe loved classical things: classical music, art, and literature.

Sometimes she and Joe recited John Greenleaf Whittier's poem "The Gift of Tritemius" together as they did house chores.

"'Tritemius of Herbipolis, one day, / While kneeling at the altar's foot to pray,'" Margaret began, and finished that stanza.

Joe took the next. "'Thereat the Abbot paused; the chain whereby / His thoughts went upward broken by that cry.'" They'd memorized it when they were in grade school.

Margaret walks to the corner of Harpster and Froman Streets. Actually she scoots, almost like a fast shuffle. People recognize Margaret's scoot from two blocks away. She crosses to the other side of the street to avoid a stretch of particularly wobbly cobblestones in front of Thelma Wurdock's house and then returns to her side of the street and climbs the four steps to Saint Anthony Chapel.

Now eighty-three, she has made the same trip every Tuesday for decades, although decades ago she wore a dress and some sort of hat. All women and girls had to wear a hat, veil, or scarf in church. If a schoolgirl didn't have anything on her head, a nun took a white Kleenex and a hairpin and pinned it to the girl's hair. Boys had it easy. Nothing on their heads to ruin their slicked-down hair. They even got to be altar boys. As a young girl Margaret sat in her pew and watched those lucky robed boys, standing like angels, and wished she could be up there, too. A few years ago she finally got her chance. She and Joe were at a retreat for couples. The priest asked for volunteers. Joe nudged her. "Aren't you going to raise your hand?" he whispered. Margaret's hand shot up. The other wives came up after and congratulated Margaret. "We were so proud of you," they told her, and embraced her hand in theirs.

The church has relaxed, for better or worse. Her granddaughters can be altar girls if they like. Margaret wears a hat only when it's cold or rainy, and pants all year round. Today she wears deep pink pants, a rose-colored jacket, and round pink earrings, the size of a nickel, that clip on her ears. Her purse is embroidered with roses. Everything blends. Her home is that way, too. Rooms come in ensembles. A wine-colored swag above the front door matches one above the entrance to the living room and is the same color as the wooden trim on the steps and the dried flowers clinging to a heart-shaped wreath above the living-room doorway. The little china candy dish is always full and in season. Candy corn comes in pastel pink for Easter and orange-and-yellow for Halloween. A tiny silver spoon sits in the candy.

Pink, being cheery, becomes her, even when she is not feeling great, like today. This weekend she made a special new recipe for chicken lasagna and spinach. It sounded wonderful and tasted wonderful but had too much milk. Milk doesn't sit well with the Kunzmanns, which she was before she married Joe. Her father drank a crème-de-menthe-like concoction at meals. When that didn't work, he'd roll around on the floor with stomach pains.

With that history, she knows better. "No fool like an old fool," she whispers, scooting into the chapel.

Margaret slides into her pew in the chapel, which is not really hers, but it is where she typically sits. She nods to Ethel White, whose place is the other end of the pew. People sit in the same spot not because they are rigid. It is part of their identity. "You know, the one who sits in the third pew next to Rose" is as handy a description as "the one who lives in the orange-brick house at the corner." When someone is absent, that person is missed. Should he or she be missing the next day, and the next, the phone rings. "Are you OK? Do you need something from the grocery store?"

The Guehl sisters walk down the aisle. Cecilia leads and raises her hand to Margaret—a still wave. It's more like a salute. An active wave would be inappropriate in church. Margaret was a couple years ahead of Cecilia and a couple behind

Loretta in school. Margaret's father-in-law was a good friend of their father, John, and gave him an oil painting of a winter landscape that hangs in the Guehl home. A companion summer scene is in Margaret's front hallway.

The sisters pass Margaret and head to the front of the chapel. They sit among the relics, their pew between the two reclining plaster statues of slain soldiers.

Margaret sits in the back section with the stations of the cross. To her left, Jesus picks up his cross. To her right, the thirteenth station, Jesus is taken down from the cross.

Margaret doesn't kneel down. It is the privilege, or curse, of getting older and arthritic. No matter how generous the padding on the kneeler, after eighty years, kneeling can be painful. Still it is not abandoned casually. Kneeling is a sign of humility and sacrifice. Those who can't kneel remain humble, maybe even more so, and still want to sacrifice. So Margaret and many others half kneel, sitting at the edge of the wooden seat. Sitting completely would be too relaxing. Kneeling completely is too painful or impossible. Half kneeling is the least, and the most, they can do.

Last week the temperature reached eighty-four degrees, a record high for spring. A woman in her eighties, who lives two doors down from the chapel, was outside in her work boots, pushing an electric lawn mower around her islands of daffodils. Farther down the street, a man opened a folding chair on the sidewalk and sat listening to the radio, with no shirt on. In the school's little courtyard across the street, three young trees, white with blossoms, held private ticker-tape parades, dropping soft petals as thin as parchment to the daffodils below.

Given the heat the chapel windows were opened earlier than usual. The fourteen windows are about thirty feet off the ground and must be opened by hand. Once open they remain so until October. On sweltering days metal pedestal fans stand in the aisles like a row of skinny flowers with overgrown whirling petals.

Unfortunately, after the windows were opened, it turned cooler. This morning white smoke rests frozen like cotton candy above the stacks of the Heinz Company. A time-and-temperature clock blinks below an illuminated ketchup bottle that empties and fills every few minutes. Thirty-six degrees. Blink. Eight o'clock.

Inside the stone chapel, those who have arrived early say the rosary, led by a woman two pews in front of Margaret. The woman begins promptly at 8:10. As people come in, they kneel down, pull out their beads, and join her. If they miss half, they will make it up later in the day. They think nothing of saying the rosary every day, sometimes twice a day. The five decades of Hail Marys and five Our Fathers never become redundant. When they were children, the radio broadcast the rosary daily at 7 A.M. and 7 P.M. Their mothers and grandmothers pulled out their rosary beads and knelt down, resting their folded hands on a chair or couch, and prayed along.

Margaret joins at the third decade. Her breath clouds before her.

The altar is still dark. A glow rises from a table in the middle of the chapel where tall white votive candles stand twenty across and ten deep, nearly all lit and shimmering the air above. One woman takes a long wooden match and lights a candle.

After she is done, she slips a small envelope containing a few dollars and marked with her specific intention—HAPPY MARRIAGE, POOR SOULS, SUCCESS IN STUDIES, GOOD HEALTH, or EMPLOYMENT—into a box. Two more women wait behind her, their envelopes in their hands.

Margaret doesn't sit back after the rosary. She opens her purse and pulls out a white card, small enough to fit in a pocket and sturdy enough to withstand being pulled out twice a day, 365 days a year.

One side bears the evening prayer. The flip side carries the morning prayer. It begins, "Bless each one at home." Only one of her nine children lives at home, but that doesn't matter. A mother never stops praying for her children, whether they are five or fifty. The requests for health, success, guidance, strength, continue daily in their behalf. Should they die, the invocations continue. Her oldest son died when he was forty-two. He remains in her prayers. She continues reading quietly.

" 'My dearest Lord, what do You send me today? Humiliations, contradictions, physical sufferings, bad news which I do not expect; an aching heart, a failure? Shall I see myself misjudged, wrong suspected, despised? All that You wish, O my God; I accept it all in advance.' "

Every morning she says that prayer. "It gets me through the day," she tells a friend. She returns the card to her purse.

At 8:30 sharp, the bell named for Saint Anthony sounds deeply and slowly, the echo of each rich toll emptying into silence before another begins fresh. Seconds later, softer sweeter bells chime in, swinging back and forth across the linear *clangs*. They are the bells of Saint Francis of Assisi and Saint Clare of Assisi. When bells are blessed, they are named, christened like a boat, with the name of a saint.

The altar lights up.

Every pew is filled. While the chapel is not huge, such a crowd is notable for a weekday morning. Most are women. But there are a fair number of men who have retired and now have Tuesday mornings free. They pass the collection baskets. Two men always sit in the back. When the priest asks the congregation for specific intentions, one of the men intones, "For the crippled, the mentally retarded, and the handicapped." The other follows, "In Thanksgiving." If those petitions aren't heard, people up front know the two men aren't in chapel today. They don't even have to turn around and look.

Nearly all of these people grew up on Troy Hill. As children they had no choice but to attend mass daily. It was as much a part of their grade school day as the Pledge of Allegiance. The choice is theirs now and they choose to continue.

Habit begets faith; faith begets habit. Neither is acquired. Faith is something they work on. At daylight they pick up where they left off the night before, to see how it will figure into the next twenty-four-hours. Often, believing is a struggle. All of them have lost someone dear. Parents, brothers, sisters, husbands, or children. Privately they might ask why and feel unduly punished. Still, faith remains a source of strength and, at times, their only consolation.

Margaret will never forget when she was just about to give birth to her eighth child. Doctors found something on her husband's lungs that looked like tuberculosis and ordered him to go immediately to a sanitarium. The cab came. Margaret went into her bedroom and stood before a statue of Jesus. She said a quick prayer asking for the strength to smile for Joe and not break down in tears. They parted at the door. He couldn't even give her a kiss and hug. She gave him a big cheery smile, waved good-bye. When the cab disappeared from sight, she ran to her bedroom, flung herself across the bed, and sobbed. Joe returned home after the baby was born.

This morning the priest talks about signs and how people always want signs. They wanted signs centuries ago when Jesus was alive. They want them now. Something definite, like an extravagant magic show without sleight of hand. Turn this rock into a loaf of bread. Dry up this river. Open the heavens so we can see Moses and the others up there. Then we can fall to our knees and believe.

"Why," he asks, "are we always looking beyond that which is already there? Look around. The signs are there." He doesn't elaborate. Doing so wouldn't work. Signs are in the eye, heart, or mind of the beholder.

At the sign of peace, people shake hands with those on either side and directly in front of or behind them. The practice is a standard part of all Catholic masses. At most churches it ends there. Here it continues. After shaking Ethel's hand, Margaret turns slowly, scanning the seats around her, offering a nod, a smile, and a raised hand in greeting to those whose hands she cannot reach but whose names and faces she grew up with. She nods to Thelma Wurdock, who sits across the aisle, and to Loretta Grindel, a fellow Lady of Charity.

"You know everybody," says Margaret. "And when they

shake your hand and extend a few words, you know they really mean it. It's a good feeling. It starts your day off real good."

After mass, Margaret waits on the sidewalk for Loretta Grindel. Loretta is quiet and soft-spoken and several years younger than Margaret. Her husband, also named Joe, is the lector every Tuesday morning. On Sundays he pauses to gently pat Margaret's shoulder on the way to their pew.

When Margaret's husband was sick and in a wheelchair, Joe Grindel dropped by to visit. Margaret's Joe was carving a small tavern to add to the Christmas village under their tree, using a board propped across the arms of his wheelchair as a table. A few days later, Joe Grindel came back again with a board that hooked onto the arms of the wheelchair so Joe's work surface wouldn't slide back and forth. The board was stained and varnished. Joe Grindel is like that. One time Mary Wohleber asked him to fix her husband's forty-year-old radio. Joe told her he didn't think it was possible because the radio was too old, so Mary told him to keep it for parts. A month or so later he knocked at her door and handed her Alan's radio, completely repaired. He didn't give up, because he knew it was important to her.

Margaret and Loretta are among the five Ladies of Charity left, all older. They visit shut-ins, some of whom are younger, with a small gift or conversation, and occasionally take those who are mentally retarded out shopping for shoes. The group meets the third Monday of the month.

Years ago charity was handled by the Catholic Women's Union, a national group formed locally in 1923 as the Frauenbund, German meaning "women's union." The union sought empowerment as much as charity, urging Catholic women to be self-reliant and to vote, as well as to hear the cry of the stricken. Such mandates were revolutionary for the time and the church. In the late twenties, the local union had 350 members. The women's union disbanded and the Ladies of Charity, a far tamer group, was organized in its place.

Margaret joined in 1982. She was in charge of organizing people to attend funeral masses for the homeless. She wrote notes asking folks to come and then sent her daughters up and down the streets to drop them off. Her husband, Joe, knew which neighbors worked the night shift and called to line up pallbearers.

Between the two of them, they would get about fifty people to fill the front of the church for the funeral of a friendless person. Joe belonged to the Saint Vincent de Paul Society, as does Joe Grindel. The society provides food and clothes to needy families and is the men's equivalent of the Ladies of Charity. Margaret recently attended a lecture about the saint. It turns out that Vincent de Paul was a rather immodest young man. His father was missing a few teeth, and Vincent was so ashamed that he walked several steps behind his father, pretending they weren't together.

"That little stinker," Margaret says. "He turned out OK after a while, though."

"You ready?" Margaret asks Loretta. They are delivering little gift plates this morning. The two women walk down the sidewalk to Margaret's house, where a half dozen Styrofoam plates covered in purple plastic wrap dot her dining-room table. On each is a hard-boiled egg, a white cookie sprinkled with colored sugar, a small loaf of bread, a cluster of grapes, and a plastic container of holy water. Loretta had braided the palms from Palm Sunday into little crosses for each plate.

Margaret is pleased with the plates. "Don't these look nice?" she asks Loretta, and then continues. " 'Make it look nice.' That's what my mother always said, and she learned it from her mother. 'Even if you're just going to serve coffee and jelly bread, make the table look nice.' " Margaret's grandson, a chef, says people eat first with their eyes and then with their nose. Same thing, really. But he had to go to school to find that out.

Margaret would resurrect that handy little chorus many times in the course of raising nine children in a small home on a working-class wage. Setting a pretty table has a way of lifting the spirits. Her dining-room table wears cloth and a simple centerpiece. Cups have saucers and tiny spoons. Cream comes in a pitcher, not a carton.

"My old grandmother, she was born out on a farm. She had no education—well, minimum education—but she had more horse sense than anybody," Margaret tells Loretta. "She said to her daughters, 'If you have a fight with your husband, don't tell me. I don't want to hear it, because you will kiss and make up, but I will remember the hurt.' "

They walk outside, each holding plates. Margaret locks her door. Loretta waits on the front walk, admiring the sundial.

Three of the shut-ins on their list live within a block of Margaret's house. She knows them because she has lived on this street for sixty years.

Each home is familiar, not simply the one with the yellow-and-white-striped awning or the iron fence, but the one where the widow Bea lived. If Bea got lonely, she walked out her front door and strolled down the street. In no time she'd be in someone's living room sipping tea and feeling refreshed. Every morning, Margaret came downstairs and looked out her kitchen window to check on Bea's blinds. If they weren't open, Margaret called to make sure she was OK. When it was Margaret's turn to bring the offertory gifts up to the altar at Sunday mass, she asked Bea to share the honor and walk down the aisle with her.

The Republican Lady lived farther down. Most people on the hill were Democrats or reserved Republicans. Not the Republican Lady. She went door to door, dropping off literature. Margaret invited her in. They sat and chatted. The Republican Lady left and Margaret continued to vote Democratic.

In the 1970s a large poster of Democratic presidential candidate George McGovern hung out front of the Fichter home. A couple of her younger children became active in his campaign during the Vietnam War and set up local headquarters in the Fichter basement. After Sunday morning mass they handed out leaflets. Margaret made pancakes. McGovern later wrote the Fichters, thanking them for their support. Margaret keeps the letter in her scrapbook. At the time, she and Joe were close to sixty years old. Most of their friends had children in their thirties and forties. Having politically active college-age children during the Vietnam War gave them a different perspective.

The pale yellow house cloaked in tall pine trees is the Fichter homestead. Joe grew up there, and he and Margaret rented the first floor shortly after they married. The rest of his family lived upstairs. Joe and Margaret stayed there for nearly twenty years and had eight of their nine children before they could afford to buy their own house, across the street and three doors down. It remains home for Margaret and her daughter Molly who just turned sixty and is a social worker. Margaret's brother-in-law, Bill Fichter, still lives in the homestead.

"Is this where we are going?" Loretta asks, as they approach a cream-colored home that was on their shut-in list.

"No, she is in a nursing home. And there," Margaret says, pointing to a house across the street, "she died." The woman's brother had taken care of her. Margaret remembers that he set the table nicely, changing the place mats according to the seasons. She admires that in a man and on a table. At one time the Ladies had sixty shut-ins on their list. It has narrowed to thirty.

Margaret leads the way, a step or two ahead of Loretta, down a narrow brick walk. In between the bricks, soft green moss rises like leavened bread. Children call it fairy carpet.

A note is taped to the door. "Watch cat doesn't go out." Margaret opens the door and walks into the kitchen. Loretta follows quickly. The cat is nowhere to be seen. A television blares in the corner of the next room. On the screen, a child in a cowboy hat just dropped a bowl of spaghetti. Margaret peeks around the corner. "Don't get up. We've got something here for you. I'll just leave it on the table and I'll see you Sunday." Margaret knows with a glance when to stay and talk for a while and when someone needs rest.

While walking back down the path, Margaret cautions, "Now, this next one has a dog. But it's a nice one. He's always waiting at the door for me on Sundays. I forget his name."

On the front door hangs a wreath made of tiny wood hearts painted pink. Margaret knocks. A woman opens the door and invites Margaret and Loretta in. Loretta tells her she likes the cheery wreath. The woman says her daughter picked it up for her in a country store.

A little Shetland sheepdog appears with a bright green tennis ball and drops it at Margaret's feet. After a few seconds, he picks it up and drops it at Loretta's feet, to no avail. Who would throw a ball in the house? The woman collects beautiful tiny china teacups and displays them on a glass-topped table. Loretta admires them but at a safe distance. They talk for a while, the three of them, standing in the living room. The woman announces that she is a great-grandmother. "Spread the word," she tells them.

Margaret hands her the plate. "Oh dear, I hate to take this," the woman says.

"Aw, c'mon. There's nothing to it. It just looks pretty," says Margaret.

Down the street, Margaret rings the bell. This last plate has two hard-boiled eggs and two cookies. Both the mother and daughter are shut-ins. The daughter, short, round, and stooped, answers the door. The mother hears voices and comes from the kitchen to the living room. Her husband died in January 1994, only a month before Joe died. She and Margaret have that loss in common. It makes them more familiar. The mother goes to the dining-room table and picks up a five-by-seven-inch photograph that was propped up in front of a white china bowl and brings it out to show Margaret.

"Here he is," she says. She wrote in pencil on the back of the photograph "Last Picture of Dad, Christmas 1993." A daughter-in-law cooked a Christmas feast of turkey, potatoes, and gravy, and drove it to their house. He sits at the head of the table, in a red plaid shirt. The four-year-old photograph remains out, unframed, on the table, to show to visitors. It's not something to be put away or to have in an album, or even to hang on a wall. Rather, it is to be presented.

"We still miss him," the woman says to Margaret and Loretta.

"You just have to put your best foot forward like all of us," Margaret tells her.

"He looks good," the woman says, looking at the picture. Presiding over the bountiful holiday table, he is smiling. "He lived up until the end."

"So did Joe," Margaret says. "He played cards the Saturday night before he died."

"Did he really?" Loretta asks.

"Yep." Margaret nods and grins.

More than one hundred years ago, Margaret's grandfather helped dig the foundation of Most Holy Name of Jesus Church on the corner of Claim and Harpster Streets, two blocks away from where she now lives. His was one of seventy families to attend the first mass in 1868 in that small hundred-foot-long building. The front half was the church. The priest lived in the back half. Later it was expanded, and a convent and school were added. The family of Most Holy Name buildings now covers an entire block. Priests live in a splendid home across the street. Cases filled with crystal sherry glasses line the dining-room walls of the house. The walls themselves are bound in maroon leather, like a fine book.

Two decades after Most Holy Name was dedicated, and two blocks over, Grace Lutheran Church opened its doors. Services lasted for three hours. If anyone fell asleep, the designated tickler waved a feather under the weary nose. In 1930 lightning toppled the steeple, which was finally replaced forty years later. It was never a grand church, but beside the altar hangs a large and rich tableau of Jesus praying in the garden of Gethsemane.

In 1901 the little redbrick Troy Hill Presbyterian Church in Bohemian Hill was dedicated, replacing the tent that blew over in a violent storm. Sitting on the western precipice at the head of the two-block enclave, the church became Bohemian Hill's physical and spiritual center. To this day, when the sun rises, it comes down the center of Goettmann Street, up the church's front walk, warms the double red doors, and then greets the simple white cross above them. Only then does it turn its attention to the houses.

Inside are twenty pews and an altar. Decades ago a minister took his wood hobby kit and burned a Bohemian phrase in the front of the Communion table. The translation is kept on a slip of white paper in the minister's desk drawer in case anyone wants to know. It means "This do in My remembrance." Though tiny, the church had a Sunday school, a manse, and a dedicated women's group that baked rye bread to raise money for new ceilings and floors.

All three churches remain, though the Presbyterian church just barely, serving only a dozen members, nearly all older women who live within these two blocks. The Husaks—Alois Jr. and Ellen—who live on neighboring Mount Troy, join them. Alois, eighty-seven, is the head elder and always wears a suit and tie. His father was a respected minister here. Ellen is an organist.

The small congregation gives the church a reason to exist, and the church gives them a sense of belonging.

The little trinity of churches anchored the community, trying to keep their congregations not just pure and holy but entertained as well. Young men bowled in the basement of the Catholic church, played pool in the kitchen of the Presbyterian church and Ping-Pong at the Lutheran church. Adult drama clubs performed *The Rosary* and *Pollyanna* to packed halls. As grade-schoolers, Cecilia Guehl and Thelma Wurdock provided entertainment during the intermissions, tap dancing on stage. A church festival welcomed every season and celebrated every food. Summer and fall. Strawberry and bratwurst. Religion didn't matter. Anyone could buy a chance to win bacon and wine at the Maria Mission Circle booth. As children, Troy Hill residents knew that if Santa couldn't produce the bicycle, maybe the church raffle would.

Then, too, the churches provided needed solace and beauty during gloomy times of war and the Depression. No matter how somber the events on the streets below or the world beyond, the people of Troy Hill could walk through the front doors of their protected hilltop churches and find comfort. The stained-glass windows, hundreds of flickering candles, and the triumphant march of the organ wrapped them in a comforting reassurance that some greater force was in charge during those times, which, though simpler, were far less certain.

Robed priests swinging golden balls filled with sweet burning incense led grand processions through the streets to mark special holy days. Garlands of flowers dangled from windows. Neighbors joined one another on the sidewalks. Even if the procession was a solemn rite, marching two miles to a cemetery and singing the liturgical dirge *Miserere* so that the poor souls in purgatory could finally be lifted to heaven, it was nonetheless much anticipated. Mothers, fathers, and children dressed up. Every May a young girl in a white dress crowned Mary with a wreath of flowers. Once though, the year that Cecilia Guehl's little sister, Mary Margaret, was supposed to crown Mary, the ceremony was cut short. The eighth graders carrying the statue failed to lower it enough to clear the choir loft, knocking Mary's head off.

Those occasions provided a welcome break in the routine. So it's not surprising that they stand out among childhood memories. It was the church that officially declared Troy Hill's children young men or young women, with a sacrament and a ritual fitting of the transformation, and often a keepsake. While other mementos, outfits, and papers have over time been given away or discarded, the parchment-covered pamphlet for the newly confirmed remains carefully packed in the cedar chest. A delicately embroidered First Communion dress rests seventy years between folds of white tissue paper.

Church figured most prominently in the lives of the women of Troy Hill. They didn't, for the most part, have paying jobs. They had their families and their church. Their church, in turn, had clubs for every age and interest. Sewers stitched altar vestments. Singers sang in the choir. One group raised money for the missions and offered life insurance. During the war, the women wrote letters to servicemen overseas. The Semper Fideles group bought pots and pans for the kitchen of Grace Lutheran Church. When girls or women outgrew one club, another was waiting to

embrace them. Junior Maria Mission Circle members sewed ki-
monos for babies and then graduated to full-fledged members
who hosted card parties and held an annual flea market.

Over the years, these groups provided their respective
churches with significant gifts, such as stained-glass windows
and a ramp for the handicapped. Every time the organist played
"The Church's One Foundation," the young Presbyterian
ladies of the Friendly Circle couldn't help but feel pride and satisfaction knowing that their $1,325 went to such a worthy cause.

As their churches benefited, so did the women, though in
far less tangible ways. Within these circles their singular skills,
which might otherwise go unnoticed, were tapped. One woman
organized fish dinners like no other. Another woman could
raise a few thousand dollars through a rummage sale, knowing
what doesn't sell and what does and for how much. If a piano
needed to be moved, ladies looked around for Ethel Brendel to
move it. Whatever the need, someone with a special talent or
strength emerged and rose to fill it. Everyone could have a role.
The star baker and the meticulous cleaner. The leaders and the
dedicated followers.

Mary Kaule, who lived two doors down from the Guehls
and was a good friend of their mother, baked bread so tall that it
didn't fit in the toaster. She made a few loaves for church festivals. When the fresh bread arrived, everyone would say, "*Who*
made that?" It got to the point that people would call her and
say, "Well, Mrs. Kaule, if you are sending bread to the festival,
would you please put my name on it?" It was sold before it ever
reached the booth.

Only Mildred Mares was gutsy enough to host hush-hush
Wednesday afternoon bingo parties in her living room. The

Presbyterian Church frowned on bingo, viewing it as a form of gambling, and gambling as a sin. The ladies, though, had pure motives. They were sending the money to a six-year-old Korean orphan, who wrote grateful notes in response, saying he was in good health, liked to sing hymns and listen to the story of Jesus. On every third Wednesday, at 12:30, dozens of women would file down the street and stream into Mildred's living room. Some arrived earlier to help move the furniture out of the way and set up tables and chairs. Mildred had a car and drove around picking up big boxes of blue soap flakes—made down below in Spring Garden—and canned goods for prizes.

The value of those Wednesday afternoon gatherings rested as much in the intangibles as in buying the boy shoes. "It kept these women together," says Mildred. It was the same for all. It didn't matter if the group was Catholic, Lutheran, or Presbyterian; whether they were sewing, cleaning, baking, or playing cards. The same forces were at work.

Those clubs provided a framework for initiating and nurturing friendships. Week after week the ladies met at the same place, saw the same faces, and engaged in a common goal. Membership in one group often led to another, thus broadening their circle while tightening it. Without anyone having to say a word, they knew they shared something very personal. As Christian Mothers, they solemnly pledged to uphold the home and the sanctity of the family above all else. They could be open with one another.

For many, these meetings were their only extravagance. On meeting nights, they walked out of their houses and down the streets alone, leaving behind—for a few hours at least—worries about money or bills. Friends called them by their first names, or childhood nicknames. In the course of listening to a treasurer's report and signing up to work at a festival, they might exchange news or jokes, enjoy cups of coffee while they were still hot, and eat sweet rolls without interruption. It was refreshing, like an afternoon nap.

Those monthly meetings became, and remained, anchors as their lives and circumstances changed. At first the meetings were a refuge from the early anxieties of motherhood and later from the greater anxieties of their childrens' teen years. Together the women watched, with both dismay and hope, changes in their community and the world, the transient lifestyles of their children, and the dramatic march of feminism. They tried to make some sense of it or find some peace with it. In general the women of Troy Hill think women should be feminine. Let men open the doors and pick up the check. Of course, that doesn't mean a woman can't be strong or competent; and they certainly wouldn't want anything denied their daughters or granddaughters.

A small white sign just inside the chain-link fence of the Troy Hill Presbyterian Church welcomes all to a strawberry festival at 1 P.M. Sunday. Visitors are also welcome at the 9:30 A.M. service. This morning the Reverend Harry R. Heidrich will preach on the light within us.

The half dozen ladies of the church spent yesterday baking rectangular pans of rich yellow shortcake. Edna McKinney, who lives around the corner from the church, baked a round angel food cake for those who might want something lighter.

Earlier in the day, Florence Klingman came up to the church, washed off the long metal folding tables in the community room downstairs, and put chairs around. It's a nice sunny day, but people would rather eat inside on level ground and away from bugs. She swept the floor, although there wasn't much to sweep. In the ladies' room, she wiped the vanity table. On it, she arranged a hairbrush, comb, box of tissues, and a little vase filled with small plastic flowers in an arc like a fan.

She is essentially the caretaker of the little church. Every day she walks over, unlocks the door, gets a small Sunday-school chair from the minister's office, and steps up on it to reach the mailbox. She leaves the mail on the minister's desk. She dusts the pews, weeds between the cracks of the sidewalk, takes out the garbage weekly. She marks the change in seasons by replacing the summer's pink, red, and white plastic roses in little vases on the altar with autumn's orange and yellow mums.

The church and the people in it mean much to her. Her happiest childhood memories are of Sunday school with the adored Miss Wilma Owens, who taught school for fifty years. When Miss Owens retired, the church threw her a farewell dinner and sang "Blest be the tie that binds." Florence and her sister, Lil, who lived on the same street, were confirmed and married in the church. Lil died a few years ago. An outdoor illuminated cross, dedicated in her name, hangs on the back wall of the church so it shines at night to the streets below.

"Our number one spark plug," says Mr. Husak, the head elder, referring to Florence.

The praise embarrasses her. "I don't do anything," she insists.

The first strawberry festival was organized by the Ladies Aid Society in the 1950s. It was a big success and became an annual event. The ladies used the money to help pay church bills.

The society disbanded as the congregation grew smaller. But this year the church session—which includes Mr. Husak,

Edna, and Florence—decided to resurrect the festival and combine it with a hot-dog roast. Sunday, June 15, was picked as the date, which would be in the middle of the local strawberry-picking season.

Each member of the congregation has a job. Bob Leder takes care of buying the strawberries. He picked up a dozen tiny jars of Heinz ketchup and mustard for the hot dogs, too. Bob retired from Heinz after forty years but can still shop at the employee store. His wife, Ruth, the one who makes all the church decorations, isn't there. She is confined to a wheelchair. He will relate the afternoon—who was there, what they ate, and how good everyone looked—to Ruth when he gets home. Bob's mother used to play bingo in Mildred's living room.

John Novak, a retired police officer, is outside, grilling hot dogs. He brought a small radio and some polka tapes, which play on the raffle table, by the kitchen door.

Florence is in the kitchen, a flowered apron tied to her waist, standing in front of a huge stove with a dozen gas burners. A pot of water boils on one burner. Florence tosses in a half dozen hot dogs for those who prefer theirs with softer, ungrilled skin. The hot dogs bob on top of the bubbling hot water. Florence watches until they bloat as wide as their skin will allow without exploding. Then she rescues them. The red light on the coffeepot glows. Rose Ptacek, Florence's sister-in-law, who lives across the street from her, wanders into the kitchen to see if Florence needs help. Florence asks her to test the coffee.

Reverend Heidrich mills around, moving from the kitchen to the community room. He doesn't live in the manse next door, which is now abandoned. He lives at another church, a hill away. The two churches have shared the fifty-one-year-old

Reverend Heidrich for about twenty years because on their own neither could afford him and also pay for church upkeep. Not that his compensation is all that high. It's less than twenty thousand dollars. For that, he preaches weekly services at both churches, visits the sick, and helps with shoveling the snow, mowing the lawn, and fixing broken windows.

Edna McKinney sits at a card table by the door, selling tickets. She keeps the money in a square Marsh Wheeling cigar box. In front of her, cosmetic samples and little packets of shampoo fill two small wicker baskets. "Try this one," Edna says, fishing out a little sample of Timeless Pink lipstick. "That'll look nice on you."

Tickets are $3.50 for adults and $1.75 for children, of which there are none. She sells thirty-one tickets. Everyone fits comfortably at the six long folding tables inside. Edna invited her daughter-in-law Anna. Anna knows everyone here. She grew up down the street from Edna, was baptized, confirmed, and married Edna's oldest son, Art, in the church. Ellen Husak played the organ at their wedding.

The door opens. Mildred Mares enters slowly, holding on to a walker. Her niece holds the door open for her. Edna looks up. "Hey, look who's here." Conversation stops at the tables. Heads turn toward the door. A warm chorus of "It's Mildred" sounds.

Mildred didn't tell anyone she was coming. She wanted it to be a surprise. Mildred shook Bohemian Hill and her fellow church members when she announced last Christmas that she was leaving Troy Hill. She had always said it would take an atom bomb to get her off the hill, but it was the house that did it. It was simply too big. Her husband, Bob, died several years earlier. They never had children. So at the age of eighty-one, she decided to move from the only home she'd ever known to a retirement center close to her nieces and nephews.

Her friends and neighbors were stunned. They were losing the grand dame of Bohemian Hill. Mildred's family had seniority. Her first-grade teacher was Miss Dillon, who also had Mildred's father in first grade. Her uncle Steve was a barber. Mothers sent shaggy-haired children and a quarter to Uncle Steve, who sat them on the front porch and gave them all the same bowl cut. Look at a class picture from Troy Hill Elementary School. It looks as if the photographer simply rotated faces through a single cardboard cutout of hair. Bowl cuts were practical. No long hair. No head lice.

Mildred's cousin was the neighborhood midwife. Her father, a tailor, worked out of their home. As a little girl Edna McKinney walked down to Mildred's house with a dress or suit that needed to be fixed or altered. Mildred went to school with Edna's older sister, Helen, who has since died. Little did Edna know that she and Mildred would end up such close friends. They talk on the phone and go on for hours, laughing, swapping stories. Before they hang up, Edna tells her, "I'm still watching your house," which is just around the corner from Edna's.

"Why, it's not going anyplace," Mildred answers. They both laugh.

The crowd is festive but not loud. Everyone stops by to say hello to Mildred, who sits at the table with the Husaks. They ask how she likes her new place. She takes knitting and art classes and won a string of pearls at a card game. "Did you make that, Mildred?" someone asks, pointing to her orange-flowered vest and matching purse. "Yes," she says. Mildred made everything, even sofa and chair covers that fit so perfectly the furniture looks as if it was born with them.

The beer barrel polka plays over a tape recorder. Rose Ptacek and Emma Jesek, a widow who lives at the end of the street, grab each other, spin twice, and smile for a camera.

The hot dogs are ready. Two plates of them, one grilled and one boiled, sit on the table with buns, macaroni salad, a tray of deviled eggs, and the tiny ketchup and mustard jars, each with a plastic knife sticking out.

Florence watches to make sure everyone is going through the line. A few linger at the tables, talking. She walks up and urges them to get the hot dogs while they're hot. Only when everyone has eaten does she get her own plate. She eats quickly, standing at the stove. She wants to get the shortbread and straw-berries ready. This is the special attraction. The half dozen pans of shortbread sit on the counter with two angel food cakes. Ear-lier in the day Florence came over and cut the strawberries, put half in a bowl with sugar and half in a bowl without in case any-one is diabetic.

She begins cutting cake into squares. The pieces are so big they can't lie flat in the bowl but sit at an angle like they're sink-ing. Each is topped with a big spoonful of strawberries and a dollop of Cool Whip. She fills a tray with several bowls and hands it to Rose. Rose walks out to the tables. From in the kitchen Florence hears exclamations of "Oh my."

It feels good to offer such plenty. "I won't have to eat for a week," one woman exclaims. The others at her table nod in agreement. While everyone is eating, Florence looks out, lean-ing against the doorway, rubbing her hands with a towel.

Florence washes each dirty fork as it comes in. She is the last one to leave. The tables are cleared, the garbage emptied, the floors swept, the counters wiped. The coffeepot is back under its plastic cover. She sets it on the metal counter, next to the old institutional mixer, which the women use to make rye bread, and the manual typewriter. During the Depression, the men's society used this typewriter to send letters to its members, saying they could maintain their membership and insurance by signing the letter and sending in a reduced amount.

The turnout this afternoon is bigger than that at the social after the Christmas Eve candlelight services last December. That night about twenty people came downstairs for coffee and strudel in three flavors, apricot, poppy seed, and nut. It was a bitter night. Florence walked around the tables. "Would you like a heated seat?" she asked, extending crocheted circles of wool. A few ladies nodded. They placed them on the seats of their cold metal folding chairs and sat back down. That night, they almost didn't have coffee. Florence plugged in the pot before services and the fuse blew. It was too late to call an electrician, so she picked up the huge pot and carried it to the minister's office. She set it on a folding chair close to an outlet and plugged it in. Everyone took home a Norman Rockwell calendar, courtesy of the Troy Hill Federal Savings Bank, "Your Neighborhood Bank." The scenes were from the 1930s, Depression years, although there wasn't a hint of hardship in this calendar other than two boys scrubbing the sidewalk, where they had written "Nuts Old Brown," while a balding and stout man, presumably Mr. Brown, stood behind them, one fist clenched and his face red.

Mary Wohleber came that night. She doesn't belong to the church, but she is welcome. Years ago when she became the unofficial historian of Troy Hill, giving tours and getting quoted in the local newspaper, one of the churchmen asked her to mention the back part of the hill, the Bohemians and the Presbyterians. Mary does. She talks proudly of the little church and the determination of the people there.

Mary doesn't make it to the strawberry festival. It falls on the same weekend as the Saint Anthony Festival but is much smaller. There are no rides or booths. But there is a wonderful raffle table filled with baskets of stationery, sewing notions, bottles of sparkling cider, and children's toys, each wrapped in yellow ribbon. "We never had this much before," Florence says. Linda Weinzetl, a new member of the church, bought all of the gifts, using her own money. She didn't ask or want to be reimbursed. She said she had fun doing it. All who came went home with a prize. Edna's sister Mary, who wasn't even there, won a prize. At the end of the raffle, Bob Leder asked for quiet. He made a little speech thanking Linda. She moved to Troy Hill only a year or so ago. "We are happy and proud to have her." Everyone clapped and she blushed.

The festival was a success. People left feeling full and cheered, which were the only goals. At this point the congregation isn't trying to raise heaps of cash for major improvements. Buoyed by the enthusiasm of the strawberry festival, the church hosts a corn roast in the fall.

The most holy Name of Jesus Christian Mothers' and Women's Guild meets the third Wednesday of each month at 12:30 in the school cafeteria. Years ago the meetings were held in the evening. But as members got older, the officers agreed to switch to the afternoon so the ladies wouldn't have to drive or walk at night. As each arrives she assumes her seat, unassigned but understood.

Margaret Fichter joined in 1938, when her oldest child, Joann, was born. Margaret leaves her house just before the noon Angelus bell rings. She scoots past the empty chapel parking lot and the three little trees outside the school. Tender green leaves have replaced the fragrant white blossoms.

If she arrives first, she will save a seat for Helen Steinmetz. When they were children, they lived next to each other. In grade school, both had postnasal drip and could sympathize with the other having to blow her nose all the time. They've been best friends since.

Inside the cafeteria, Margaret pays two dollars and picks up a glazed doughnut, a Styrofoam cup filled with coffee, and a raffle ticket. She walks past her sister Cecilia. Cecilia has already finished her doughnut and is pulling out her bingo chips. The sisters smile and wave. Margaret sees Rose Snyder down the table from Cecilia. They are fellow choir members and go together to retreats for widows. Rose had nine children, too. Margaret could count on Rose to attend the funeral of a homeless person.

Margaret doesn't join Cecilia or Rose. They are sitting at the bingo tables. Margaret doesn't play bingo. She plays cards and has done so since she learned the game of fish on Helen's back porch.

Cardplayers sit at a lone row of tables stretching along the back of the cafeteria. Helen saved Margaret a seat.

Margaret has not been feeling well but came anyway because she enjoys this group. She'll never forget the night she stayed out late after a Christian Mothers' meeting, joining a group of ladies at the widow Bea's house to look at Bea's craft work and photos. Margaret didn't get home until 12:45. Joe had gone out looking for her and tracked down the pastor who was walking his dog. They both went to the church to see if for some strange reason Margaret was locked inside. Later, Margaret would howl recounting the night to her club members.

That is how it is with these women. Through the years the crises of yesterday—the son picking up someone's discarded cigar and puffing, or children jumping off dressers, yelling, "Geronimo," and breaking bed slats—suddenly became hysterical when telling friends. All anxiety is defused. With one another they could relax. If a group of them were at Margaret's house, her children would be upstairs lying in bed, trying to imitate their laughs—a cackle here, a giggle and a guffaw there.

Margaret sits down and eats her doughnut while the treasurer reports a balance of $2,078. The Respect Life committee chairman has no report but asks everyone to say a Hail Mary to end abortion. The ladies fold their hands, bow their heads, and pray. More than 190 people attended the Friday night fish fry. The flea market is coming up. "Please donate some items for the grocery basket raffle." One member has had successful cataract surgery but could probably use some cards. "Anyone who needs the woman's address, please stop up."

The president closes the meeting with a prayer. At the final "Amen," the cards are dealt. Each person has a partner. The winning duo of one game progresses to the next foursome. One woman doesn't budge, regardless of whether she wins or loses. "I'm not moving. I'm too old to move."

"Hey, who is keeping score here?" one woman asks.

"I can't add. That is why I brought my bookkeeper," says

another, nodding to Helen. Helen never married, and she worked as a bookkeeper until she retired. During the Depression, when she couldn't find a job, the nuns kept her occupied and in good typing form. After she typed their papers, the nuns rewarded her with cookies, milk, and a "God bless you."

A card flies past a player. "Who taught you to deal?"

"Watch it. I'm taller than you."

"Yeah, but I'm heavier than you."

"Yeah, but not by much." All is said with a straight face and without a pause, as if rehearsed.

Margaret is grinning.

After cards, Margaret walks home, past the sundial, and up to her front porch. A white basket hangs from the awning, filled with tiny strawberry plants that have yet to bear fruit. Just beyond the corner of the porch is a holly tree. At Christmas she cuts a few branches filled with clusters of bright red berries and brings them inside. If visitors want a branch for their home, she snips two and puts them in a bag for them to carry home.

Out back is a tangerine tree with three fruits, none bigger than a plum. Joe had a small garden there. In the corner of the little yard, he built a shrine. He shaped a piece of wire mesh into an alcove and covered it with cement and stones. A statue of Mary stands inside. Some of the stones have fallen off. Margaret and Molly will fix it one of these days. Molly just finished painting the fence white. Margaret painted the bench.

A pussy willow bush grows by the fence. Joe planted it after they bought this house. Every February he looked for fresh gray velvet orbs—catkins—to appear. He'd snip a few branches and bring them inside and put them in a vase. Their arrival was perhaps the most anticipated of the garden's offerings, providing the first vague hint that winter might be flagging. More often than not it was right around Ash Wednesday, the beginning of Lent, the forty-day period of fast and abstinence in preparation for Easter. They seemed to arrive in tandem. Pussy willows. Ash Wednesday. Ash Wednesday, pussy willows.

The pussy willows became part of the family's Lenten observance, sitting in the vases around the house, on tabletops, and on top of the piano. Appropriately, they are soft, gray, and quiet—more winter than spring. Other flowers and blossoms are too brash and festive for a period meant for reflection and penitence. Once Easter arrives, you can shout with lilies. Until then, the pussy willow sits quietly, unassuming enough to be sprinkled here and there, upstaging nothing, content to serve as background. Humble.

A few branches lay beside Joe's black violin case on top of the tall china cabinet. The violin case is there not for lack of closet space or for lack of a better place. The top of the china cabinet is its place, presiding literally over the dining-room table. Joe loved music. It became not only a part of his identity but the family's. If the violin is present, he is present.

After dinner, Joe and Margaret gathered their children around the piano. He picked the violin up. Margaret sat down at the piano. They assigned parts. "OK, you're alto. You're soprano." Then they taught the young Fichters "Little Red Schoolhouse" and "Oh, What a Beautiful Morning" in harmony. The Fichter family singers performed one year at the Saint Anthony Festival and were featured entertainment at

Troy Hill's American Revolution Bicentennial Celebration in 1976. Mary Wohleber gave a speech on the hill's history.

On Valentine's Day, Joe's case is draped with red lights, and at Christmas, with garland. It always joins the celebration.

Holidays were more than days at the Fichter home. They were seasons, time spans with distinct beginnings and endings, filled not with an expanse of routine but with activities. Though much of what they did was church related, Margaret and Joe went beyond the standard rituals and practices to make those holy times merry. At Easter they pulled out a record with Gene Autry singing "I have jelly beans for Tommy and colored eggs for sister Sue."

They wanted to give their children tradition, something distinctly Fichter that belonged to and defined them. They didn't go out and buy trappings off store shelves and slap a Fichter name on them. They couldn't afford to. They had a houseful of children, and Joe worked overtime around the holidays.

Even so, Margaret and Joe spent two weeks before Christmas preparing an elaborate handmade village beneath the tree, unveiling it only on Christmas Eve. Joe carved a new building each year. His last one was a bandstand like the one he remembered from the orphan picnic. A thick blanket of forest green moss served as the grass for the little village. Margaret and Joe gathered that moss on their honeymoon in 1937, and every year, Joe would carefully roll it and unroll it.

Those decorations were barely in their boxes when it was time to get ready for Lent. Margaret stayed up mixing twelve cups of flour to make one hundred doughnuts, so they would be fresh on Fastnacht. Many people know it as Mardi Gras, a day traditionally set aside for one final indulgence before Lent. Germans indulge in doughnuts. She made them every year, even the year she had a mastectomy.

Joe walked around the neighborhood with paper bags filled with doughnuts, dropping off one to Helen Steinmetz; one to Margaret's sister Cecilia and her daughter Selma; and another to Joe's brother Bill and sister Dolly. Joe took four doughnuts to a bowling partner, who lives two doors down, and the blind woman who lives out back, calling ahead to make sure she was awake. Soon after Joe dropped off the bags, the phone would ring. Margaret answered. "The delivery boy was here," her neighbors would say, and then thank Margaret. Now Helen or Molly delivers the doughnuts.

Four Fichter children have taken cuttings from Joe's pussy-willow bush and planted them in their own yards. They look for the fresh catkins at Lent and bring them inside. Margaret's granddaughter memorized a poem about them. "Although he is a pussy, he will never be a cat." Her three sons, two in Virginia and one in Cleveland, and their families eat doughnuts on Fast-nacht. It makes her feel good to see them continue the family traditions, validating what she and Joe valued. This year Margaret ran across the Gene Autry record with the jelly-bean song and made tapes for all her children.

Margaret unlocks the door. A small picture of a beggar hangs just above her doorbell. Below it reads, "Do not neglect to show hospitality to strangers, for thereby some have entertained angels unaware." Anyone selling magazines, floor wax, and shoelaces came here. Even if she wasn't interested, Margaret invited them in to sit down and rest their feet.

A neighbor dubbed Margaret's family the Waltons of Troy Hill. Nice, wholesome. Churchgoing. Before going to bed the children dipped their hands in a font of holy water at the bottom of the steps and blessed themselves. Before Joe went to bed he went back and blessed each of them again. When her children got in trouble for jumping on the beds and breaking the slats, they began feverishly saying Hail Marys. They had learned from a young age to seek divine assistance in all things.

Meat was forbidden on Fridays for all Catholics. But in the Fichter house, Joe enforced the stricture with agonizing attention, as he did all church orders. Just to make sure nothing meat related entered any Fichter mouth on that day, the family had a special butter knife that never touched meat. Only butter and cheese. That pure knife was the only one used on Friday.

He drove Margaret crazy sometimes. Even when the church relaxed some of its rules, Joe stuck by the old ones. Once he turned fifty-nine years old, he didn't have to fast between meals during Lent. But he still did. Sacrifice is sacrifice. It doesn't have an age limit. Margaret would try to get him to lighten up. "I would say, 'Oh, I'm sorry. I thought you were fifty-nine already.'"

Their daughter Molly once told a group on Troy Hill it was a curse to grow up Catholic and German; the rules, expectations, and standards so rigid and unwavering. People buzzed about that for weeks and even longer. A woman approached Molly a year later and asked, "Just what did you mean by that?"

"Just what I said," Molly told the woman. German Catholics

want to relax but are always walking a tightrope trying to do everything expected of them. There is no time or place to be out of step. Everything is perfect. When Molly was four, Joe's father had her memorize the entire tale of *Little Orphant Annie* and stood her up on a chair in the living room to recite it.

Molly is the only of the nine Fichter children living on Troy Hill. Joe dreamed that each of them would marry and buy a house on the hill. It would have been nice, and some of them did live there for a short while after they married. But Margaret knew they had different lives and needs. She told one daughter who was leaving the hill not to worry or feel bad. Don't regret it. "You have what I wanted," she told her. "A nice big yard."

Margaret and Molly Fichter.

Molly works at the Vincentian Home, a residence for older adults. She balances Margaret's energy, much as her father did. She is soft-spoken; talking quietly, and slowly enunciating with purpose and deliberation. She could sit contentedly in a chair, reading and listening to classical music for hours.

They both like to entertain. Margaret bakes an apple pie and Molly puts out a tray of tiny sweet seedless tangerines, the first of the season, fiery orange, and no bigger than an egg. They serve tea in delicate china cups with saucers and tiny silver spoons. A few years ago they started a tradition of having each guest sign and write a short message on a blue tablecloth underneath the white lace cloth. At the end of the year, they look to see who sat at their table. They recall memorable dinners and conversations. After, they cover the table with a fresh cloth and tuck the past year away.

Molly never wanted to live anywhere else but Troy Hill. The other day, she was talking to one of her sisters. "Sometimes I feel like one born out of time," Molly told her. She has no desire to be plugged into computers or television. She would rather walk than drive, and visit in person than on the telephone. Troy Hill allows her to do that. The bank, pharmacy, church, chapel, convenience store, doctors, and two restaurants are all within a few blocks. She walks, and on her way sees her cousin Selma, Cecilia's daughter, who is six months younger. At one point Molly counted five cousins in her grade school class.

What she values most of all, though, is the bonding of the community. "It is hard to explain," she says. Words like belonging and kinship are so airy and meringuelike, they almost seem to disappear in the explanation. But there's closeness without invasiveness. People don't run in and out of one another's houses. They practically live in each other's lap but respect each other's privacy. They might call out to one another and keep an eye on the house and get someone's mail but they don't interfere in one another's lives. Yet they remain concerned and interested. The news travels whether it is joyful—the birth of a healthy grandchild—or sad, as in death and sickness. In some places only bad news spreads, surrounded by *tsk*s. In other places only good news, because the spreaders don't want to get involved or take a stake in the hardships or become too familiar.

"There is genuine concern and helping out. It is almost like one large family," Molly says. A friend of hers, an anthropology professor, came for dinner and commented about this hill being a throwback to a village culture. It was not said disparagingly. The wealth of extended friendships and family support, the very things that engender concern for one another, struck him as admirable, as well as singular. These days individual communities and the sense of belonging they provide seem to be evaporating.

On Sundays after mass at Most Holy Name, Margaret and Molly deliver Communion to shut-ins on the hill. Each has a list, and a little case to carry the Communion wafers. They walk from house to house. Margaret climbs the steps to the second-floor apartment, where one woman has a small bed and drawers, and a loveseat in the kitchen. Margaret often finds the woman sitting in the front of the house, where the sun pours through the window. The woman makes lovely crafts and Margaret marvels over them. She talks much of her children and how they take her out. Margaret marvels over that, too.

Often Molly and Margaret's presence is most appreciated and needed by the shut-in's husband or wife who rarely leaves the home. To them it's a relief to put aside, if just for a half hour, discussion of illness. Tell me what's going on at church, or the school, or Christian Mothers, they ask, relying on those visits to make them feel connected. Sometimes they talk about baseball or grade school nuns or long-gone stores. Once Margaret wasn't feeling well. One of her daughters told her, "Mom, you don't have to go. Even priests and nuns take breaks." But Margaret insisted, saying her neighbors look forward to her arrival.

On a recent Sunday Molly visited an older couple. The man is in the early stages of Alzheimer's. Molly has been bringing Communion to the couple for a while and knows them fairly well. During Molly's visit the wife said she had been having stomach problems and the doctor found a spot that he suspected was cancer on her liver.

"Tell your mother," the woman told Molly, "so she can pray for me."

It struck Molly. Their families know each other but not intimately. Their ties date to some blur, a decade rather than a day or year. A brother married a girl who lived across the street, or something like that.

But there was nothing awkward, fearful, or unnatural about the request. Her mother and this woman share something intangible. This woman felt comfortable asking Margaret to pray for her, saying in effect, "I'm vulnerable. I am concerned. I need help." And not only that, she knew Margaret would respond. Her plea wouldn't be rejected. That is trust. There's an assumption—and not at all presumptuous—that you will understand because you have suffered loss, sought help, and received help, too.

"The bonds are so strong," says Molly. "When people aren't in their places, they are *missed*."

Margaret wasn't in church on Tuesday morning. Molly was there in her place. It was not a major change, but enough to make Selma come up quietly after mass, sit in the pew behind her, lean over, and ask, "How is your mom?"

Selma, who never married, recently retired from the telephone company and purchased one of the few ranch homes on Troy Hill, for herself and her mother.

Molly says Margaret feels better, but the doctor wants her to drink more fluid. Her children are always after her about that. Drink some water. Drink some juice. Margaret has never been a thirsty person. Joe and her son could drain an eighteen-cup coffeepot in one day. She's like a camel. Eat a bland diet for a while. Pasta. Rice. No spices. No dairy, not even any butter or margarine, the doctor said.

At one point the doctor asked Margaret if she ever got short of breath. "Only when I mow the lawn," Margaret told him. Margaret likes the lawn done a certain way. In straight even rows, and along the edges so no long strands stick up. Margaret can't stand that. It looks like a bad haircut. When the snow falls, she shovels. Just a path, she reassures her daughter, failing to mention it's a two-shovel-wide path.

The next day the phone rang. One of Margaret's friends was on the other end. "You weren't in church Monday, you weren't in church Tuesday, and when it came to Wednesday, I thought I better give a call," the friend told her. Then Ev, her bowling partner, called and asked if she needed anything at the store.

CHAPTER THREE

True Harmony, the Story of Margaret and Joe

ROSE M. GOETTMANN'S photograph holds a place of honor in the front hallway of the Fichter home, hanging alongside the family portraits and next to a painting of a cottage sitting in the lap of a lush green hillside, a well-traveled path outside its front door. Margaret's father-in-law painted it. German men, as a rule, were not demonstrative, and if they were, they needed an outlet—a respectable one—to express themselves. Painting was acceptable. His son Joseph found expression in music.

That is where and how Rose Goettmann comes in. Miss Goettmann was choir director at Most Holy Name from 1902 to 1952. After she died, a friend of hers was going through her belongings and came across this black-and-white studio photograph taken somewhere in downtown Pittsburgh. Rose's silken dark hair ripples in soft waves to her chin. Her face is wide, round, and white like a pearl onion. She is wearing a dark dress and a white necklace. She is a grand woman, physically and musically, with the cut and voice of an opera singer.

This particular friend wanted Joe and Margaret to have the photo, knowing that they would cherish it. They shared Rose's passion and respect for music. In their home, music is carefully chosen, not relegated to the background but invited as an honored guest. Melody fills the entire room, not just the corners.

Margaret was in the eighth-grade choir at Most Holy Name School, while Miss Goettmann was director. The eighth graders had the privilege of singing at funerals and weddings. For weddings they sang all of the songs except for "Ave Maria."

That was Miss Goettmann's song, hers and hers alone. Miss Goettmann was a sight to behold anytime she sang, but particularly singing this song. The eighth graders sat tall, straining their necks, like anxious baby birds, to capture the magnificent sight of Miss Goettmann as she lifted her head and gently cradled the word *Maria* along the passage. Her thick white arms rose to accompany each crescendo. Her eyes gently genuflected. She looked as if she could go to heaven, right then and there. No one, it seemed, but Rose could raise a C to such great heights and then hold and fill the note until it pushed against the walls and ceilings. She didn't even turn red. That's what was amazing. You either had to turn red or explode, and she did neither.

Everyone watched her from the pews and instinctively held their breath. When she finally exhaled, they did, too.

Her specialty at funerals was the song "Face-to-Face."

Face to face with Christ my Savior,
Face to face what will it be?
When with rapture I behold Him,
Jesus Christ who died for me?

"When she sang that, everybody in the whole church cried," Margaret says. "You had to pay five dollars for that one." For a smaller amount, Rose would sing a lesser hymn, with no guarantee of tears.

Margaret always loved to sing.

"I think I was born singing," she told Molly the other day at supper.

"I think you were," Molly replied.

Margaret's earliest memory involves song. She was three, maybe four, and sitting on her father's knee on the family farm, north of Troy Hill, where she was born and her family lived for only a short time. He was trying to teach her to sing a song in German. The words sounded so strange and harsh at first. She couldn't do it and began to cry. He looked at her and said gently, "You don't have to cry." She doesn't remember the song or what happened before or after. Just that one snatch on her father's knee, her tears and his consolation.

A few years passed and the family moved back to Troy Hill, where her parents had both been born and raised, into a home just off Lowrie Street. Her father joined the Saint Cecilia choir at Most Holy Name. He had a deep and distinctive voice. If he was missing on Sunday, the nuns would approach the children the next day, saying, "Oh, I didn't hear your dad up there."

Margaret sang at home, belting out tunes while washing the dishes, the windows and doors wide open. She didn't give a hoot who was walking by. Her older and more proper sister Emma was horrified. "What will the people think when they pass?" Emma would say.

Many of the songs, Margaret learned next door at Helen Steinmetz's house. Helen's family had a Victrola and dozens of records, which came with little songbooks. Margaret sat on the back porch, paging through them and memorizing the lyrics, which she found as fascinating as any storybook. Ballads told of poor little Mary Fagan and her grisly murder. Children could turn the gruesome tale silly by dragging out the last word as long as they could.

She went to town one day.
She went to the pencil factory to get her little pay.
She left her home at seven and she kissed her mother good-bye.
Little did the poor child think that she was going to die.
Just then the villain met her with a brutal heart, you know,
And said to Mary Fagan, "You will go home no mooooeeeeee."

For hours Margaret and Helen sat on the Steinmetz's back-porch swing, listening to the songs and watching the Allegheny River three hundred feet below. Huge barges slid across the river as slowly as melting ice cubes, giving daydreamers plenty of time to dwell on them and guess whether they were coming or going, loaded with coal or stowaways, and turning up or down the Ohio or Monongahela Rivers. Houseboats docked at small gardens growing along the shore. In the heat of summer, children and adults jumped sixty feet from riverbanks into the river, yelping and hollering the whole way down. The river provided something to think and wonder about. George Washington himself fell off a raft and almost drowned in the river in 1753.

Prosperous factories lined the banks. Keystone Cones made crunchy melt-in-your-mouth yellow ice-cream cones and Lutz

& Schramm packed dill pickles into huge wooden barrels. In the big flood, Saint Patrick's Day 1936, barrels filled with pickles bobbed down the river.

Stockyards sat on Herrs Island, right below Troy Hill. It was once the tenth largest livestock terminal, and second largest east of the Mississippi in terms of volume of animals processed—pigs in Margaret and Helen's time, and cows before then.

Once a wood bridge going across to the island collapsed, dropping a truck filled with pigs into the river. One man drowned. But the driver grabbed hold of a pig and the pig swam to shore, saving the driver's life.

Margaret will never forget that day and its dual wonders, one horrifying and one fascinating. The bridge, there one minute and gone the next. It wasn't the biggest bridge and was never the sturdiest. Anyone crossing it could look down between the wooden planks and see the muddy river lolling beneath. But it was a bridge nonetheless, and such structures were supposed to be dependable. Trucks, people, and pigs relied on that bridge. It had no business collapsing. And if that bridge fell apart, what about the rest? Here they were in Pittsburgh, the little Venice, the city of bridges, with three healthy rivers. Mary Wohleber said there were more than five hundred in the city. What if they all just gave up, sighed, and shrugged themselves into the river? That was the horrifying part of the day.

"I was always afraid of bridges after that. Every time I would cross one, riding the bus or streetcar, I would just pray," says Margaret.

But then, this pig—this squat squealing pig destined for the packinghouse—becomes a hero. What a marvelous thing! And as a child you can't help but think the pig was put on that truck for a reason. God put it there and made sure it was good and strong to save that man. The other man, who drowned, well, he must not have prayed for help.

Hero pig, pig of mercy, aside, most kids growing up on Troy Hill lived in fear of pigs. Margaret was about six years old when her neighbor, an older woman, routinely sent her to the butcher's shop, which happened to be on the pigs' route. The pigs ran right past that shop, grunting and slobbering. She dreaded those trips. On her way she would whisper over and over, "Please, God, don't let it be time for the pigs. Please, God, don't let it be time for the pigs." In all things, she relied on God. *Please, Lord, get me across the bridge. Please, Lord, hold off the pigs.*

Joe was a sickly boy, plagued by asthma, bronchitis, and frail nerves. When he was about six, his mother mentioned to the doctor that she planned to send him to school. The doctor said that wasn't a good idea. His mother protested. "What about his cousins? They'll be ahead of him at Most Holy Name. He'll be left behind." Cousins the same age should be in the same grade. That was the natural order of things, the way things should go. His mother lived by the rules, whether the Golden Rule, the church rule, the school rule. Things should be done as they had been done. Forevermore.

The doctor hollered, "That boy is a wreck. Keep him back another year."

She did. Doctors, like priests, were esteemed. Each blessed with some special power—one, shepherd over the body; the other, over the soul. Ignore their advice and you might kill your child or yourself or go straight to hell.

Joe ended up in the same class as his brother Francis, who

was two years younger. Francis died of blood poisoning when he was fourteen years old. A wall in their home had caved in, and while he was helping to repair it, a dirty two-by-four cut Francis's leg. His leg began to swell. He was taken to the hospital, but died of the infection.

Margaret has a studio photograph of the two brothers standing next to each other on their First Holy Communion day. Joe is a full head taller than Francis, his black wavy hair slicked back. His eyes are huge, bulging as if the white starched collar and huge black bow at his neck are choking him. Any minute now and he will jump out of his sallow skin or faint. He and his brother are weighted down with accoutrements of the First Holy Communion. A tall white candle in one hand, a rosary and prayer book in the other. The more blessed things to hold, the more significant the day. On confirmation day, children aren't nearly as encumbered.

Joe isn't smiling. It was a holy, solemn occasion, and he was a holy boy, although he was never an altar boy like his brothers. He missed out on that rite and privilege of Catholic boyhood because he was sickly. Altar boys were the priest's right-hand men, and since the priest was the Lord's right-hand man, an altar boy must be only once removed from the Lord. At Communion, altar boys would position the little round gold plate beneath each person's chin. In case the host fell, they could catch it and be heroes. Such an important task could not be left to someone who might have a bronchitis attack and have to miss his Sunday obligation, stay at home, and inhale some smoky powder from a cup that looked like a chalice.

The nuns at Most Holy Name never thought he would make it out of school. Poor boy. People routinely died of pneumonia.

Only a matter of time, they thought. If by the grace of God he did graduate from grade school, he surely would never be able to do much.

Joe did graduate from eighth grade and later got a job at a local candy company. Most of his paycheck went to his parents. He spent his few remaining dollars on sheet music and music classes. He had been taking violin lessons since he was seven years old. After just a few notes, he could identify the name of a song coming from a music box, even if it was a jazzed-up, nearly unrecognizable version of a classic piece. His family couldn't understand it. Money was so scarce. Why not use what little you have for clothes or an occasional movie? But to him it was no sacrifice. Only those who shared the same passion for music could understand.

He belonged to a quartet of young fellows who played various instruments. One of the very first songs they mastered was "Over the Waves," the common title for the classic "Blue Danube." That was music. Joe was happy. Soon the other fellows began experimenting with popular music, and when they did, Joe refused and dropped out. The group disbanded. Why waste precious time on things that didn't last? Popular music doesn't last. Classical does. That's why they call it classical. He was so practical. His standards rigid and unwavering. Refusing to go along with the gang left him somewhat of a loner.

Margaret was a bit of a loner, too. Her older sister, Emma, was petite and graceful in all things. She tried to teach Margaret how to be ladylike and sociable, especially after their mother died, when Margaret was seventeen.

Emma would nudge her and whisper, "Don't sit off by yourself. Go on over with them."

Margaret wasn't interested. " 'If you think I want to be hanging on to a guy all day, you are badly mistaken. I want to be free.' My sister said I was supposed to be sociable. I tried. But I think she sort of gave up on me as far as being ladylike. I wanted to be me, you know?"

The lives of Margaret and Joe ultimately converged at Helen's house.

On Sunday nights, Joe's family got together with Helen's family. The young men knew each other from choir. The young women from Sodality.

Joe brought his violin. Helen's brother and sister played the guitar, and another brother, the harmonica. The men gathered around the piano and sang in four-part harmony. The women played cards in the kitchen. At the end of the night, they gathered at the dining-room table for pineapple upside-down cake. Helen's mother baked it in a cast-iron skillet and then upended it onto a milky white china plate so the circles of yellow fruit rested on top.

Margaret, being Helen's best friend and a music lover, was included. She remembered Joe from grade school. He was the kid who made her miss recess in Sister Hubertina's class.

Sister Hubertina had called on Joe to read out loud from the Bible history book. He read well but quietly, his face down. Margaret was on the other side of the room and could barely hear him. "That's enough, Joseph." Sister Hubertina pointed to Margaret, which meant Margaret was to continue. Margaret picked up where she thought Joe had left off. She was wrong.

The nun frowned and scolded her for not paying attention. Margaret was sentenced to her desk for recess. "I would think, 'Well I didn't get recess on account of that Joe Fichter.'"

Their friends realized they belonged to each other. Both were independent and loved music. Each had high values and standards. But they were a little shy. So Helen and the others in their gang had a plan. When the group went out for a walk, everyone held back, leaving Joe and Margaret ahead and alone together. Finally Joe had the nerve to walk Margaret home.

He sent her an Easter card. She was nineteen years old. She opened and read it. It was in German, which made it even more special, like a secret message to her. Not everyone, he knew, would be able to read and appreciate it. It was completely aboveboard. He could have sent it to an aunt or teacher. Outside were a few simple flowers. Inside, it read, "As the spring flowers are blooming over the fields and moon. May this Eastertide enrich your joyousness." He signed his name in the corner, "Joe." Not "Love, Joe." Just "Joe."

She ran and showed it to her father. He would be pleased, she knew. Her father was proud of his German heritage. Joe came from a good family and sang in the choir. After, she went to the store and bought Joe an Easter card, also in German.

Sometime around then, Joe began keeping a journal in a small black binder. Men didn't generally keep journals. Feelings and emotions were private things, barely acknowledged to themselves, let alone preserved on paper.

His few entries, written in pencil, are self-conscious and formal, as if recorded for someone other than himself. Taking the part of a narrator, he introduces and tries to explain himself, reviewing and evaluating his behavior and his feelings. That would be in keeping with him. An examination of conscience, deliberate like he was. He wouldn't write with abandon, no matter how private the pages. At times he is almost professorial, explaining the meaning of certain German syllables.

"Once upon a time I was alone, just a serious thinker not interested in anything enough from which to get much enjoyment. Life is just routine day in and day out. I had no one I could honestly call a true friend, perhaps my own fault. But to go out evenings and associate with anybody was not my idea of a good time.

"I did not care much about girls because there was a certain type of girl for whom I was looking and for whom I had decided to wait. She must be a good old-fashioned girl, must understand my ideas and disposition. There were girls in a crowd to which I belonged and I must say they were all good girls, but even in this crowd, I seemed to be alone. It seemed that my idea of a girlfriend was a little too different from what one could expect in these times. But I was set on waiting and wait I did, much to my happiness.

"There is a girl who when I was a kid in school I knew only as Emma Kunzmann's younger sister. Occasionally at evening services at church, I would see her enter. She was then a little girl with long dark curls. Well, this very girl was a member of our crowd at its beginning, but I must have been asleep to the fact that she was every bit and even more the type of girl I was waiting for.

"She is Gretchen as I sometimes think of her. For anyone reading this, and most not understanding the meaning of Gretchen, let me explain. Her name is really Margaret, but the

German language of which she and I are both very fond has the name for Margaret, which makes it endearing. It is Gretchen, which is often used when referring to girls who are called Marguerite. The use of *-chen* as a suffix to a German word causes it to become a word of admiration.

"Now, on with my story. It seems the starting point was a birthday party for one of the girls. Margaret was present at this gathering, which I might mention was held at our house. On this occasion, I teased her considerably... This crowd grew, keeping its original members. We met quite often for birthdays, and on Sunday evenings. When I think it over, I must have had an interest for Margaret from the time the crowd formed. If I recall correctly it was shortly after our organization that I took a liking to her, and I believe I even gave thought to the idea of having such a girl for a wife." Abruptly it ends there, as if he finally did it. He finally realized that this is the girl I want to marry. I've said it. I've written it. No need to go further.

One summer evening while Joe and Margaret were dating, they walked up to Mount Troy, the neighboring hilltop, to visit two of their girlfriends, who played guitar. The girls' mother said they were at an abandoned school down the road.

Joe and Margaret walked over. It was the middle of the Depression. Two families were living in the old school building because they had no other place to go. Sheets hung from ropes and nails, creating makeshift rooms, one for sleeping, one for living. Margaret doesn't remember what else they had, maybe a few boxes, stools, and mattresses. She doesn't recall names or numbers.

But this she remembers clearly: Everyone sat in a circle.

Margaret and Joe's two friends played their guitars. One by one each person was invited to sing or play a song. Joe and Margaret sang a duet, "Whispering Hope." They spent the evening singing and laughing. Walking home, the young couple felt exuberant and optimistic.

"We were uplifted. These people didn't have anything. They were so happy. They were filled with music. Money didn't mean much. They seemed so content. It just left us with a different feeling when we left that place," she says.

She looks back on that night so fondly. She and Joe were innocent and naive. They had no clue how life would treat them, about the grief and disappointments, the struggles and rewards of raising nine children, the sorrow at the death of their oldest son.

She's wiser now. Yet, when she thinks about it, she still believes it is true. "If you have love you can get through anything. Love and music. That's a good bond." That duet was their constant companion. After dinner, as Margaret washed the dishes and Joe dried them, they harmonized together.

It was conversation with a melody attached. Often the lyrics were in German. Their children might be able to catch a word or two, but only the two of them understood what was being said. Singing was a proper way, an acceptable way to express their love. Though the song was someone else's words, their voices gave it life.

Joe and Margaret had similar backgrounds. Both were raised in large, close-knit, working-class German Catholic families. Margaret's maternal and Joe's paternal grandmother were neighbors on Lowrie Street, by the orphanage.

But Joe and Margaret came from completely different households, which is apparent from two pages of Margaret's scrapbook. On one page Joe's parents sit facing each other in front of a fireplace. Joe's father wears a white shirt and tie. His legs are crossed. Joe's mother sits in an upholstered chair across from him, in a black dress. Her legs are not crossed. Women didn't cross their legs but kept them firmly planted on the ground. They are not smiling. American Gothic, minus the pitchfork, comes to mind. His toe could touch her leg if he extended it, but he dare not. They look cemented there.

On the opposite page is a small faded picture of Margaret's parents. They are outside at a farm, in a field, sitting on something that could have been a bale of hay, or tree stump, or chair. Her father's dungarees look worn by the sun and earth, as does her mother's light cotton dress. Her mother's arm is draped over his shoulder, as natural as if it were a leaf that floated down from some heavenly tree and came to rest there. They're smiling. There's no angst in their expression, no worry about being caught touching each other not only in public but in front of a camera, preserving that lark, that easiness, forever. The tiny square looks as if it drifted into the room, riding a hot summer breeze, landed on that page, and was thankfully glued into place before it had a chance to blow away again.

When she was little, Margaret remembers her dad teasing her mother. He pulled her down into his arms as she was walking to the kitchen. Margaret looked up. Her mother scolded her father, "Pete, the children."

After Margaret and Joe married and were living on the first floor of the Fichter family home, Joe's younger sister Dolly came downstairs and found Margaret sitting on Joe's lap. She

Margaret and Joe on their wedding day.

rushed upstairs to tell her mother. Seconds later Joe's mother came down to see for herself.

Families were larger forty and fifty years ago, and homes, smaller. Households had rules and routines—that or chaos. The Fichters had rules. Slamming doors was not permitted.

Doors have knobs. Use them, Joe told his children. Anyone who ran up the steps, or took two at a time, had to come back down and climb the steps properly.

The Fichter children began preparing for their father's arrival home from work at about four-thirty. The younger ones picked up cars, dolls, puzzle pieces, and cards, while the older ones swept the front walk. Chores done, they filed upstairs, where they took turns in the bathroom, washing their faces and combing their hair. Play clothes were hung up and dinner clothes put on.

They came down the steps, took one last look to make sure everything was in order, and walked down to the corner of Froman and Hatteras Streets. They sat on the front three steps of Helen the Cleaner's, which was also a front seat to commerce and activity.

Across the street, Barney Michael's Troy Hill Department Store carried hardware, gloves, and Communion dresses. Mrs. Michael, a wise businesswoman, would stage a little fashion show, bringing a few Communion dresses to the school so the girls could try them on for their mothers. On the other corner, a late-afternoon crowd gathered on the sidewalk in front of Fire Station No. 39.

The Fichter children sat on the steps, waiting for the Woodic bus, which took their father to and from work. Joe worked across the river in downtown Pittsburgh, in the Reymer Building on Fifth Avenue, by Murphy's Five-and-Ten. Inside the building was a fancy restaurant called Reymer's Tea Room. But Reymer's was best known for its chocolate candy and a concentrated lemon blend that came in jugs. Just add water.

It was the dawn of convenience, and no one could get

enough things like dryers, frost-free refrigerators, permanent press, and Reymer's Blennd, spelled with a double *n* to make it unique. A friend of Margaret's uncle Pete knew the recipe and when he was dying, people came to his bed and tried to pry it from him.

Joe worked in the shipping department. One of his jobs was to pack candy being sent by parents to their sons during World War II. Boys wrote home saying Reymer's candy held up. It wasn't broken and crushed. Joe was careful. What he did, he did well.

He took the bus every morning and every afternoon. No need for a car when you had the perfectly acceptable, perfectly reliable Woodic bus. At 6 P.M., the Woodic bus—with its long sleek hood, blue-and-white trim, and REAL LEMON IS GOOD on the side—rounded the corner and deposited Joe in front of his

children. Real Lemon was another of the marvelous conveniences. Every house had bottled Real Lemon in the refrigerator. A little splash keeps bananas from turning brown and gives apple pies tang.

Joe stepped off the bus and grinned. He had a large grin for such a small man. It occupied half his face; his thick black glasses occupied the other half. His ears dominated the sides of his head. At Halloween he and Margaret

The Fichter children on a Christmas card.

dressed up as the Pillsbury Doughboy and Little Bo Peep. Margaret told Joe to cover his ears or people would know who he was.

If the children were lucky, Joe carried a bag of employee mix—candy not good enough to be sold to the public because the chocolate coating missed a few peanuts. He loved chocolate as much as the kids, but only quality chocolate. He never got sick of it. That and cookies.

One day he brought home a tin box as big as a briefcase and the color of a new copper penny. It was sturdy and airtight, and too good to simply toss away. The white label on the lid read VEAL CUTLETS, a specialty at Reymer's Tea Room.

Over the years the box served many purposes. At one time Margaret kept thread and needles there. It eventually became the card box and remains so today, the veal cutlet label remaining, though faded. Actually, it's the first of two card boxes. One wasn't enough to hold all the cards that Joe sent to Margaret.

Margaret pulls out a small card, no bigger than the palm of her hand. It's the Easter card Joe sent Margaret in 1934. Once white, it now bears a rich ivory color.

From that holiday on, Joe bought Margaret a card. He marked not just the greater holidays of Christmas and Valentine's Day, but the lesser ones as well, such as the Epiphany and Saint Nicholas Day. After reading the card Margaret propped it open on the piano in the living room and left it until the holiday season was over. Then she took it down and put it inside the veal cutlet box.

On rainy days when her children were a little older and bored, they pleaded to look at the box of cards. Margaret pulled off the lid, and they sat on the floor going through them.

Each card took time to appreciate and explore. Her children could run their fingers over the smooth satin bows that gathered bouquets of roses on Valentine's Day, or the outlines of frilly lace Easter umbrellas.

One birthday card had a half dozen little books on the cover, each of which opened to a message. "May each chapter bring joys that are new to bless the years ahead of you." "Happy Birthday and wishing you the dearest joys life sends and happiness that never ends."

Inside, in the corner, Joe signed his name. Just "Joe" in the early ones. Later he wrote, "With my deepest love, Joe." For their wedding, he bought a card and wrote Margaret a note. "To the most wonderful girl in the world from the most happiest and most fortunate fellow in the world on our wedding date, September 8, 1937." They picked that date for two reasons. Margaret's parents were married on September 8 and it's the birthday of Mary the mother of Jesus. On that special day, prayers, which are traditionally recited at mass, are sung. Margaret and Joe wanted their ceremony filled with song. "You get the works because it's Mary's birthday," says Margaret.

After reading a half dozen cards, all the "Sweetheart," "Darling," "My love," "My dear," "Forever yours," messages seemed to blur for her children. What really stood out to them was when they turned the cards over to see how much their father spent.

"Dad spent a dollar on a card?!" This couldn't be the same Mr. Frugal they knew.

"Why stop for a cup of coffee, or ice cream, when we have it at home?" he routinely asked. Yet he must have marched right past the twenty-five-cent cards that essentially offered the same sentiment without satin bows, to the rows of three-dimensional, deluxe cards that cost seventy-five cents more. He shopped for them with deliberation, looking for the perfect one. Each had to have "To my dearest wife" on the cover or "From your loving husband." To the day he died, his big complaint was that he could no longer find New Year's cards that said, "To my wife."

Margaret told him, "You don't have to spend that much." But he did. He was allowed to indulge her, but she had a heck of a time buying anything for him for birthdays or anniversaries. "I don't need it," he'd say. He wasn't being a martyr. It never occurred to him to receive anything he didn't need.

He wouldn't even buy himself a hat. He had a pair of ear-muffs before he got married and lost them. Margaret finally got fed up and said, "If you don't buy yourself a hat, I will." So he went to the store and bought one. The next day, he was walking across the Thirty-first Street Bridge and the wind blew his brand-new hat into the river. That became a family joke. Joe would never say, "So there." The good Lord said it for him.

But for Margaret, he could and would indulge. And while purple lace on a card may not seem much of an indulgence, it was at the time—and through the times. With nine children, anything beyond necessity was extravagant. Even when he was between jobs after Reymer's closed, he bought her Valentine's Day and Easter cards that didn't just open but unfolded once or twice, with raised gold lettering that begged to be touched.

Cecilia, the youngest of the nine Fichter children, never considered her parents romantic. Not many children do. Parents exist solely as mother and father, to serve their sons and daughters. Romance, or the concept of husband and wife, isn't part of that picture.

In Cecilia's case it seemed even less so. By the time she was born, her father was forty-four and her mother was forty-two. They were staid and settled in their relationship. They were incredibly committed to each other and loved one another. She knew that.

If Margaret needed to make an elaborate table decoration for the Christian Mothers' dinner, she came home and told Joe about it. "What can I do to help?" he asked. They bowled at the Pines Bowling Lanes. Margaret was on one team. Joe was on another. In between their turns, they ran back and forth to cheer or moan. Margaret made the Fastnacht doughnuts. Joe delivered them. He grew tomatoes. She canned them. A friend told her, "You guys just mesh." Like something woven together, two separate reeds, one horizontal and the other vertical. Together they make one thing. Alone they are just two sticks.

But none of that seemed romantic. Just comfortable. They called each other Boots. How romantic was that?

Her father was cautious and predictable, especially when it came to his children dating. "Make sure you know what you're doing," he warned again and again. "Will this last?" "Don't rush into things." If Cecilia had a date the first question was "Is he Catholic?"; the second, "What's his family like?"

She sat in the living room and rolled her eyes as he lectured her dates about long hair, dungarees, and staying out past 11 P.M. "What could be open that late?" he questioned, both rhetorically and literally. Her brothers gave one of her dates— her dad's favorite—the nickname Briefcase because he was so conservative. "This should be safe," she envisioned him think-ing. "Here is a person who acts like he's sixty."

Affection seemed ritualized and practiced. Parents kiss each other before leaving home and upon returning. Children kiss parents before going upstairs to bed, which follows putting on pajamas, brushing teeth, and saying prayers. Things were in order, in order to make sense. That's how Germans do it. One of her closest friends was Italian. In that house, people hugged and kissed everyone without a schedule.

Even the holiday cards seemed prescribed. Those sanc-tioned sentiments delivered in third-party verse were expected like candles on a birthday cake.

It didn't dawn on Cecilia until later, when she was an adult living on her own and giving talks on relationships, that not every father or husband did the same. Some wives or husbands or girlfriends or boyfriends would give anything for one year's worth of those cards, let alone fifty-six.

The importance of that rite, the love and romance that gave it life and nurtured it, only came clear when her father was dying.

Joe was diagnosed with congestive heart failure in the spring of 1992. He finished the bowling season that spring but thereafter simply went to watch Margaret play. Most of the time, he dozed off, but he was always behind her. Over the next two years, his body began to swell and he had problems breathing.

By October 1993 he had to wheel a little oxygen cart around with him wherever he went. Sweetest Day is in October. Half the world has never heard of Sweetest Day. A greeting-card company invented it as a way to boost sluggish autumn sales.

But Joe knew it existed and had been giving Margaret a card every year for Sweetest Day.

One particular evening, Margaret needed to go to the North Hills shopping mall. Joe wanted to go. Molly went along to keep her dad company on a bench while Margaret shopped. After Margaret left to run her errands, Joe told Molly that he wanted to buy Margaret a Sweetest Day card. He wheeled his little cart from one card shop to another in the mall. Molly was at his side. None of them had a Sweetest Day card, or even a trace of one, such as an empty Sweetest Day rack. Molly wondered.

"Finally I looked at him and I said 'Are you sure that it's not in September?'" says Molly. It was like asking Santa if he was sure about December 25. Joe had bought dozens of the cards over the years. He was sure. Out of luck, but sure.

On the way home, Margaret had to stop at Kuhn's supermarket. "I'll only be a minute," she told them. Joe was too sick to go in and said he would wait in the car. Molly went with Margaret and decided to take a quick look at the card aisle, which was at the very back of the store. There she found three Sweetest Day cards. She memorized the verses on each and ran out to the car.

"Dad, they have those cards in there," she told him, and then proceeded to describe the types of flowers on the front and recite the verses inside. When she was done, she looked at him and said, "Now which one do you want?"

"'Never mind, I'm going in and I'll get it myself,'" Molly says he told her. "He could hardly breathe and walk. It took him forever to walk from the entrance to the back of the store, but he had to pick that card."

It wasn't that he was being stubborn. If he was, she says, she would have insisted, in delicate terms, or even not-so-delicate terms, that he be reasonable. She couldn't say, "It doesn't make a difference if I pick out the card, or if you do," because it made all the difference.

"He had to do it. It was one of the last things that we could possibly do was to allow him to do that. And he was carrying his tank of oxygen," she says.

In the following months, he grew weaker and could not make it out to the stores at all. As each holiday approached, he pulled one of his children aside. He took out his wallet, describing carefully what he wanted. He refused to let them pay for it. It had to be from him.

His children picked Margaret's birthday card, her Thanksgiving card, her Saint Nicholas Day and Christmas and New Year's cards. Cecilia was ready to relax after New Year's Day, counting on a hiatus in the card-giving season. Then she remembered Valentine's Day.

She later wrote about this card and her father's final days in a moving letter that she gave to her brothers and sisters. "Never one to be late and ever conscious of his tenuous hold on life, Dad began planning for Valentine's Day in mid-January. He was so afraid, as the days slipped one into another, he might forget or miss this all-important holiday. One evening, late in January, he called me aside and commissioned me to buy Mom's Valentine's card. I was given explicit instructions. It must say, "To my wife" or "From your husband," printed on the face of the card. There was to be no doubt as to whom this was for or whom it was from.

"Dad shared these specifications with me as if I had never seen any other cards he had sent to Mom during my thirty-eight years of existence. What I knew as the top-of-the-piano greeting card ritual was an intensely private communication."

She bought four Valentine's Day cards and brought them home for her father to pick the one he liked. It has flowers on the cover. "For my wife, with love . . . Life is beautiful for those who share love." The bottom unfolds. Up pops a three-dimensional garden of paper flowers.

Inside it reads: "I just wanted to tell you thanks for sharing and caring, and most of all for your love. Happy Valentine's Day." He wrote "Marge" on the envelope, but that exhausted him. He never got to sign "Love, Joe" on the inside.

The night before Valentine's Day, Cecilia, Molly, Margaret, and Joe sat down to watch the classic movie *An Affair to Remember*. A friend dropped it off as a birthday gift. Joe was turning eighty-two February 18.

It couldn't be a more romantic movie. Cary Grant and Deborah Kerr meet on an ocean liner. They were both engaged to others but, over sunsets and pink champagne, fall in love.

As the ship prepares to dock, their betrotheds waiting anxiously on the dock, Cary and Deborah vow to meet in six months on the 102nd floor of the Empire State Building.

The six months pass. They have broken off their engagements. Cary, a painter, is finally selling some of his work and figures he will be able to support Deborah.

She rushes to meet her intended. Anxiously gazing up at the Empire State Building, she doesn't see an oncoming car. Cary Grant is waiting on the 102nd floor, unaware that Deborah is lying in the street below. He stays until midnight and then, dejected, leaves. Deborah Kerr ends up in the hospital, her legs crushed, unable to walk. She doesn't call him to explain, hoping to get back on her feet before contacting him. Finally, he tracks her down and goes to her apartment. She sits on the couch, reading a book, her maimed legs covered by an afghan. She doesn't mention the accident and seems rather cold and distant. He is disgusted and begins walking away.

At the doorway he turns around and tells her about a woman who went into a studio and fell in love with a portrait of Deborah Kerr that he had painted. The studio owner called him to tell him the woman was interested but couldn't afford it and, furthermore, was in a wheelchair. Go ahead, give it to the pathetic soul, Cary told him.

As Cary is relaying this conversation, it apparently dawns on him that the poor invalid was none other than his precious Deborah Kerr. He comes to her side, kneeling on the floor. She grabs his hand and kisses it. Tearfully, she tells him, "If you can paint, I can walk."

The movie ended. Cecilia sighed, turned to all, and said, "Wasn't that romantic?"

"No," her father told her. "It was just dumb."

His unexpected response floored her. After going through the card-buying ritual, she was convinced he was romantic after all. Then he says Cary Grant and Deborah Kerr are unromantic and dumb. Well, she thought, I was right all along. "Where is the man who bought mushy valentines? How could he not think true love romantic? Ever the storyteller, he patiently explained it to me. True to his style, this part took longer than the movie," Cecilia wrote.

Her father told her that Cary Grant and Deborah Kerr had wasted precious time carefully weighing the odds instead of taking the risk to love.

" 'If they knew they were in love all along, why didn't they do something about it? It wasn't romantic to play it safe,' " he told Cecilia.

"It was incredibly sad as I listened to this man who had been married to our mother for more than half a century and knew that as good and plentiful as it had been, it would never be enough.... His message was simple: 'Don't waste it, don't be afraid to love.' "

That night he told Cecilia something she had not heard before, though she'd heard dozens of stories over the years of how her parents had met and courted.

He and Margaret had been dating only a short time when he had the nerve to ask her whether she was interested in him. "If you are not serious about this, then I'll move on," he told Margaret.

Cecilia recalls, "I was, like, 'You? Mr. Cautious?' He said, 'Well, yeah. I knew what I wanted, and if she wasn't interested, then I would just have to move on.' "

Joe once told Cecilia that he wouldn't know what he would do if Margaret died before him. It wasn't so much the fear of being alone as the fear of being without her. His strength lay with her. Retirement was such a joy because they could spend more time together. Margaret played volleyball at the senior center. Helen Steinmetz was always there, too. Joe went once after he retired. His fingers got smashed, and he didn't want to go anymore. Margaret didn't want to go without him. He had nightmares about going back to work.

Cecilia stopped by on occasion to see if Margaret wanted to go shopping. When Cecilia left the room, Joe would come over and whisper to Margaret, "Can I come, too?"

At one point Joe was in intensive care. Cecilia, her mother, and her sister Marge, who is a nurse, went to visit. They were allowed in for only a few minutes. During that time, her father talked to all of them, but it became clear through his tone, expression, and focused gaze on Margaret, that he was really only talking to her. Cecilia felt like a voyeur. As their grown child, she thought she knew everything about her parents. But she saw something different.

He was explaining what the nurses had said and done. "It wasn't that he was saying anything that he didn't want my sister or me to hear. It was just very clear that he needed to talk to my mother. It wasn't meant for us. That's when I thought that, as public and open as they are, they have something very private."

She was able to see their relationship, their love for one another, as theirs alone. She and her brothers and sisters were a part of it. But her parents had something independent of the children and independent of the children's interpretation of them as parents. Yes, they were parents and grandparents. But above all, they were a couple who loved each other dearly.

Joe came home. Margaret and Molly set up a hospital bed in the living room. Cecilia stopped by the house on her way home from work. One time Joe wanted to get out of bed and into the wheelchair. Usually her mother, or Cecilia's sister or niece, both of whom are nurses, handled those things. Give Cecilia a grocery list, the vacuum cleaner, a dinner menu. Those she could handle.

But she was the only one in the room when he needed help. So by default she helped him up. It was a struggle.

"I thought to myself, How does my mother do this? because it was hard. I was saying things like 'I won't drop you, I won't hurt you.' He was real, real cool about it, but I could also tell he was thinking, Oh no. I have this person, who is clueless, helping me." She laughs.

A while later she watched her mother do the same thing. Margaret is hardly frail, but she is small and at the time, in 1994, was seventy-nine years old. Given the circumstances, she was also probably physically and emotionally weary.

Although Joe wasn't very big, either, he was bigger than she was, and his body was swollen with fluids. Lifting him should have been awkward. But it was smooth, almost fluid or musical. They moved in practiced harmony. They meshed.

"It was the trust factor. He trusted exactly what she was telling him and what she would do. They had this rhythm that was really part of their relationship. There was something about it," Cecilia says.

Margaret thought Joe would pull through. Though he was largely confined to the hospital bed beginning in December 1993, she got him up and dressed every day but the last two.

"They said he wasn't going to get better, but I was in denial. I just thought it couldn't happen. I watched the diet. The doctor even commented that the swelling was going down in his ankles and knees."

A priest, who had visited Joe throughout his illness, saw him in those last few weeks and told Margaret that he was ready to die. "My stomach went all over the place when he told me that. I thought that can't be. I thought this is a bad dream and I'm going to wake up. But I didn't wake up."

It didn't seem fair, she told the priest. "I thought we would grow old together. And he said, 'You are old.' And I said, 'We are not old.'" Codgers are old. The maid that everyone tries to get rid of when playing cards—that prune-faced lady with glasses and a boxy black hat—now, *that* lady is old.

Joe fought death. He didn't want to leave her alone, but it was getting to be so painful. The pastor of Most Holy Name was sitting in Margaret's kitchen. He told her that some people need to be told it is OK to die. Especially someone like Joe, who was always seeking permission and wanting to do the right thing.

"Joe didn't want to let go. He held on," Margaret says.

On February 24, Joe was dying. Margaret, Molly, and Cecilia were at his side. Cecilia wrote about those final hours in her letter.

"Hours before he died, I had the privilege to stand by with Molly as he asked Mom to pray for him. I watched him struggle out of his morphine haze to tell her he loved her and to smile as he called her Boot.

"Mom prayed, sang, and told Dad he was her first and only love. They held hands as she told him they had traveled as far as they could together and it was OK for him to leave her. I wasn't there to see Dad die. Mom and Molly tell us his last hour was torturous.

"Mercifully his final moment was peaceful. Arriving shortly thereafter I saw a wondrous look of serenity on his face, illuminating a life well loved. This is my gift I will carry with me always. It's not the only one I received. As a member of this family, I have been given a share in the legacy of love."

He died that day. Cecilia calls her father's sickness and dying, though painful and sorrowful, "one of the most graced experiences I think that I have ever had."

Margaret and Molly found a poem that Joe wrote before he and Margaret married.

> *You are to me a sweetheart*
> *Like no other has known.*
> *You will make for me*
> *What I will always probably call home.*
>
> *You are always in my thoughts dear,*
> *Regardless of where I am,*
> *But to make you a happy angel*
> *Will always be my plan.*
>
> *There is only one such sweetheart*
> *Who is so loyal, true blue,*
> *And I know who this sweetheart is,*
> *Gretchen, only you.*

When Joe was sick, he sat on the couch and listened to music. Margaret washed the dishes, cleaned, and baked. Sometimes he would look up and see her. "Come in and sit with me," he said.

She did. They held hands on the couch and sang in harmony. He took the bass. She took soprano. Music soothed his soul.

"When he was singing, he was a different person. He was relaxed," Margaret says. "We sang till the very end, 'How Can I Leave Thee, How Can I From Thee Part.'"

Margaret tries to translate the song from memory. She is so accustomed to singing it in German that she needs to see the words to figure the English equivalent. She goes upstairs to get an old German songbook. The binding is gone. Pages are simply stacked between the front cover and the back.

After glancing down at the words, Margaret closes her eyes to translate. With her eyes still closed, she tells the story of the song. She doesn't sing it. Its melody belongs to German words. In song, the abrupt "*Ach, wie ist's möglich dann*" has no beginning or end. It flows.

"How can I leave thee? How can I from thee part?" She stops. "That is the first line," she says. She is instructing, not singing. Without Joe, it is words and notes.

"Thou only hast my heart, Dear One, believe. Thou hast this soul of mine so closely bound to thine, No other can I love, Save thee alone."

Again she stops. "Can you believe we sang that?" she asks, surprised that either of them found the strength physically and emotionally to sing such a song when Joe was dying. Maybe it just seems so sad in retrospect. At the time, they were singing and filling their home with a beautiful song.

She and Molly sing. She sings with her children. She sings with the choir. But the harmony, the voice answering, matching and following hers, is gone. "That is what I miss now. Even to the very end we would sing and harmonize, and I have nobody to harmonize with now. Sometimes the days just seem to, you know..." She trails off.

A few months after Joe died, Margaret went into a greeting card store. Rows of cards bearing "To my husband," "To my sweetheart," "To my love," brought her to tears.

"I really thought I was doing well and I just broke down," she told her daughter.

"There's nothing wrong with that. You are doing well," her daughter told her.

People assume it's easier for an older woman to be a widow than for a younger woman. And in certain respects it is. Margaret doesn't have to worry about sending children to college, or paying their health care. She doesn't have to go out and get a job, or a better paying one.

Then, too, older women have often lost both parents and in-laws. Margaret and Joe's oldest son died suddenly of an aneurysm. Older women see their friends lose husbands. They should be prepared, especially if their husband has been sick. The insurance plans have been reviewed, cemetery plots bought, and wills finalized.

But nothing, she says, can prepare for the loss of a partner and best friend. It can't be explained. "He was my pal. We did everything together," she says. "I miss the dumb things we did with each other." They were shopping at a mall when they passed a display of papier-mâché bunnies that looked as solid as concrete. "We looked at them, we stared at them, we walked past, we went back. And we splurged. We each bought a bunny for each other," she says. "We really didn't need these things, but this was only a couple of years ago, we could do it then." Joe and Margaret were tickled every Easter when they set the little bunny couple on the porch.

Every year for thirty years, she and Joe went to Saint Emma's, a retreat for married couples. Faith was something they openly shared. They didn't withdraw to a tiny dark space between folded hands, locking out the other with closed eyes. There were times for private and silent prayer, but faith was an integral part of their relationship, adding another dimension so complex and evolving that Margaret and Joe were always in a state of discovery. They came back from Saint Emma's energized.

The year after Joe died, Margaret went to Saint Emma's alone. A nun asked her a couple of times, "Are you OK?"

The nine Fichter children.

"I'm fine," Margaret answered. She would go outside and take a walk and say the rosary. "I would just pretend that he was going along with me. I thought, *Well, this is where we were.*" Still, it was hard being with all those couples and not having Joe at her side. As much as she wanted it to be the same, it wasn't and never would be. After that she decided to go to special retreats for widows.

Margaret remains connected to Joe. Not just in the ritualistic and formal sense of visiting the cemetery, planting tulips in the fall, bringing fresh pussy willows up in the late winter. But daily as well. There isn't a minute of the day that she doesn't think of him. They cleaned, cooked, and shopped together.

She told Helen she was talking to Joe recently. "'Well, I said to Joe, 'You *have* to do this,'" Margaret told her.

Helen looked at her and replied, "You don't let that man rest."

CHAPTER FOUR

The Sound of Bells

THE BELL OF MARY rings slowly this Wednesday morning, its clear, deliberate toll rising from the corner of Claim and Harpster Streets, where Most Holy Name Church sits, and spreading down the streets, through the yards, and into the narrow open windows of the homes on Troy Hill. It is one of five bells in the belltower of Most Holy Name, each inscribed with its own name and purpose. The largest bell, with the deepest tone, is Jesus. He rings before mass on Sunday.

The bells of Saint Joseph and Saint Aloysius ring together at noon and 6 P.M. Years ago, upon hearing those bells, Catholic children dropped their jacks or hopped off their bikes, ran into the house, and said a prayer, called the Angelus, before dashing back out. To this day, when those bells ring, some people look up from their books, turn off their sweepers, or dry their hands and begin, "The angel of the Lord."

It takes a practiced ear to notice the difference between the bells' chimes, but those who recognize Mary's call know there is a funeral mass on Troy Hill at Most Holy Name Church this morning. Dolly Fichter, Margaret's sister-in-law, is being buried today.

This is the second time in days that Mary has rung for the Fichter family. Last week, Margaret's brother-in-law Paul Fichter died. The week has been exhausting for Margaret and the entire Fichter family.

Paul and Joe were close. Joe had watched out for his little brother. Paul, eleven years younger, idolized his big brother. When Joe and Margaret were married but still living in the Fichter homestead, Paul spent much of his free time downstairs with them and their young children. At dinner, his mother would open the door and yell down the steps, "Paul, come on home."

Paul was in the army during World War II. Margaret baked him cakes and cookies. Joe carefully wrapped them and shipped them off. All the men in his unit huddled around lucky Paul when the legendary goodies arrived, fresh and intact. One Christmas, Margaret and Joe sat down with their four oldest children, rehearsed Christmas carols, and cut a record. At the end, the children shouted sweetly, "Merry Christmas, Uncle Pauly." It took him a year to find a record player, but he didn't give up until he did.

In 1944, while stationed in the Gilbert Islands, Paul wrote Margaret and Joe a letter. "It just came to my mind that today is February 18, which means that another milestone has passed in your life, Joe. Being that it's your birthday, I thought I'd write both of you a few lines to leave you know that I'm thinking about you. Joe, as long as I've known you, all I can say is that you've been one of my best pals and you're a fellow that I'm proud to be able to call my brother. . . . Wishing you loads of luck, health, and happiness, and may God bless all of you. Your loving brother, Paul." At the time, he was twenty-one, the age when many young men disavow sentimentality in the name of masculinity.

It was a simple letter, not very long or particularly poetic. But Joe and Margaret were touched. Paul was a lot like Joe. Both were sensitive, sweet guys. Joe had kept the letter. Margaret's son stumbled across it just a few days before Paul died among some of his father's papers. Margaret was struck by the timing. Her son brought it with him to the funeral. Margaret then made copies and gave them to her children, proud of the tribute to their father and their uncle.

Paul died of congestive heart failure, as had Joe. Margaret and Molly visited and brought him Communion while he was in the hospital. They watched as his ankles swelled up in the same way as Joe's. They heard the familiar prognosis from the doctors. Watching him die brought back many of Margaret's memories of Joe dying; it was draining. Then, to have Dolly die. Dolly never married and had lived all but the last year of her life in the Fichter homestead with her brother Bill, now the only living member of the Fichter family. It was Dolly who saw Margaret sitting on Joe's lap and went running to tell her mother. One of Margaret's daughters has Dolly's wooden sled.

A year ago, Dolly went to live in the nursing home where Molly works. One day Dolly would be feeling good and the next day, bad. Lately, though, she had been doing well. Her favorite nurse and the nurse's children came with peanut-butter pie for a long-awaited visit. That very weekend, Dolly died.

With a big family, chances are higher that a brother and sister might die within a short period of time as they grow older. But two in one week, and at a relatively young age? Dolly was only seventy-one and Paul seventy-five. That seemed unfair. Anyone who knew the Fichters would privately say so. They had so little time to grieve one loss before having to face another. The family, though, is more prosaic. It's the Lord's will that on this sunny but windy and cool morning the bell of Mary sounds for Dolly. If she were here, Dolly would agree. Just before she died she told the pastor, "I'm ready to go." She had no fear. She had faith that she had lived a good life and would not be forgotten. Her blessings, she believed, would continue.

The corner where the church sits is known to long-timers, who have walked every street and just about every foot of this hill, as the windiest on Troy Hill. A thin purple ribbon circling a wreath of tangled grapevines on the church door flutters wildly. Across the street two concrete geese stand steadfast, impervious to the wind, although the blue-flowered dress on one goose billows. Her partner wears a sturdy raincoat and rain hat that don't budge. The geese change outfits regularly. When they do, churchgoers nudge each other, point, and smile.

Dolly's friends and neighbors begin arriving twenty minutes before the 10 A.M. service, wishing some quiet time. One woman lights a candle at the feet of Mary.

Most of them arrive alone, passing through the side and front doors, which close firmly behind them from the weight and wind. They walked the handful of blocks from their homes. Those who live at the far end of the hill, or who have bad knees, take the bus. They don't make arrangements to meet and come together. They come on their own for Dolly. Nor is it necessary to call and ask, "Are you going?" They know they will see one another. Nearly all are older women. One woman, baby-sitting for her working daughter, rocks her three-month-old granddaughter, who has fallen asleep, the infant's tender pink cheek resting on a blanket draped over her grandmother's shoulder.

Many served on a church committee, which is why and how they know Dolly. Their paths crossed and merged within these walls or down the street in the rectory, the chapel, or the chapel gift store. Dolly spent more time in these places than she did at home it seemed. Cecilia and Loretta Guehl slip into one row quietly and are joined by Thelma Wurdock. Dolly and Cecilia served on the Saint Anthony Chapel committee. Thelma lives across the street from Dolly and Bill's house. They exchanged good-mornings across the blacktopped street.

Dozens of friends fill the front left-hand side of the church. That is where Dolly sat, too, among them. At one point the priest points to her pew, saying that was her place. No one sits in her spot now because it is Dolly's place and because they have their own. After placing their purses on the wooden bench, those who can kneel do so. All bow their heads. When they finish their silent private prayers, they sit back, fold their hands, and look up. Purple cloths drape the altar. A yellow banner reading COME FOLLOW ME hangs to the right of the altar.

Ernestine Hepp, eighty-seven, kneels down. A chiffon scarf circles her head and gathers in a snug knot under her chin. She unties it and puts it in her purse. Resting in the bottom of her raincoat pocket is a silver rosary. She reaches in, pulls it out. Her daughter, Annamae Ubinger, bought it in Rome. "It was blessed by the Pope," she says when anyone comments on it. She has never been to Rome. She has been to Cleveland to visit her sister Bernadette Shurman and has made several trips to the East Coast for baptisms and First Communions of grand- and now great-grandchildren. At last count she had about thirty grandchildren and forty great-grandchildren.

Ernestine didn't serve on any committees with Dolly or work in the rectory. She was and is a homebody. But having lived here all her life, she knows the Fichter family and just about everyone else on the hill. "I was born and raised here and will die here," she says resolutely. Any death touches her in some way, directly or indirectly. She went to Paul's funeral last week. Paul's daughter and son-in-law live next door. Dolly was a familiar face at church.

When a friend or a neighbor, or even any of their relatives, dies, Ernestine bakes for the family. Last week she baked apple pie for Paul's family. For Dolly she made a batch of pizzelles, thin, pale yellow anise cookies that look like snowflakes and melt in your mouth. Pizzelles are her specialty. She parcels them out to visitors, friends, grandchildren, and children, layering them carefully between sheets of waxed paper in round sturdy metal tins, labeled with a piece of masking tape: BELONGS TO GRANDMA HEPP.

"I like doing something for neighbors," she says. It seems that at precisely those moments when others feel helpless, Ernestine quietly appears with some small offering. For her bed-bound friend who lives on the street behind her, she made stuffed peppers. She calls the woman to talk, and visits on Sundays after church, doing the work of the Ladies of Charity, though not officially a member. The day a cousin came home from the hospital, she walked a pot of chicken soup five blocks to the woman's home, even though the temperature that February morning was twenty degrees.

Margaret stands in the choir loft at the back of the church. She belongs there, rather than below with her children. Singing is the best gift she can offer her sister-in-law. Music should accompany the soul to heaven, she thinks; the soprano lifting it, the bass supporting it. Were Joe alive, he would be there, too, a few seats away with the rest of the basses, singing "Gentle Woman," which Dolly was, according to all who knew her. Strong but gentle.

Family members fill the right side of the church. Dolly had fifty nieces and nephews. She remembered each on their birthdays, sending a Peanuts birthday card signed Aunt Dolly. Margaret's three sons, two from Virginia and one from Cleveland, returned this week for their aunt's funeral. They made the same trip last week for their uncle's service. Margaret and Molly had changed the sheets on the beds and put fresh towels out. Her sons are pallbearers. Her daughters read prayers. Molly distributes Communion.

Margaret is proud of how her children help without being asked. Once, Margaret was on a weekend retreat when a neighbor died. Her children, though young then, knew they should do something, so they pulled one of Margaret's cakes out of the freezer and gave the frozen square to the family. To this day, Margaret doesn't know if it was frosted.

The night before the funeral, they divvied up dishes for the luncheon to be held after the funeral in the church basement. Margaret doesn't want anyone driving home on an empty stomach. Besides, sharing a meal is comforting. Margaret made the rigatoni.

Cecilia approaches the lectern to deliver her aunt's eulogy. She is a poised and gifted speaker. She graduated with two majors. Someone must have once mentioned to Margaret that when mothers have children later in life, those children aren't as smart. Baloney. "I don't know how much smarter she could have gotten," Margaret often says of Cecilia.

Cecilia speaks slowly and deliberately, with quiet emotion, which would be like her father. The fact that she can stand before a crowd and speak with confidence, though, is more like her mother. As a young girl, Cecilia tagged along to Christian Mothers' meetings. Margaret was president of the organization. Cecilia, her hair in braids, sat at a little desk and colored. Her mother stood at the front table and ran things.

Her aunt Dolly could be a take-charge person, too. She marched into the pastor's office and organized his desk, which he says has been in disarray since Dolly left. If Dolly spotted a single wrinkle on a banner or altar cloth, she insisted, "You can't hang that up. There are wrinkles in it." Then, she remained in the church until midnight ironing. Carrying a small knife in her hand, she walked around the altar scraping up bits of wax that had fallen from candles to the carpet and floor, and dropped the scraps into a bag. An African priest, assigned to Most Holy Name parish, was trying to learn English. In the evenings, Dolly paged through magazines, cutting out a picture of a monk and a monkey to show him the difference.

Dolly was always busy. People can be busy at things but flit from one thing to another, flitting being both the end and the means, neither grounded in purpose. Dolly, though, was motivated by something profoundly personal, a devotion to her church and, by extension, the people belonging to it.

Everyone knew her. Her brother Bill placed a full-page ad in the Saint Anthony Festival booklet in her memory. No one had to wonder who she was or what she looked like, or who Bill was. All were touched. Her friends remember the weeks before she went into the nursing home. They saw her at church and thought, Oh dear, Dolly doesn't look good, and kept her silently in their prayers. They didn't mention it to others or discuss probable maladies. They wouldn't want someone else dissecting their skin tone. Why do it to others?

At the end of the funeral, as the casket is being carried out, Margaret and the choir sing "How Great Thou Art." After, Margaret tells a friend how the choir sang the same song at Joe's funeral. While it did, her children flashed slides of his photographs of new blossoms and his children sleeping. He would carefully stack jars of Margaret's homemade grape jelly on a round table, creating a beautiful, simple still life, and take a picture.

While the family attends a short service at the cemetery on Mount Troy, three of the nine members of the bereavement committee gather in the basement of the church hall to prepare for the luncheon. Metal-legged folding tables stand in four rows, covered with white plastic tablecloths. Positioned perfectly in the middle of each table is a tall milky vase holding a single red carnation. Remembering her grandmother's words, Margaret wanted to make sure the tables look nice.

Two front tables are filled with Margaret's rigatoni, her children's seven-layer salad, tuna fish salad, and pasta salad. Ernestine's pizzelles sit on the dessert table.

The bereavement committee doesn't cook. Members brew the coffee and put the food out so it's ready when the family returns from the cemetery. They replenish the coffeepot, cream, and sugar, and clean up. The committee also visits grieving relatives at home. Cecilia Guehl stands by the sixty-cup coffeepot. Her sister Loretta has gone home. Yet, if you ask anyone which of the two sisters would be more comfortable in the kitchen, the answer would be Loretta. Cecilia would starve if she had to cook for herself, and says as much. Loretta cooks. Cecilia washes the dishes. They make a good team.

Cecilia isn't a member of the bereavement group, but she was close to the Fichter family and wanted to help. She stands quietly at her place. Other members stand in the kitchen. When the pile of napkins begins to dwindle, one woman quickly replenishes it.

After the family has gone through the line, Cecilia and the other workers fix plates for themselves and sit at a table by the door.

Last week, they attended the funeral of an eighteen-year-old from Troy Hill who died in an airplane crash. They met at the funeral home and said the rosary. One woman sent a sympathy card on behalf of the committee and the church. Though only three years old, the group was cited for outstanding voluntary efforts by Catholic Charities. This year alone, they have assisted sixty families in the parish. After mass on All Souls' Day, the day set aside to pray for those who have died, the bereavement committee hosts a social with sweet rolls and coffee.

A less formal support group works quietly on the backstreets of Troy Hill. In the morning, many of these women read the obituaries. If a neighbor dies, they alert others. The news is spread in a considerate way, so each person can respond by either baking a pie or finding a piece of stationery to write a note of comfort. They arrive at front doors with roasts and homemade soups. They pass the news because they themselves would want to know. It would bother them to find out that someone had died and they didn't have a chance to attend the service. All have suffered loss and know the importance of being there for each other. One eighty-five-year-old woman attended the wake of the eighteen-year-old boy simply because her daughter had taught him in school and said he was such a fine young man.

On some streets, a woman goes door-to-door, knocking to see if anyone is home and whether they would like to donate a dollar to buy flowers. Beautiful bouquets arrive at the funeral home bearing cards that read "From the neighbors" or "From your friends on Brabec Street." Even if they didn't know the family well, they contribute. Their fathers or mothers might have been close friends.

Recently, a woman in her seventies died. She never married, had few family members, and was very independent. She belonged to Grace Lutheran Church, and was always behind some church dinner or school reunion, or working at the church's Red Door thrift shop. She had been seriously ill for about a year and knew she was dying, but kept it largely to herself. Others could see she was failing and tried to reach out to her. She refused much help, saying she could manage. It frustrated them at times.

Before she died, she arranged a small and private service. But her friends didn't want to let her go uncelebrated and decided to hold a memorial. Flyers were posted in the church and thrift shop. They printed a four-page program. Miss Bowen, her fifth-grade and Sunday-school teacher came. Most walked, carrying folding umbrellas in case they got caught in the downpour expected later that afternoon. A few women who knew her only from shopping at the Red Door sat off to the side of the church. At the service, friends approached the microphone and eulogized her, telling stories of how she told off the mayor once.

Several of the church members baked marble cakes. Before the service, they cut the cakes and set the pieces on a long table in the downstairs community room. Red punch waited in a fancy glass bowl. At the close of the service, the minister invited everyone downstairs.

One woman took home an extra program for a friend who was out of town. It listed all the songs and readings. Psalm 90 was included. "Teach us to number our days, that we may apply our hearts unto wisdom." The friend was grateful. Instinctively they know that such seemingly small acts hold great value. It doesn't take much to be generous.

Years ago, Margaret Fichter was singing the funeral mass for an older woman who'd died. Margaret knew the woman's daughter was in the hospital and couldn't attend the service. So Margaret brought a small tape recorder and asked the priest to speak loudly. The daughter was so touched as she listened to the priest talk about her mother and the choir's glorious songs. She could even hear the clang of the incense burner.

Most of the Fichters have finished eating their lunches. Toddlers prance on the linoleum floor, fall, push themselves up, and prance again. Adults linger over white Styrofoam plates with a remnant of a roll or a small piece of lettuce, drinking another cup of coffee. It could be any family reunion, a graduation, or First Communion party.

Margaret gets up and begins walking around, visiting tables and telling people to take seconds if they want.

She introduces family members to friends. Two sons are sitting next to each other. "This is Bill. He lives in Cleveland. This is Ed. He's from Virginia." They each nod and say hello. Bob is with Cathy Trimble, her fifth child. Bob drove in from Virginia, too. They come for their aunt and their uncle, but perhaps more for their mother.

Ed wrote Margaret a letter for Mother's Day. His own young son had gone to bed, expecting his uniform to be washed, his lunch packed, his gear together. It struck Ed how often his parents had done these same things and more for him. Margaret packed a half dozen lunches, remembering who liked peanut butter, who liked mayonnaise, or mustard, or butter. Each child was assigned a lunch spot. One on each side of the piano, one on the edge of the table, one in the middle.

Like most children, it seems, Ed waited until bedtime to mention that he desperately needed something for school the next day. Chances are, his brothers and sisters did the same. Nine kids. *Mom, Dad, I need this.* Margaret would tell them, "I'm not a magician," yet she always came through. The next morning, whatever they needed was there.

"Countless times I went to bed with things left to do only to wake up and find that you had mended a shirt or packed a lunch, or Dad had rummaged through the basement to find something that I needed for a school assignment," he wrote to her. "Sometimes when I'm tired at the end of the day, what keeps me going is remembering how often you and Dad did that for us. So I thank you," he wrote. "And Matt and Luke [his sons] thank you as well. We think of you a lot."

As people finish, they get up to stretch, and visit with those who sat a table over. Small clusters form. Margaret's daughter Cecilia is congratulated for her poise. Her sister Marge takes full credit, saying she conditioned Cecilia to be a public speaker, co-incidentally enough at funeral homes. The Fichter children weren't sheltered from death. They went to wakes and were instructed to approach grieving family members and offer condolences. When Margaret's own mother died, a neighbor woman came up, put her arm around Margaret, then only seventeen, and said she was sorry. Margaret remembered how good that little gesture made her feel. She wanted her children to do the same for others. Maybe not put their arms around people, but go up and say something. Tell them, Margaret suggested, "You have our sympathy."

Cecilia and Marge decided as children to offer their sympathy together. Two are better than one, especially in a funeral home.

They rehearsed at home, taking their mother's line and inserting the word *deepest*. *Deepest* added a little flourish and sounded better, more sincere, they decided. Again and again they practiced, walking side-by-side up to the imaginary family member.

"You have," Cecilia rehearsed. "Our deepest sympathy," Marge followed on cue. They smiled and retreated. They could tell their mother, yes, indeed, they offered their sympathy, their *deepest* sympathy.

Once at the funeral home, they held back, reviewing their lines again. Together they approached the leading grieving family member.

As rehearsed, Cecilia opened with, "You have"—she stopped. Silence. Marge stood beside her, her mouth resolutely closed in a polite smile. Cecilia, who had started the sentence, had no choice but to complete it or look like a fool. She blurted out, "*Our deepest sympathy.*"

Then they both retreated. Cecilia quietly fumed at Marge about how she was supposed to finish the sentence and she better not back out again. Next funeral, they rehearsed. Cecilia made Marge promise she would do her part and not leave Cecilia hanging. "I promise. I promise," Marge vowed.

At the appropriate time, they approached the family member. Cecilia began, "You have." Silence. Marge, stood next to her with that same sweet, but clearly pursed, smile. Cecilia blurted out, "*Our deepest sympathy.*" Cecilia stood there like a gullible Charlie Brown, having sped toward that football to give it a good whack, only to have Lucy pull it away.

A few feet away Molly stands with Cecilia Guehl recounting the morning at the funeral home, which used to be the Guehl Funeral Home, but is now the Robert Hughes Funeral Home. Molly was sitting in the room when the funeral director was about to close the casket. She finds that particular moment difficult and didn't want to look. Instead, she glanced at the wall above, focusing on an oil painting of the sun shining on a snow-covered walk. If Dolly could and would open her eyes, the sun would be glimmering in her face. There was no signature on the painting. But Molly recognized it. Dolly's father painted it decades earlier and gave it to John Guehl, Loretta and Cecilia's father. Mr. Guehl ran the funeral business at that time and hung it in the viewing room. It's still there.

"I couldn't believe it," says Molly. Decades had passed. And then, this morning, Dolly was lying perfectly positioned below her father's painting, bathed in the sun's warm glow.

Margaret's younger sister, Cecilia Uhlig, remains in her seat. The two girls are the youngest in their family. Their older brothers and sisters have died. Margaret taught Cecilia how to harmonize and make doughnuts, taking over that chore when their mother died. Cecilia was twelve at the time.

The sisters now live only a few blocks apart. But they have had completely different lives.

Cecilia's husband died suddenly of a stroke, leaving her a widow at the age of thirty-five with six children. The oldest was sixteen years and four months; the youngest was ten years old the day after the funeral. Cecilia had to get a job. At one point she worked in an office until 4:30. From there she went to a department store and worked until 9 P.M., came home, and put six children to bed. She didn't have time to join clubs or make the doughnuts for Fastnacht.

"As you are doing it, you don't think about it," she says. "I just figured that this is what the Lord had for me. I accepted it. Some have it a lot worse than I did. A lot of people. They're busy taking their children to the doctors, and I was fortunate that I had healthy children."

The kids took care of one another. If during the day they argued or got into scrapes with the neighborhood kids, the older ones washed bloody noses or cuts before their mother got home. "Don't say a word," they told the younger ones. They were protective. The last thing their mother needed was someone running up as soon as she walked in the house from working two jobs, saying, "He hit me."

"We felt sorry for her, but we wouldn't tell her that," says Selma. "We would say, 'C'mon, you know Mom is going to get upset, so don't do this.' We protected her because she had enough on her mind just trying to raise us kids." Four of her six children still live on Troy Hill.

If Selma's friends wanted her to go to the movies, Selma would ask. When her mother said no, she would report back that she couldn't go. "Well you only asked her once. You didn't beg yet," they said.

"I would never think of begging. I figured she had her reason. Maybe she couldn't afford it. We all knew how poor we were. If she said no, that meant she didn't have money. She didn't have to explain. We just accepted it."

Her children wanted to do something special for their mother when she retired. Cecilia had always said she wanted to see Germany, so they pooled their money and sent her on a twenty-one-day trip to Europe.

Sometimes her children try to think what it would have been like to be a thirty-five-year-old widow with six young children. They simply can't imagine it. Nothing, it seems, was presented to her and so many of the women here that they couldn't handle. If they doubted their own abilities, they never betrayed that doubt. They did what had to be done with a quiet confidence and ability that empowered their own children.

To this day, when Cecilia isn't feeling well, she still gets up and straightens the house. "It's hard to keep these women down," says Selma. Not that anyone would want to.

When Margaret was fifty-seven, she decided to get her driver's license. It was after the doctor told her she had to have a hysterectomy.

"I cried. I always tried to do what was right, and all I ever wanted to do was drive a car," she says. "I thought I was going to be dead and never have a chance to drive, and my son-in-law said, 'Well, why don't you drive?' I said, 'Well, I'm too old.' He told me that I wasn't."

So she got her license and drove Joe around because he didn't have one yet. When he retired, he learned to drive and took over as chauffeur. Margaret gladly let him. Joe drove her to the grocery store and sat while Margaret shopped.

When Joe died, she was going to sell the car, but her children convinced her not to. You've always been independent. Stay that way. Don't rely on the bus or us, they said.

But I haven't driven in seventeen years, she said.

Learn again, they responded.

At my age? Margaret said. She was seventy-nine.

Yes.

Her son-in-law took her down to a parking lot and reviewed the basics. She passed her test. She drives in nontraffic hours, taking her little white Dodge Colt a mile down the hill to the Shop 'n Save, and to the hospital on Fridays to distribute Communion. Her neighbor, Ev, drives her to the Pines Bowling Alley on Tuesday afternoons so she doesn't have to deal with school-bus traffic.

CHAPTER FIVE

Emma Mae or
Emma May Not

E MMA HILDENBRAND went to Dolly's wake the night before. She doesn't go to funerals unless she really knows the person well, which she didn't. Emma doesn't belong to Most Holy Name. She isn't Catholic, although her husband and his family were devout Catholics and she raised her two daughters in that faith. Her oldest daughter, Jeanne, is a nun and now lives with her.

Emma knew nothing about Troy Hill until she started dating Leo. He picked her up one night to meet his family. Once they got to Rialto Street, Leo had to pull his car over to the side of the road to make room for the pigs. Emma stared, amused at their squeals, and amazed. Her eyes must have chanced upon Troy Hill at some point in her life, walking to school, looking up and surveying the horizon east to west. Somewhere in that sweep sat this little plateau. But who would have thought pigs would be running through the streets here, or on any city hilltop, for that matter? "I had never seen anything like that in my life," she says.

Leo was twenty-four. Emma had just turned eighteen when they met at a circle of summer cottages north of Pittsburgh. Emma was with her high school sweetheart, an Irish boy named Pete. Leo and his friends were at the cottage next door. They heard the music playing and came over. Everyone was dancing. Emma loved to dance. On summer evenings, she and her girlfriends spent hours dancing in a nearby park that had a lake and a small confection shop with a jukebox.

Her older sister Sadie lent her a two-piece bouclé suit to wear that night at the cottage. Emma was striking, her creamy fair Irish skin, soft blue eyes, and heart-shaped face circled by waves of dark hair. Dimples deepened when she smiled, which was often

Emma Hildenbrand,
summer of 1935.

and with ease. It still is. In her yearbook, someone wrote a poem describing Emma as a fair maiden, seeing in her the quintessential beauty that would cause lovestruck knights to joust.

> *Emma is a maiden fair,*
> *With never a worry, never a care.*
> *In big warm smiles, she does excel,*
> *And to all who know her, she's a charming belle.*

She probably seemed older to Leo, and more sophisticated, out there spinning on the floor, looking happy and relaxed. He was a quiet young man who had lived his whole life on Troy Hill. Emma grew up in a neighborhood a few miles away, with blacks, Italians, and Jews. She graduated from high school. Leo didn't. A group of her best friends called themselves the Hot Shots. They were daring. Emma was the first to dive off the high board at the swimming pool. Every once in a while they smoked and wore halter tops. Her middle name was Mae. Later Leo would say "Emma Mae, you can never tell." As in Emma may or may not. You can never tell. She was so carefree.

By the end of the night she was dancing with Leo. "Poor Pete, I don't know how I explained anything, but I went home with Leo." She felt bad about that. Pete was a nice guy. He had taken Emma to their senior prom and had bought her a black onyx ring with the letter *E* engraved in the stone. The following year Emma's father died, and Pete sent her the most beautiful card, even though they were no longer dating.

Leo was tall, slender, and fair. He was older and had his own car. Emma's parents could never afford one. At one time her family moved to another house simply to be closer to the streetcar because her father had phlebitis in his legs and couldn't walk far.

On their first date, Leo wore a gray suit and a coat with a velvet collar. A derby sat smartly on his blond hair. Emma's father and Sadie were impressed. So was she. Emma always was particular about clothes, influenced, no doubt, by her mother's sisters, Mame, Tillie, and Flo, who dressed in long stylish coats and wore their hair tied up in perfect knots, set off with delicate little black bows. Clothes stick with her, more so than dates or names. Hand Emma a picture, and no matter how old or faded, she can describe in detail the weave of the fabric;

whether it was linen, cotton, or taffeta; whether the sleeves were scalloped or straight, the buttons covered. She knows whether she made or bought it, for how much and where. Watershed moments are defined by outfits. Baptism was a rose jumper with a cape, and the end of World War II was a white eyelet dress, with matching ones for her two daughters. She didn't have a lot, and everything was handmade. But what she did have, she cherished.

To top it off, Leo had a wonderful smile. "I kind of fell for him," she says. He fell for her, too, but was too shy to ask her out. His best friend called Emma on his behalf.

They dated for five years before Leo proposed. It was the Depression. Neither had much money to buy furniture or pay rent. Leo worked in a garage fixing cars. His check went to his parents. Emma didn't have steady work. At holidays she wrapped gifts at a downtown department store. Her girlfriend helped get her a job at a brass company, but she didn't type fast enough. At one job her boss told her to stay late to take inventory. "I have to catch a bus," Emma told him, and left. The next day, she came back and her boss told her she no longer worked there. The only real money Emma had was the three hundred dollars she received at the age of nineteen when her father died.

Then, there was the issue of religion, which was the prevailing issue—and Catholicism the prevailing religion. Children knew better than to date a non-Catholic, and if they did, the hope, prayer, and even assumption was that the non-Catholic would convert. Especially women. They would be mothers, and mothers were the caretakers of the soul as well as the body. Leo grew up here. He knew the expectations. His parents listened to the rosary on the radio. His father woke early, went to mass, then work. Sometimes, after work, he took a nap and then went back to church. And here Leo was, dating a Methodist. There wasn't even a Methodist church on Troy Hill. Lutheran, yes. Presbyterian, yes. But no Methodist. Some kids were adults before they knew such a thing existed.

To Emma, differences in religion were just that: differences. One wasn't better. One wasn't worse. That is how she was raised. She doesn't remember her parents sitting down and explicitly saying so. It was the way they lived their lives. They were generous in thought and didn't distinguish people by race, creed, or color. By example they endowed their daughter Emma with a rare sensitivity. A girl down the street was Jewish. Emma didn't know her well and hadn't known she was Jewish until the girl told her how cruel people had been because of her religion. "I wish I would have known," Emma said, "so I could have been a better friend." Once, her nephew, then a small boy of about seven, came home, his arm proudly resting on the shoulder of a black boy who lived down the street. Emma's nephew announced to his mother and her card party, "Mom, this is my new boyfriend." No one flinched.

Time and years have simply strengthened that perspective. Once you get to know people, Emma says, there are few differences. Everyone shares the same basic needs and wants. What a person looks like or where they go to church on Sundays has nothing to do with it.

Leo was in an accident while they were dating. He was working beneath a car when a coworker, unaware that Leo was below, lowered the car on top of him. Leo's skull was crushed. Doctors kept him in the hospital for a month. One side of his face was paralyzed. His eyes teared uncontrollably. Every day, Emma took a streetcar to see him. A happy person by nature, her spirits uplifted him. He struggled to smile for her. Her devotion and concern touched Leo's parents.

Leo didn't want to lose Emma, Methodist or not. He proposed on Christmas, 1935. It was important to Leo and his family to have a priest perform the ceremony. That was fine with Emma. The priest made the couple sign a form promising their children would be baptized Catholic. The church wanted assurances the children would be raised properly. Properly, in the church's eyes, was Catholic.

Emma had no intention of converting and Leo never pushed. It wasn't out of stubbornness and defiance but rather personal need. Every Sunday, her dear sister Sadie took her to Allegheny United Methodist Church, where they belonged. Her friends were there. It was a part of her past and identity. Leo understood that. They never discussed it but, instead, quietly respected each other's beliefs. Both were spiritual people. In that way, their lives followed parallel paths, just not the same one. They may not have shared religion, but they shared faith.

Leo promised to drive Emma every Sunday to her church. That weekly drive was probably considered an act of defiance. If Leo wasn't encouraging Emma, he was at least enabling her to continue being Methodist.

Though their marriage was allowed, it wasn't particularly celebrated. They exchanged vows in a simple ceremony in the priest's office. Emma wore a white dress she'd bought for $5.98, blue shoes, and a blue purse, blue hat, and blue gloves. Leo wore a dark suit. No one took pictures or sang songs. Only Leo's cousin Marie dared to throw rice on the couple when they came outside the rectory. Emma loved Marie for that. To this day Emma puts fresh flowers on Marie's grave when she goes to the cemetery. Leo's mother had noodle soup waiting for them in her kitchen. After, the newlyweds drove to Niagara Falls for a short honeymoon. The first morning there, Leo went to mass. Emma stayed in their hotel room.

They came home to Troy Hill and moved into the first floor of the house Leo grew up in. His parents moved upstairs.

There was little question where they would live. Leo belonged here. His father and grandfather lived on Troy Hill and knew other longtime families like the Fichters, the Kunzmanns, and the Guehls. His sister lived on the next hill, Mount Troy. Leo had roots. By then Emma had lived in seven houses. Both her parents had died. Her five older brothers and sisters were starting their own lives and households in different parts of the city.

Up until her mother's death, Emma's life had been relatively stable. She was born across the street from her grandparents' house. Her grandfather was a brilliant inventor and had three patents. They lived there until she was five. Their next house was only a block away. Her family lived there for ten years, the bulk of her childhood. Kids took sheets of cardboard and sledded down the middle of Shields Alley. A lookout was stationed below to check for streetcars. Summers were spent on porch steps and playing on the sidewalk because they had no yard.

Her mother was protective of all the children, particularly Emma, the youngest. When she was a young girl, her father, who was a fireman, worked the night shift. On those nights,

Emma would sleep with her mother. Her mother never had Emma do chores around the house.

Every so often her mother's sisters, Tillie, Mame, and Flo, would visit. Emma would sit with the ladies and listen to their stories. One Wednesday night in December, when Emma was fifteen years old, her aunts came over. They sat in the kitchen by the woodstove. It was getting dark. The sisters put on their long winter coats and got up to leave. Emma and her mother walked them to the front door and stood in the drafty doorway, lingering over farewells. Emma glanced at her mother's face. In the pale hallway light, she could tell it was flushed. The next day, her mother wasn't feeling well. The doctor came and said she had pneumonia.

On Saturday Emma ran to the drugstore to get a prescription filled. Back home, the house was cold. Her mother told her to light the woodstove. Emma had never done that before and was afraid something might pop or explode. She told her mother she couldn't. And then her mother did something Emma has never forgotten. She slapped her. It was the only time Emma remembers her mother striking her. That night Emma's mother died. Pneumonia was like that then. It would kill someone in days.

A few days later Emma's chest began to hurt. Terrified that she had pneumonia and was going to die, she took a spoonful of Vicks vapor rub and swallowed it. She ran tearfully to Sadie, who was ten years older. "I have pneumonia," Emma cried, telling her sister how her chest hurt, and that she was going to die, too. "You're not sick," Sadie told her. "It's sorrow. It's your broken heart."

Sadie had always watched out for her baby sister, but even more so after their mother died. Sadie had a good job and bought Emma a dress and took her to the beauty parlor for her first permanent when Emma was about sixteen years old. In 1933 the two sisters rode a train to the World's Fair in Chicago, where an artist made a miniature black-and-white silhouette of Emma's profile. It hangs next to her mirror in her bedroom. Across from it, on the mantel, a little rose-cheeked china doll curtsies. Sadie gave it to Emma and Leo shortly after they married.

With all the moving around, Emma wasn't bound to one piece of land. She welcomed a place to call home.

Emma felt particularly lucky. Her mother-in-law gave the two rooms a fresh coat of paint and hung venetian blinds in the window. Emma had admired such blinds in magazines, but never thought she would have her own. A bed sat in one corner. A sofa in another. When Jeanne and Joan were born, Emma made room for a crib and twin bed. The second room was the kitchen. Sadie gave them a table and chairs. Emma and Leo bought two extra chairs for six dollars apiece. The family lived in those two rooms until the girls were in grade school, and then moved upstairs and had four rooms including the attic. Emma's in-laws moved downstairs.

Out back was a yard. A chicken coop sat in the dirt. Emma had such wonderful plans for it. Gardening seemed to come naturally to her. "You should have an acre," her mother-in-law told her after Emma came in with a freshly picked bouquet to take to the cemetery.

She loved that little plot and her home. She was happy. Neither she nor Leo had the greatest voice. But together they would sing, "Troy Hill will shine tonight, Troy Hill will shine. Troy Hill will shine tonight won't that be fine." She sang it as proudly as if she were born and raised right there on Lautner Street.

But, of course, she wasn't, which everyone knew.

Emma was different from her neighbors in many ways. There were the obvious ones. Emma wasn't native, Catholic, or German. Maybe a smidgen of German, but she was really more Irish and English. Her maiden name was Caskey. Her Scottish grandmother taught her how to drink tea and tell fortunes from the leaves. Turn the cup upside down, spin it three times. Stand it back up and look in the loose tea leaves for images of dogs, houses, or babies.

She was not the least bit stoic. To Emma, emotions were for expressing, not for keeping in check. She was not a dramatic or loud person. She was very comfortable saying she loved something, and not just safe objects like a pair of shoes or a piece of cake, but people, her friends and neighbors. "I love him" or "I love her," she would say. It wasn't empty or saccharine, but natural and genuine. That is who she was. A friend down the street, Helen Lindenfelser, uses one word to describe her. *Effervescent*.

Pulling weeds or hanging wash, Emma chatted with neighbors. She made friends at the butcher, the baker, and the local thrift shop. Men, women, and children sat silently in their chairs at the doctor's office, reading, knitting, or just waiting. Emma sat down, turned to the person next to her, and began talking. Minutes later another person across the room joined in and then another. The once-sterile waiting office became animated.

After Leo died Emma started going to the local bank to pay the utility bills. Leo had handled that. She chatted with the teller and soon knew her name. With every visit, Emma shared some little bit of news about where she had been and how her family was doing. Sometimes she brought a photograph. They talked about the weather. Emma seemed so bright. When the bank celebrated its hundredth anniversary and featured some of its customers with large photographs in the lobby, the teller suggested using Emma. Emma had just the image the bank wanted to convey. Warm and friendly.

She was delighted. A photographer took her picture. She was asked for a quote. "I've been coming here for, oh, at least fifty years. I like coming here because everyone at Troy Hill does a lot of little things for their customers. I like seeing my friends, my neighbors, and all the tellers." A poster with her picture and her comments hung in the lobby for months. Some of the older men, who bring their wives to the Red Door thrift shop, where Emma goes on Wednesdays with her friend Ernestine Hepp, joked with her good-naturedly, calling her a star.

Emma and her children.

Over the years winds would change, bringing to Emma the unexpected and unfamiliar. When they did, Emma didn't turn her back. While carefree, she is remarkably steadfast in tolerance. Maybe that, too, is from her parents not being critical, or judgmental, of others.

Somewhere along her way she had learned to find contentment in what she had. When her daughters would long one moment for snow and the next for spring, she told them to enjoy the day at hand. "You're wishing your life away," she said to them.

Emma was true to her promise to raise her children Catholic. When she became pregnant, she assumed the baby had to be named after a saint. The whole notion of saints was foreign to her. Methodists don't have saints or martyrs, relics or rosaries. So, she went into her kitchen and looked at the Most Holy Name calendar hanging on a nail on her pantry door. Each month listed major holidays, religious and secular, and the feast days of saints. Emma flipped through the months looking for a nice name. She found Saints Dolores and Jeanne. Her daughter was baptized Dolores Jeanne. Everyone called her Jeanne.

Joan was named after the saint Joan of Arc and the actress Joan Crawford. "I didn't know much about Joan of Arc. I knew Joan Crawford," Emma says. "I didn't like her when she got older, but I did when she started out."

At each point in her daughters' lives, when they received a sacrament or were in a special procession, Emma anticipated the celebrated day with equal excitement. She found the perfect radiant white taffeta dress for Jeanne's first Holy Communion and gathered flowers for the May crowning. Emma became familiar with the Catholic abstinence and fasting rules and the holy days when Catholics had to attend mass. All these things, she did, but not instinctively. She had to consult the calendar, Leo's family, or neighbors.

None of that bothered her. But the fact that she wasn't Catholic made an impression on her daughters. Their whole little world was Catholic. Their only grandmother, Leo's mother, prayed that she would live to see Jeanne make her First Communion, as if after that day, she would be ready to die.

Every Sunday morning, doors opened up and down the street like a string of cuckoo clocks, and families filed out for morning mass. Their door opened, too. All the Hildenbrands, but Emma, came out. After mass Leo and the girls drove Emma to her church, dropped her off at the bottom of the concrete steps, and left for an outing to the zoo, the cemetery, or to visit one of Leo's aunts. One time, they rode the incline up and down a hillside across the river.

After an hour or so, they came back and waited outside. They wouldn't dare step inside her church. The Catholic Church forbade entering a non-Catholic church. No one said what would happen, whether they would be struck down by lightning, or a corner of their once-pure soul smudged. But no one wanted to find out.

In grade school they had come to see the world divided neatly into two—Catholics and non-Catholics. There weren't even degrees of non-Catholics. Lutherans, Presbyterians, and Methodists were all lumped together on the other side, the wrong side. Catholics were never just Catholics. In describing someone, it was, "He is a good Catholic." Or, "She is a good Catholic." No one was ever a bad Catholic. *Good Catholic* was one long word.

"It was a tight little world. I felt very much a part of it," says Joan. Joan and her girlfriend built a little altar in the woods and decorated it with statues of Mary and Jesus, and flowers. They could play priest and nun and take turns crowning Mary.

"We were sure we were right. That was the impression of adults, nuns, and priests. We had God's way and message. This was a conflict for me growing up. We tended to look down on the others. Mother was in the part that was not right."

The last thing a child wants is to be different, or to have anyone in her family be different. In high school one of the nuns asked the class, "How many of you have parents who are non-Catholics?" Joan raised her hand. Only one other girl raised her hand. The girl's father was non-Catholic, which at the time seemed more typical and acceptable. Some thirty years later that girl remembered Joan's name because she was so impressed that a non-Catholic mother could raise Catholic children.

It couldn't have been easy for either of her parents, says Jeanne. Her father, a conservative by-the-rules man, defied authority in a more rigid time and place. Her mother, seemingly so carefree, remained true to herself, when it might have been easier to convert and avoid distinction.

"I think it's amazing that my dad actually broke convention in marrying my mother. He was raised here. He was the one in the middle of the Catholic environment. In 1936 that was still not the thing to do. I think it took some members of the family a while to adjust to the idea. As for my mother, she has always been a person in her own right.

"I've only thought of all this recently. You know, as an adult, you start looking at them and trying to see how they made their decisions and how it affected them," she says.

Emma raised her daughters Catholic for Leo, his family, and the girls. Only once was she troubled. For some reason Emma wasn't allowed to attend the baptisms of Jeanne and Joan. She can't recall why. She would have offered to sit in the back, she says. That was the only thing she ever felt bad about.

Leo became a firefighter, as his father and grandfather had been. When he worked nights, Emma lay in bed and told the girls stories. During the day, they sat on the floor dressing paper doll cutouts in different cardboard outfits. They played with other children in the neighborhood but kept somewhat to themselves, usually reading. Like Leo, they were more private and introspective.

Both did well in school. Joan was particularly intense. In first grade she raced home and proudly printed "Puff" and "Scottie" on the blackboard that hung on the wall in their kitchen, so she wouldn't forget that day's lesson.

When Jeanne was in high school, Leo told her she should consider being a pharmacist or a dietitian because they seemed like good, secure professions. Perhaps he never meant anything more, but implicit in that suggestion was the notion that she didn't have to pursue the traditional careers of nursing, teaching, and shorthand or be a homemaker. Other possibilities and options existed.

He left it at that. He didn't explore what it would take to be a pharmacist, or mention college. Neither did Emma. It didn't really occur to Emma that her daughters would want to go to college, or that it would even be possible. She had no reason to think they would want a life different from her own. She was content. It was reasonable to assume they would be, too.

At the same time, she was very proud of their accomplishments. When they received honors or were class officers, she marveled and noted their achievements to family and friends. That encouragement and praise couldn't help but build the confidence needed to pursue dreams, as different as they may be. Emma was protective but not possessive. She would never say they couldn't do something, or stand in their way.

Up until then, the only family members who had gone past high school were Leo's niece, who was a nurse, and Emma's nephew, who attended college on a football scholarship and became a high school teacher. If the girls wanted to go to college, the initiative would have to come from them. Jeanne was first.

"I'm going to college," she told Emma and Leo one day during her senior year in high school. She didn't ask if she could or what they thought. It was a statement of fact. Her father made a respectable living, and helped out some. But the girls wanted to do it on their own. Both had had jobs since they were sixteen. "I was sure that I was going to find a way to go, and I did," says Jeanne.

Jeanne researched a program at Duquesne University, a respected Catholic university in Pittsburgh, which reduced the tuition for elementary education majors who agreed to teach at a parochial school.

Joan went to the same university because she could get tuition half price since Jeanne was a student there. She studied English.

One night Joan's sorority was performing in Greek Sing, a festive annual choral competition between the local sororities. Jeanne and Emma decided to go.

By this time Jeanne was twenty-three and teaching. On the way over Jeanne told her mother she wanted to stop at the Most Holy Name convent, which was only a block out of the way. Emma didn't question. Jeanne knew the nuns from growing up and through teaching. Jeanne got out. Emma waited in the car. After a few minutes Jeanne came back and got inside the car. They drove off.

As they were driving, Jeanne said she had something to tell her. She was entering the convent.

Emma was stunned. She didn't know what to say. Jeanne had never mentioned that she was considering becoming a nun nor had she given the impression that she was wrestling with such an important decision. Jeanne seemed happy teaching and living at home. All of her friends were getting married. In time, Emma and Leo thought, Jeanne might, too—and that they would be grandparents. "I just couldn't believe it," Emma says. They drove to the concert in silence.

Emma sat through the evening vaguely aware of a blur of song and people. All she could think about was that her daughter Jeanne was going away for good. The rules were much more strict then. Women entered the convent, and the convent became their whole life. Family ties were downplayed, if not discouraged. Emma had heard stories about nuns who couldn't go to visit their own parents without a chaperone. Or the nun who couldn't personally deliver a wedding gift to her cousin, but had to leave it at the front gate. Emma's entire life was home and family. That is what made her happy. Jeanne would be deprived of the very things that gave Emma joy.

Those first few days, Emma remained uncharacteristically quiet. Privately she searched for reasons and clues. Should she have seen it coming so she wouldn't be so shocked? Jeanne dressed up as a nun one day for something in school when she was sixteen. Was that it? But then, Jeanne did what everyone else did. She wore bobby socks and saddle shoes. Her scrapbook is filled with black-and-white pictures of her going to basketball and football games, PJ parties, and driving around in a friend's blue Plymouth. In college she pledged a sorority and stayed up until 2 A.M. making paper flowers for a parade float. Emma didn't know anything about sororities, but everyone seemed to be having fun, Jeanne included. Emma loved hearing the stories about their adventures.

What made it more difficult was that Emma couldn't understand Jeanne's decision, intellectually or spiritually. There are no Methodist nuns and convents, no vows of poverty and celibacy and obedience. Prunes for breakfast and for dinner, all in the name of obedience. Scrubbing woodwork in the name of humility. None of it made sense to her.

And those starched headdresses and sweeping robes. Jeanne loved pretty clothes, like her mother did. Now she was ordering styleless black shoes and dark nylons. On the order form, she couldn't even find a small enough size. Everything came in huge. Those towering, hulking robed women would dwarf Jeanne. Emma was torn with ambivalence. Part of her was proud of Jeanne's dedication and willingness to surrender to something she believed in. The other part was sad, grieving the loss of her. If Jeanne had married, she would be leaving home, too, but she could come back to visit, spend the night, join them for holidays and birthdays. The two of them could go shopping together. Jeanne couldn't even keep her name. Everyone would be calling their Jeanne, Sister Monica.

Emma felt alone. Having a priest or nun in the family was considered a badge of honor and a tribute to the faith and goodness of the parents. "You know how good a mother she must be," one woman says of Emma. "Her daughter is a nun." Leo's sister wished one of her children would be a nun or priest.

Leo was more familiar with the notion of nuns. Yet, he felt a similar loss. "I was a daughter leaving," says Jeanne. "I was not going to come home. That is how it was then." Leo tried to talk Jeanne into waiting a year, but she had already spent so much time thinking about her decision. She didn't want to go back and rehash why and how. It was not an easy choice for her, either. A determined and strong-willed twenty-three-year-old, she had to take vows of obedience. A very private person, she had to wear a habit, which thrust her into the public and made her a magnet for people who wanted to talk. "It took a lot of courage to commit, and once I did, I didn't want to step back from it," says Jeanne.

Emma turned to her older sister Sadie. Sadie had always been there for her, offering wisdom and support. Sadie helped Emma see the value in what Jeanne was doing.

"Well, Emma, if Jeanne wanted to be a Methodist missionary, you would think that was wonderful. It's just like being a missionary," Sadie told Emma. "She's doing God's work. This is what she learned, and she'll be good at it." After Sadie put it that way, Emma said, she felt better. "I could accept it."

That first year, Emma and Leo drove to Baltimore anytime Jeanne was allowed visitors. They made the five-hour trip up and back in one day. The second year, Jeanne couldn't have visitors and could write home only once a month. Emma missed her so much. She began teaching Sunday school to give her something to do, and she joined a card club with her friends from church, even though she doesn't like playing cards. It gave her a night out. She became neighborhood chairman of the Girl Scouts.

She would never tell Jeanne she was sad and burden her daughter with her own personal struggles. It wasn't the life she would have chosen. But she would accept it, hoping Jeanne would be happy and fulfilled. Her own words guided her. She wouldn't wish her life away or cling to what would never be.

Becoming a nun was the last thing Joan wanted.

She and Jeanne were close as young girls but grew apart during their teenage years. Instead of following Jeanne to Saint Benedict's, Joan went to Saint Peter's. Her friends were going there. In Latin class she got 100 percent, and the nun praised her in front of everyone. "I never got a hundred again. I had learned a lesson. I wanted to be with the group and not stand out," Joan said.

After two years her good friend switched to Allegheny High School, a public school. Joan wanted to go, too. Her father didn't like the idea. Public schools and public-school children were unknown quantities. Who knows what she would be exposed to, what the other kids would be like, what kind of morals or beliefs their parents or teachers held and taught? On the first page of the yearbook of Saint Benedict's, where Jeanne went, girls kneel and wear white veils. The school motto was in Latin, *Ut in omnibus glorificetum deus*, which means, "In all things God may be glorified." The public school had a dance called the Witchdoctor Stomp. Allegheny High's motto was Onward and Upward.

Emma was Joan's ally. Emma had graduated from Allegheny High School and had only warm memories of it. She petitioned

Leo on Joan's behalf. Finally, Leo consented. "You can go to Allegheny, but you better do well," Leo told Joan. She took it as a command. Do well.

She did. Every semester she was on the honor roll. She joined the college club, the yearbook staff, aligning herself with the school leaders. On the service squad, she guided visitors through the building, and she was a member of her class's hall of fame.

Like her mother, she was outgoing, though far more driven. Her mother was a fair maiden. Joan was a worker. "Effervescent Joanie will long be remembered by her classmates for her sparkling personality and initiative. Her willingness to work will surely be a great asset to her when she enters college," her yearbook said of her.

In 1958, the summer she graduated from high school, Joan told her parents she wanted to spend the summer in New Jersey, working as a waitress at a fancy hotel by the ocean. She could make more money than she could at home, and that money could be used for college tuition, she reasoned. And she would be free, although that was left unsaid. Her parents had to sign a form allowing her to go.

Leo said no. He refused to sign it.

Emma did. She admired Joan's independence. "I don't think it was rebellion. She wanted to earn her money. She was going to go to college," Emma says.

Joan was outgrowing her home and childhood. Emma could see it coming and didn't stop it. "Going to Allegheny was the start of a lot of stuff for her," Emma says. "We were very quiet people." Joan wrote a prize-winning essay in high school, was given twenty-five dollars and invited to lunch with television star Jane Powell. Emma couldn't believe it. Her daughter eating lunch with a well-known star! A picture of Joan standing alongside Jane Powell appeared in the local newspaper. Emma clipped and saved it.

Joan wasn't sure what she wanted to do, but she knew she wanted a different life than her mother, her sister, and even her classmates. "I looked at what my other friends were doing—going to work and taking shorthand. I didn't think I would like that. I didn't know what I wanted to do. The only thing I knew was I was good in was English."

She followed Jeanne to Duquesne, but joined a different sorority, seeking one that seemed more sophisticated and worldly. Her sorority sisters didn't commute. They came from different cities and states, and every year honored outstanding women in the United States.

Joan was elected president her senior year. During a dinner to recognize mothers, Joan stood up and gave a speech. Emma sat in the audience, watching her at the podium, overwhelmed that her daughter had risen to that position and spoke so beautifully. "I was sitting at the table. I don't remember what she said or anything, but I thought, *Oh my god, that is my daughter,*" Emma says.

After graduation, and still somewhat rudderless, Joan obtained her master's degree and then began traveling and pursuing other degrees. She studied in England on a Fulbright scholarship. At one point she joined VISTA, a volunteer jobs program. She went to graduate school in Denver, obtained a second master's degree from Vanderbilt University. She worked in San Francisco as a temporary worker, and with the welfare department in New York.

"Joan is a free spirit. She's been to, I think, ten colleges. She's been to China, and spent nine days in a Jewish kibbutz. I never knew anyone who did that. She's so smart," says Emma.

Her youngest daughter, too, was choosing a life completely different from her own. Emma felt no desire to roam. The more Joan traveled, the bigger her world became, and the smaller Emma and Leo's world seemed. Some people who travel can't wait to get back home. Joan wasn't like that.

When she was home, she still seemed far away. Between trips or schools, she ate dinner with her parents, then went up to her room. Emma and Leo would hear her practicing Japanese or Chinese upstairs. She didn't bring home photographs of the exotic places she visited because she never bothered with a camera. At Christmas they would listen to her conversations with relatives and learn more about her adventures then than from Joan herself.

At some point in the early 1960s, Joan quit going to church. Traditions and rituals that she loved as a child seemed cold and remote. She knew she couldn't abide by the Church's conservative rules and standards.

Instead of telling her parents, she just stopped going and left it for them to notice. Emma and Leo wondered but didn't ask. She was an adult. Young people were breaking away from institutions. She was independent. Emma wouldn't consume herself with worry. Not that she didn't care, but Joan was smart. She was a good person. Emma knew that. Sadie always told her not to worry about things she had no control over.

When Joan was forty-three, she was in New York, working toward her doctorate. She sent a letter to Jeanne. After seven years in Baltimore, Jeanne was assigned to Most Holy Name on Troy Hill and lived in the convent there. Emma and Leo were thrilled. The church had begun relaxing its rules. Jeanne could be Sister Jeanne, and she didn't have to wear robes. The daughter they thought was gone for good was just a few blocks away.

In the letter, Joan said she was pregnant and had no intentions of getting married. She asked Jeanne to tell her parents, because she was afraid of how they would react. Jeanne was shocked.

After she read the letter, she called Joan. They talked. Joan explained that she felt as if she had so much to give and so much that she wanted to share.

It was up to Jeanne to break the news. She decided to tell Emma first. They were going to an arts festival downtown and stopped at a restaurant for lunch. During lunch, Jeanne gave Emma the letter. Emma read it. Her first thought was, Oh, how am I ever going to tell Leo?

But she couldn't help but be thrilled, too. She was seventy years old and had given up hopes of ever having a grandchild. Jeanne was a nun. Joan was traveling all over the world. Finally she was going to be a grandmother. It wasn't the way she expected it would be, but she was going to be a grandmother nonetheless. Having a grandchild was more important to her than whether Joan was married or not.

"Jeannie was going to be an aunt and I was going to be a grandmother and Leo was going to be a grandfather and we were going to have this dear little child. And I think that is the way you are supposed to feel," she says. "It was wonderful. And I even thought about the Bible. Who was it that was so old and had a child? Sarah? And I thought, Here I am, oh my gosh. I was so happy."

She looked at Jeanne and said, "If only I were ten years younger."

Emma said she would take care of telling Leo. Again she would be the buffer. He wanted a grandchild, but he was so moral and rigid when it came to rules of the Church, she wasn't sure how he would react. He was standing in the kitchen, by the cabinet between the two back windows, getting dinner ready. She told him. "He was upset but he wasn't a crying type. He didn't get mad. But then I told my friends. I didn't hide it," says Emma.

At some point Emma called Joan. She remembers asking about what nationality the baby would be. Joan had traveled so much. It was possible, she thought, the baby might be Asian. No, Joan told her. The baby's father was African American. Emma felt bad. Not so much about the answer but about her own question.

She had told her daughters a story about when she was in high school. She and her best friend, Dorothy, were walking down the street to go to the Kenyon Theater on Federal Street. Hot-dog shops and shoe-shine places lined the walk. One of her classmates, a black student who was on the football team, was sitting outside one of the shops. As she approached him, Emma said, "Hi, Murphy."

"He stepped out and was going to talk to me, and I ignored

him. It was ignorant, but I guess I was afraid. I didn't know what I was going to say. I was friendly enough to say hi to him, but I didn't want to go any further." She was ashamed. She told the story to her daughters, hoping they might learn from her. She wanted to teach them what her own parents had taught her. To accept others, no matter how different.

When their daughters were babies, Emma remembers Leo standing outside a five-and-ten, cradling one of the girls. Emma had been inside shopping and came outside just as an older man approached Leo.

"You think you love that child, don't you?" the man said to Leo.

"Sure I do," Leo answered.

And the man said, "Well, wait until that child has a child."

"I always remember him saying that," says Emma.

The following Christmas, Joan brought her daughter, Shannon, home. Emma and Leo adored her, this tiny girl crawling all over the floor, and proudly invited relatives over. Leo baked Shannon special birthday cakes and bought her toy cars. When she got big enough to ride a bike, he got Shannon a bicycle. Emma has pictures of Leo putting a pie in the oven. Shannon is standing alongside him, covered with flour. When she got a little older, Leo would talk to her on the phone. He wasn't much of a talker and didn't know what to say. He knew Shannon had picked up some German from Joan, and he would say to her in fake gruffness, "Ich bin der Herr." I'm the boss.

Emma kept lockets of hair from Shannon's first haircut and the outline of her shoe from September 1984. It looks like a big potato.

Joan continued working on her doctorate, typing well into the night with Shannon strapped to her back. Emma worried about her staying up so late and whether she would get enough rest. Emma told her relatives and friends how hard Joan was working, so amazed at her determination.

When Shannon was about three years old, Joan decided to join a church. Emma had encouraged her. It didn't matter to Emma what church. A mother and young baby need friends and support. Emma remembers when Jeanne went to the convent, how lonely she felt, and how her friends from church would invite her over.

Joan visited a few churches. She finally found one where she felt welcome and accepted. It was Methodist. Other than Catholicism, it was the religion she was most familiar with, although even then, only remotely. When Emma visited Joan and Shannon, she went to their services. "It's so nice. It's a big church and has beautiful windows. At the end, everybody joined hands. Then afterward you went downstairs and ate." When they visit Emma, they go to her church.

Joan has her doctorate in English, teaches, and lives in Atlanta with Shannon. They usually get to Troy Hill at least once a year, often around Christmas. This Christmas Jeanne drove fifteen-year-old Shannon around the city to look at older homes and churches, because she knows her niece is interested in architecture. At one church, Jeanne explained how the congregation was trying to raise enough money to have the Tiffany windows repaired. Shannon said if she had a lot of money when she grew up, she would like to make donations to churches to help them renovate. Emma was so proud of Shannon when Jeanne told her about their conversation.

"I didn't have to hear anything else. That made my day," Emma said.

Joan knew that no matter where her life took her and how different the choices and paths, that she had Emma's love and support.

"I remember in college my mother always being proud of me. I never felt unappreciated by my mother. She values my sister for what my sister gives," Joan says. "Jeanne is very loyal, hardworking, and very dependable. I think my mother values me because I have taken an independent route. My mother is a big person and has room for everyone. She has always had that gift."

Jeanne lives at home with Emma now. During the day, she works with disabled adults, teaching them to read. On a little table is a glass angel that grateful parents gave Jeanne at Christmas. "Jeanne is such a good person," Emma says.

Emma never realized how much Jeanne and Leo were alike. They share an attention to order and detail. Clothes are neatly pressed. Plastic lawn chairs are scrubbed before they go outside in the spring. Emma is inclined to simply wipe the chairs off with a sponge. On Sundays, Jeanne drives Emma to her church, as Leo did. After dropping her off, Jeanne buys fresh bread. She goes to the cemetery and plants the irises that Emma bought for Leo's grave. Emma loves their fragrance.

They enjoy each other's company. When the power failed during one summer storm, Jeanne read to Emma by flashlight. If Jeanne comes across a humorous cartoon or passage in a book, she reads it out loud and they laugh together. At the library, she searches for biographies or histories of immigrants passing through Ellis Island for Emma to read. Emma picks up a yellow shawl at the Red Door thrift shop and shows it to Jeanne. They both know she doesn't need it, but Jeanne says it's cheery.

"I don't know what I would do without her," Emma says of Jeanne.

Yet, Jeanne says her mother is remarkably self-sufficient. A lot of people want everything. Emma isn't like that. Her mother has the ability to find delight and wonder in simple things around her, a delicate violet or the venetian blinds that pleased her as a newlywed. After Christmas Jeanne carried the tree outside and leaned it against the back wall. Later Emma was looking out the kitchen window and saw small birds flitting in and out, drawn to seeds that neither she nor Jeanne had noticed before. Emma couldn't wait to tell Jeanne when she got home.

One morning Emma woke up and told Jeanne about the most wonderful dream about a friend, who had died a few years ago. Her friend was sitting at a bus stop, wearing a straw hat with a wide brim. It was sunny. Emma walked over to her and lifted the edge of her hat. The woman looked up and smiled radiantly. Emma wanted to call the woman's daughter that very morning and share the peaceful scene with her.

Not many people would think of Emma as particularly strong, says Jeanne. It's not an obvious characteristic of someone so lighthearted.

"But she is," Jeanne says. "She came here and became a part of the community but remained true to herself. She didn't feel she had to be the way somebody else was."

Perhaps the greater, yet more subtle, demonstration of strength is that she allowed her daughters to be themselves.

"I'm sure she would have wanted me to be like my friends. To marry someday and have children to bring home. My sister studied for many years and did a lot of traveling. So I think in a sense we kind of denied our parents a lot of things that people look forward to," says Jeanne.

Emma keeps special school papers, pictures, and articles inside a stationery box covered with soft pink roses.

Inside is Joan's diploma, a half dozen index cards from high school with her grades, all As and a few Bs. A letter from the academic dean congratulates Joan on being selected as an usher for commencement and directs her to wear a pastel dress, no hat, and short white gloves.

Along with them is a thirty-year-old Sunday bulletin from Most Holy Name Church. One paragraph reads, "On Thursday, September 7, Jeanne Hildenbrand will be received as a postulate of the School Sisters of Notre Dame at 7:00 P.M. in the church. The ceremony will close with Benediction of the Blessed Sacrament. All relatives and friends are most cordially invited to attend."

"They've had an altogether different life. They always worked and were smart and on the dean's list. They did real good. I'm very proud of both of them," Emma says.

One time she and the girls were sitting in the living room. Emma was on the couch. Jeanne and Joan were reading. Both were more interested in their studies or their careers than in getting married. She told them she was going to be like a mother bird. "I'm going to put you out and let you fly."

They did.

CHAPTER SIX

Bountiful Gardens
and Friends

E MMA CARRIED HER Wandering Jew up from the cellar yesterday and took it outside to get some fresh air and sunlight. Then she replaced the dark rose sofa pillows with cream-colored ones that had little French knots resembling tiny buds, putting one on either end of the couch.

She marks a new season with little changes around the house. Bringing out the lightweight bedspreads, the pillows, the pink tablecloth, makes rooms fresher and livelier. Jeanne moved the couch to the other side of the living room so it faces the window. From there Emma can look up and see the afternoon sun.

Early spring is Emma's favorite time of year. The days, edged in cold and warm in the middle, draw her outside to the little backyard garden. She works in short bursts, sometimes going in and out a half dozen times a day. In the hot summer she stays inside between 10 A.M. and 2 P.M. and takes frequent breaks.

"I know when to quit. Leo wasn't like that. Once he started something, he would finish it. My girls are the same way," says Emma. At Easter Jeanne baked a cake and Emma was going to ice it. Emma leafed through her cookbook and found the recipe for seven-minute icing, which she made years ago. Something came up. A phone call or a knock at the door. Emma never got around to making icing. She put the cookbook away. She and Jeanne ate the cake unadorned and declared it delicious.

If Emma tires in her garden, she rests on her white plastic chair placed in the sun against the back wall. From there she can see what subtle changes the new day has brought in the flowers, plants, and vegetables that ring her yard. One afternoon the whole yard is cast in purple with violets and pansies, and the next in the soft pink of bursting roses.

She keeps her garden immaculate. She is less fussy about the living room or kitchen. Newspapers can rest on the couch until she gets to them. She opens a closet and throws a single glove onto the top shelf. It lands in the vicinity of the other, which is enough.

But outside is different, especially now. Everything looks tidy as if the stars spent the night grooming the grass, trees, leaves, and petals to look their finest at daybreak. Even the moist dirt glistens. A few bent old sticks can make an entire backyard look disheveled.

Brittle curled brown leaves have blown over from the cemetery three doors down and wedged themselves in the chain-link fence. Emma reaches down and picks them up, working her way steadily along the fence and then through the rosebushes. One hides in the tangled feet of a shock of decorative grass. She crumbles it in her hands.

Working quietly but intently, she stoops at a small green clump just emerging from the ground and pulls it out. It doesn't belong there. She doesn't even know what it is but she knows it doesn't belong there. She spies and seizes a single leaf blemished by tiny black spots, plucks it from an otherwise immaculate rose-bush, and tosses it in a growing pile of debris on her sidewalk.

Weeds are beginning to creep up between the cobblestones of the path between her house and the one next door. They grow slowly because the sun rarely reaches the ground there. In the hot summer, children gather with their dolls and trucks on those narrow pathways between houses. The cobblestones are so cool they almost seem wet.

Her best friend, Ernestine Hepp, who lives two doors down, gave her some rock salt. Emma puts the salt in a bucket of hot water and pours it over the weeds to kill them. Cheap bleach works, too. Thelma Wurdock mentioned that once. A child-size broom rests by the back door. She climbs up the three steps, brings it down, and starts sweeping the walk.

Years ago, when the steel mills lined the riverbanks, the fine soot rose from dozens of smokestacks and came to rest on her pure white asters, turning them ashen gray. One of her relatives lived out in the country and washed her curtains once or twice a year. Emma had to wash hers almost weekly. No one would dare complain. Dirt, smoke, and soot were badges of prosperity.

Emma's garden is not wild or wanton. Nor is it tame. Tulips don't bloom lockstep in rows or march neatly along the fence but, rather, grow here and there.

She loves the grape hyacinths, which look like tiny clusters of purple fruit, because they're free-spirited. They surprise her, popping up one place and then in another spot five feet away, like they simply landed, rather than grew. Even if they could take over the yard, they wouldn't. These flowers are too generous and gracious. It's as if they glanced around and decided among themselves, "We need a dash of purple there. Oh, and a little bit by the fence would look nice, too."

An ivory-colored birdbath sits in the middle of her yard, ringed with daffodils in the spring, and pink and purple petunias in the summer. Some mornings she and Leo would wake up to find the shallow bowl lying on the ground, knocked off the pedestal by an animal. Raccoons and muskrats had come from the streets below Troy Hill looking for a drink. Leo would cement it back on.

"I always, always have a birdbath," says Emma. Gardens need birdbaths. It makes the picture complete. Flowers provide background color and fragrance. Birds make the scene come alive with movement and song. Emma bought a heart-shaped stepping-stone with a hummingbird approaching a flower and placed it between her roses.

Emma never had gardens, or even a yard, as a child. She played on the sidewalk and steps. Just a few weeks ago she heard a story from a nephew, who had heard it from his own mother, Emma's oldest sister, Annabelle. He said Emma's mother cried when the family moved to a house with no place for a garden. Emma didn't know her mother loved to garden. It makes her feel closer to her. Sadie, too, loved flowers. After Sadie married, she moved to a house with a little backyard and grew roses named Vogue, Fashion, and Peace. Emma longed to grow such beautifully named flowers, too. Once Emma and Leo married, Sadie gave her cuttings from her Crimson Glory and Peace rosebushes, and a delicate little purple flower called Live Forever.

But it was really Ana, the woman who lived next door, who guided Emma. "Anything I learned about the garden, I learned from Ana," Emma says.

Ana was born in Europe and spoke little English. She lived by herself and filled her yard with zinnias and tomatoes, onions and peppers. In the morning Ana would come outside and begin talking to Emma over the chain-link fence between their two yards. Emma smiled and listened, trying to understand what the woman was saying. Every once in a while, Emma could make out a word, like *money* or *police*.

More than anything, though, Emma watched Ana tend her plants. She noted when Ana planted, when she cut back the blossoms and branches, and by how much. By example Ana taught Emma how to start new flowers and bushes from the branch, stem, or root of an old one. Nothing in Ana's garden, or even her kitchen, went to waste. She was from the old country. Twigs, leaves, grass, and old vegetables fed the compost.

Even in the last few years of her life, when Ana was failing mentally, she remained ever aware of her garden and its needs. Her grandson came over and started planting or pulling. She scolded him, "No, no, no." It wasn't time yet.

Ana died in 1996 at the age of ninety-two. Emma clipped her death notice, a small paragraph, from the newspaper. It sits on top of her dresser. "I couldn't understand her. But I always knew she had a story to tell," says Emma.

Ana had a white statue of the Blessed Virgin Mary in her garden. Her grandson brought it over and gave it to Emma and Jeanne. Jeanne put it on the side of the garden so it could face Ana's house. The same statue is all over Troy Hill, standing in the grass of those who have yards, or on a porch. A smaller version rests on mantels or dressers. In all of them Mary is looking down, not downcast, but humble. Her arms are open at her sides, as if to welcome.

What Ana taught her, Emma passes on to others. A young mother, who lives two doors down, stops by with her daughter, a pot, and a handful of daffodil bulbs. She wants to know how many bulbs she can plant in the pot.

"You can put three in there," Emma tells her. "Just don't overcrowd them." She looks at the empty pot and says she wishes she had some good dirt to give her.

Another neighbor, working outside, overhears the conversation. He comes into Emma's yard with a bag of planting soil. They stand on the walk, talking. He spotted a turtle in his yard and it made Emma think of her father. One time he brought home turtle soup he'd cooked at the fire station. "That soup, it was so delicious. I don't think I've had it since," says Emma. She had forgotten about that until the turtle showed up in her neighbor's garden. She'll have to tell Jeanne about the turtle soup. Jeanne is fascinated by family history.

Gardens and flowers have a way of bringing people together, drawing them from their homes. That is one reason Emma loves them. She and they are both so social. Trowels or brooms in hand, neighbors busy themselves digging and weeding, then stand up, look over, and remark, "Sun is warm today. Think we'll get that rain they're promising?" They gather at the fence, praising a snapdragon. When a rosebush or flowering tree blooms with particular beauty, it is a source of pride for the gardener because it delights all.

"Your azaleas will be blooming," Emma tells the young mother.

Emma remembers when her good friend Dolores lived in the young mother's house and had beautiful azaleas. Dolores didn't have an easy life. She grew up on a farm. Her mother died when she was a girl, and she went to work cleaning for a wealthy woman. She had seven children of her own, and all were well-behaved and clean. She would see Emma enjoying her flowers, then decided to plant her own. They became fast friends, inviting each other over for birthdays, talking about gardening. Dolores's son who lives in another state stopped by recently with his wife and children to visit Emma. He said he always considered her wise.

"Dolores ended up with a beautiful garden," says Emma. She grew peach trees and a dogwood. "We all look forward to spring and that dogwood blooming," Emma says.

Nearly every flower and plant in Emma's garden has a past and an identity. The first rose to bloom is red. It was her father-in-law's favorite. He sat in their kitchen, his feet propped up on the white windowsill and a spittoon at his side, and looked out the back window, admiring it.

Her mother-in-law carried lilies of the valley in her wedding bouquet. Clusters of them grow by Emma's fence and are among the first flowers to appear in the spring. As soon as they arrive, Emma clips a few stems and brings them inside. Two or three of those delicate little white bells sweeten the entire living room.

Along the back fence, dozens of roses spill over like a silent all-pink grand finale of fireworks. Emma calls it Marianne's rosebush. Emma passed on some of Sadie's roses to help her neighbor Marianne get started. Years later and with her own garden thriving, Marianne gave Emma a cutting of her pink bush, now taller than Emma. Marianne's bush doesn't grow straight up but gushes and splays uninhibitedly with a bold fragrance. A contradiction, it seems both wild and Victorian.

Marianne has since died. Emma clipped four of the most beautiful blossoms, wrapped their stems in moist paper towels, and brought them to church. There, she gave them to a friend who knows Marianne's sons. She wanted the boys to see their mother's roses and how beautiful they were and are.

With a garden, there is always something to give and share. Emma doesn't bake or crochet. Instead of sending friends home with a plate of cookies, she fills a bag with white Shasta daisies and offers a bit of Ana-like advice.

"These are beautiful," she says. "Take some. You won't be sorry. If you don't get to plant them right away, keep them in water." She loves passing on the Live Forever.

Joe Grindel gave Emma and Jeanne tomato plants he had grown from seed. He didn't want anything in return. His only request was that they share the tomatoes with neighbors who didn't have any. Joe repaired their television set when it was broken, too.

Emma doesn't bother with gardening gloves this day because they aren't handy. Even when the gloves are hanging right by the door, she sometimes walks right past them. She loves the feel of warm dirt, or cool packed soil below the sun-drenched surface. She grabs the spiky stem of lavender. The skin on her right hand rips like paper into a small tear. Blood squirts out.

She rushes inside the kitchen and puts her hand under cold water. A ceramic square with a yellow bird sitting on a branch hangs on the tile wall above Emma's sink. Sadie bought it for her years ago. Every time she washes her hands after coming in from the garden, she sees it and thinks, Isn't that nice. Sadie got that for me.

After drying her hands, Emma puts a Band-Aid on her cut and goes back outside. If Jeanne were here, she would put ointment on it. Emma looks at her nails. They have been breaking lately. Jeanne tells her she needs more protein in her diet, or some vitamins or minerals. Maybe Jell-O would be good, Emma thinks. She doesn't watch what she eats. She eats what she wants. Jeanne likes buckwheat pancakes. Emma likes buttermilk ones with syrup and butter. She does take a good afternoon nap, though. Last time she went to the doctor, he said continue what you're doing.

Emma returns to the lavender, wearing her gloves. She wants to cut off a piece with roots to give a friend. She tussles with it. It pulls back. She picks up a tiny spade and starts digging to uncover the roots. They're thick and gnarled. She hacks at them until a piece comes free.

Lavender is hardy. No matter how many times she chops off a piece, it doesn't wince or retreat. And such sweet fragrance from an unsightly looking root. In the winter months dried lavender petals rest in an open dish on a coffee table.

A bit of her seems to be in every blossom. The tolerant lavender, the gentle violets, and the carefree tiny hyacinths. Five little green ferns, their leaves curled tight like the tips of elfin shoes, are whimsical.

Emma cuts a few stems of lavender and brings them inside the house and puts them in a vase on a small round table in the living room. This table isn't cluttered. It is free of letters, newspapers, and magazines. Everything on it has been carefully placed and is meant to be seen and noticed.

Shannon's round preschool face, wreathed in dark curls, smiles in twin heart-shaped brass frames. She smiles again a few inches away in a rectangular frame, her face slightly older, longer, and more beautiful, her hair shoulder length. A small gold jewelry box holds dried flowers. Emma bought the box because it has an *S* on it. *S* for Shannon.

Behind it is a black-and-white photograph of Emma and Leo in a reddish wood frame. They are somewhere in the country, under a tree. Leo has his arm around Emma's waist. She leans into him comfortably and naturally, wearing a tan shirt and sweater, and a flowered necklace. It was green and yellow, she remembers. Leo is in a white shirt, no tie. The collar is unbuttoned at the neck. They never had any wedding pictures to hang on their walls or frame for their mantel. Jeanne found this picture. She wanted one of her parents together and had it enlarged.

A few weeks later Emma's poppies have opened. She didn't expect them so soon, and when she sees them, she nearly squeals with delight. No other flower in the garden matches that brilliant orange. This year they are particularly splendid. Winter was mild and the poppies never died. Their stems and leaves stayed green all year round.

She hasn't been feeling well. She has a little bit of a cold, and Jeanne wanted her to stay inside. Jeanne stopped by the library and picked up a history of the president's wives. "I always like President Johnson's wife. She talks about planting entire fields of flowers. You can do it in Texas," says Emma.

Her backyard beckons. Emma puts on her coat and goes outside.

The night before, Jeanne had pulled up dozens of bachelor buttons. The little white flowers seemed to be taking over the yard. She's more aggressive than Emma when it comes to weeding and trimming. Emma is more inclined to let roses go wild.

Emma stoops at every little white clump of bachelor buttons, picks it up, and shakes the dirt still clinging to the roots into her garden. She doesn't want to lose good dirt. Ana would have a fit.

Emma transplants a violet to fill an empty space. "I hate bare spots," she says. And violets go well anywhere, those dainty threadlike stems supporting the big flapping purple petals. They're so ladylike, yet strong. For Easter Shannon sent her a card covered with violets. Shannon signed it and drew a little heart and round face with a smile.

Jeanne bought some new ground cover and planted it. Emma can't wait to see what it looks like. "I let her do what she wants," says Emma. That's the fun of gardening. Trying new things and sharing the anticipation.

A neighbor two doors down subscribes to a horticulture magazine with glossy covers of cherry red roses. When he is finished, he drops it off. Emma and Jeanne pore through it and talk about what they want to try. Jeanne suggested snapdragons and Emma was thrilled because she had them years ago and misses the way three shades of pink grace one small blossom.

Emma sits down for a rest. The Blessed Virgin Mary is up to her waist in white flowers. Cages surround three tomato plants. Shiny hot peppers dangle from a stem.

Every day there is something to be done—weeding, planting, watering, and transplanting. If a frost comes, Emma covers a bush or takes a pot inside. She puts the pot on the windowsill to get the afternoon sun. In the fall the chrysanthemum blossoms tell her winter won't be too far behind. She is ready. It doesn't sadden her. It is time for her and the earth to rest. She cuts out a picture of a beautiful garden from a magazine and puts it on her refrigerator. It stays there for the winter months. Jeanne wrote a poem in high school, called "November Duties." Emma doesn't know where it is, but she remembers that it began with a tribute to the seasons. "It's time to cover the garden / Summer has said farewell."

Once she told a friend, "I'm just as happy as can be at home. I always was. Maybe it's because of the garden and the neighbors. I always had good neighbors. You couldn't ask for better ones."

The man next door mows their yard and gave Emma a little chipmunk to set in her garden. A woman across the street reads the morning newspaper and the *New Yorker*. When she is through, she leaves them in a bag on Emma's doorknob.

Emma finishes the newspaper and walks it two houses down to Ernestine. Ernestine isn't much of a reader. But she likes to keep up with the obituaries. She has two small scrapbooks, forty pages each, filled with holy cards given out at the funerals of friends and relatives. The oldest is from 1907 when her husband's grandparents died.

Ernestine is slightly taller and slightly older than Emma. Their hair is equally white, though Ernestine's hair curls and

Ernestine Hepp and Emma Hildenbrand.

Emma's hangs straight. Ernestine wears light tan orthopedic shoes. Emma prefers white tennis shoes with Velcro fasteners instead of shoelaces.

Ernestine is out back watering her flowers with her hose. Her tulips and daffodils stand equally spaced in a nice neat row. She can't stand disorder or dirt. Twice a year, once in the spring and once in the fall, she washes every window in the house, hauling rags and buckets up to the third-floor attic, even though no one goes up there. Ernestine's daughter says she cleans with intensity.

"I want to ask you something, Emma," Ernestine says. She picks up a white plastic hanging basket and holds it up for Emma to see. "Can I leave this outside now?" she asks. "I had it down in the cellar."

"What is it?" Emma asks.

"I don't know," Ernestine answers.

"Not until at least the end of May," Emma advises.

The two of them stand at the fence, admiring the yard next door. Ernestine's neighbor grows bonsai trees in a shallow dish. Emma took a class in bonsai at the conservatory downtown but never planted any.

The man who lived in that house years ago and had moved to a nursing home just died. Ernestine went to the funeral. His wife died years earlier. She was crippled with arthritis while only in her fifties. Ernestine and Emma had watched over her while her husband was at work. Emma, more of a talker, sat and talked with the bedridden woman, keeping her spirits up. Ernestine, more of a doer, cooked and fed the woman. The couple had one son, but he didn't live close.

"Toward the end, she couldn't even hold her spoon to feed herself," says Ernestine.

"Remember the doctor?" asks Emma. "He came and sat and held her hand."

"Doctors don't do that anymore. That's the trouble," says Ernestine.

Emma and Ernestine have been neighbors—their houses on Lautner Street two doors apart—for fifty years. Their children splashed each other with a hose in Emma's backyard and went to Most Holy Name Elementary School together. Before they even met, Emma's mother-in-law and Ernestine's mother were dear friends, neighbors, and godparents to each other's children.

Still, Emma and Ernestine hadn't been particularly close. Their lives revolved around family, home, garden, and their respective churches.

While Emma tended her garden, Ernestine cared for the sick. "I wish I would have been a nurse," says Ernestine.

One of the older of ten children, she looked after younger brothers and sisters and had to stay home from grade school at Most Holy Name on Monday, laundry day, to help her mother. After Ernestine married, she cared for her elderly landlady as the woman grew frail—making her dinner and taking her to doctor appointments. Then, Ernestine's father was bedridden with throat cancer, and died in 1946. When her mother was sick in bed, Ernestine walked to her house every day, helped pay the bills, and did her grocery shopping. Two brothers had cancer. She baked apple pies and took a bus to visit them so their wives could get out and run errands. On top of that, she raised her four children and two nephews whose parents died.

And then Ray had glaucoma and was blind for the last six years of his life. She rarely left his side. She fed and dressed him. Ernestine walked him up and down the street. Neighbors, sitting on their front steps or watering their backyards, yelled out, "Hi, Ray, how are you doing?" And he smiled and returned the greeting. He knew everyone's voice.

On Saturday nights, she turned the television on to *Lawrence Welk*. When the orchestra played the polka, she pulled Ray out of the rocking chair. "We would dance in the living room, him and I. If anybody looked through the window, they would see us dancing and think we were crazy. But I thought that would make him feel good, you know. He loved to dance," says Ernestine. His favorite song was "You Are My Sunshine."

In a small box, Ernestine keeps a small newspaper article announcing that she and Ray are about to celebrate their fiftieth anniversary on June 25, 1980, with a mass at Most Holy Name and reception at the Mount Troy Fire Hall. The paper carried a picture of them. Ernestine is smiling. Ray is, too, but he's looking down, unaware of the camera's angle. She ordered a big wedding cake and white napkins embossed with FIFTIETH ANNIVERSARY, RAYMOND AND ERNESTINE, 1930 TO 1980 in gold lettering. The party was canceled. Ray was sick in the hospital. Doctors found a blood clot on his brain and operated. He went into a coma and never regained consciousness. Every day for two and a half months, Ernestine took the bus and spent the day in his room, crocheting or knitting until one of her children came for evening visiting hours. After, they drove her home.

She kept thinking he would open his eyes. He died shortly after midnight on September 27, 1980.

Emma's husband, Leo, died eleven years later, in 1991. Emma, Jeanne, and Leo had been out to the cemetery to plant new flowers for Memorial Day. Leo tried to push the shovel in the hard dirt and fell back, striking his head. He didn't seem seriously hurt. But apparently the blow caused hemorrhaging. A week later he died. Since then Emma and Ernestine have been as close as schoolgirls. A neighbor dubbed them the Gold Dust Twins. They talk on the phone daily. If one has a doctor appointment, the other will go along for company and sit in the waiting room.

"All my life I've been taking care of people," Ernestine says.

"You still are," says Emma. "You're taking care of me." When Emma's sister Sadie died, Ernestine baked a cake with cherry-and-nut flavoring for Sadie's daughter.

"That's what neighbors are for," says Ernestine. "I can't do much for my neighbors on the other side."

They look at each other and burst out laughing. Ernestine lives next to the cemetery.

"Well, at least they're quiet. I never have to argue with them," she says.

They sit at Emma's kitchen table eating cake and drinking tea. The cake is left over from Sunday, which was Ray's birthday. About fifteen of her children and grandchildren came to mass and then to Ernestine's for dinner.

Ernestine cooked a half of a boneless ham, German potato salad, and a big pot of chop suey. The pot wouldn't fit in her icebox. She put two rubber bands over the lid so animals couldn't get at it, and set it out on the porch. Chop suey is a family favorite. When she makes it she opens the windows to cool the kitchen. Outside, her neighbors know from the smell of sizzling pork, onions, and celery that Ernestine is making her chop suey. And doing it all from scratch. She'd raise the pig if she could, Emma says, and laughs.

"See," says Emma, "you can handle a crowd. Nothing seems to be too much for you, Erna."

"Funny, with all that cooking," Ernestine says, "I can't taste or smell." She can only distinguish between sweet and sour. "Out of ten children, I was the one who had to be blessed with that."

"Well, you were blessed in other ways," Emma tells her.

Emma makes people feel good about themselves. She has a special way of putting friends in their best light and holding them up to be admired. It's like her flowers. When her cosmos burst with soft violet paper-thin blossoms, she cuts a few branches and places them in a splendid cut-glass vase on the mantelpiece, flanked by purple candlesticks. Friends and flowers both flourish with devotion. In turn they grace the space around them.

"I have some of this bread I want to give you," Emma tells Ernestine. She opens her freezer door and pulls out a bag containing two thirds of a loaf of a puffy, golden yellow bread. It's slightly sweet, like Danish without icing. She and Ernestine like sweet things. Ernestine will take a bus downtown just to pick up a loaf of cinnamon bread. Emma cuts off a hunk of the yellow bread and puts it in a bag for Ernestine to take home.

Sometimes they sit and exchange stories about Ray and Leo, sharing new insights that time and reflection provide. Ernestine says her husband, Ray, was smart. He graduated from grade school and could have won a spelling contest but deliberately misspelled the last word because he didn't want to make a winning speech.

Everyone said he looked like James Cagney. He did, especially in that picture of them sitting side by side, all dressed up for the employee summer picnic at Armstrong Cork, where they met. He's wearing a dark suit and tie, and two-tone shoes, half black and half white. He wasn't a big fellow. He wore his dark hair parted straight down the middle and slicked back on both sides. His squarish face is compressed, his chin and forehead trying to meet at the nose. All he needs is a big cigar.

Ernestine sits next to him, in a sleeveless beige dress, both feet together on the floor, looking straight ahead. He looks relaxed and worldly, his legs crossed. She looks a little timid. Ray bought her that dress. On Saturdays she and Ray walked along Fifth Avenue, looking in department store windows.

One time, she saw this dress and stopped. While she was admiring it, he said, "Do you like that?"

"Yeah, but I don't have money to buy that kind of stuff," she told him.

"Come on, let's go in," he said.

They went in. She tried it on and it fit perfectly. He bought her the dress. "He bought me shoes, beige shoes. Beige was my favorite color. Later he bought me a beige coat and it had a fur collar on it. I thought I was everything when I had that coat on," she tells Emma.

"Oh, I love beige," Emma says.

"He was a nice person. A good provider and a good husband," says Ernestine. "I always said Ray was my first and only. I'll never be able to remarry again now," she says. Not because she is eighty-seven but because he was so special.

You know, Emma tells Ernestine, Leo never said anything bad about the guy who lowered the car on his head. "He never was one to hold anything against anybody. The more I think of him, now that I'm older and I have time to sit and think, the more I think he was such a good guy," she says. Leo had a good friend, a black firefighter. No one would sleep in the bed that the black firefighter used, except Leo. They were friends and remained so even after Leo retired. Leo wasn't much of a talker, but they would sit on the phone and chat.

Ernestine looks at Emma's venetian blinds covering her two kitchen windows. "Don't they get greasy from cooking?" she asks Emma.

"Oh, I don't worry about the grease," Emma answers. "Whenever they are dirty, they get washed. I can't even see that stuff anymore. I can't see it. I can't climb. So why am I going to worry about it?"

Ernestine tells Emma about a new gadget. A long rod with a soft cloth at the end that cleans the blinds. It comes in pink, blue, and yellow. "You can wash it, too, Emma," says Ernestine.

"You're the worker between the two of us. I don't do anything I don't have to," Emma says.

Like doilies. Ernestine crocheted all her doilies. Then she mixed Argo starch with cold water in a pan and cooked it on a stove until it was thick like gravy but not lumpy. She dropped in the doilies, stirred, then took them out to dry. The trick was stretching the wet doilies on the table, so they dried stiff and flat as cardboard. She doesn't have to iron them.

"I still wear doilies on all my furniture, even upstairs," says Ernestine. "And I don't even use my upstairs."

Emma would never think of making her own doilies. She bought hers for fifty cents at the Red Door, prestarched.

The Red Door, a thrift shop in the basement of the Lutheran church, is open on Wednesday, which has become Emma's and Ernestine's day to go to the bank, or drugstore, depending on whether either has checks to cash or prescriptions to fill, and then to the Red Door. They have been doing so for years. Bank tellers, bus drivers, the pharmacist, see one and look for the other.

Just after 9 A.M., Ernestine leaves her house, cane in one hand, purse in the other, and walks down to Emma's. Emma stands at the window, watching for her. As soon as she sees Ernestine, she grabs her small gray leather purse lined with suede, locks her door, and goes outside. Emma likes little purses. Ernestine likes big ones. But Ernestine is taller and bigger boned. Emma is small. Little Em they called her in high school.

The bus stop is two blocks away. They link elbows and walk arm in arm down the middle of the street because it's flatter and wider than the sidewalks. A metal folding chair sits unoccupied in the street, close to the curb, reserving a parking space. People don't have driveways.

Ernestine is a little sore today. Mornings are harder because the joints are stiffer. Yesterday she just rested, which is unusual for her. But it has been a busy few days.

Her nephew died. The wake and funeral were this weekend. Ernestine baked pizzelles and got the house ready for her sister Bernadette, who drove in from Cleveland with her husband for the funeral and spent the night. Her nephew was popular and played an accordion. Everyone called him Twisty. The man who runs the funeral home told Ernestine it was the biggest funeral he had ever seen.

"Everybody was saying, 'Oh, here is a celebrity.' He had one of the most expensive accordions and he played all by heart," Ernestine tells Emma.

They walk slowly. Doing so gives them a chance to savor Norma Weir's splendid yard, at this moment sprinkled with red, pink, and yellow tulips. Norma lives on the next street over and is Ernestine's niece. A homemade windmill stands four feet tall. Two plaster squirrels wearing hats peek over the top of a picket fence that lines her walk. The lady squirrel wears a flowered hat. The male, a derby. Norma's yard is a showcase, especially during the holidays, when she has lights, figurines, and inflatable bunnies and Santas. After the tulips, red and pink roses will blossom.

As they walk, Emma and Ernestine catch up from the day before.

"I didn't sleep so good last night," Ernestine says.

"Hmm," says Emma. "I never have that problem." Emma hits the pillow and she's out. She takes naps during the day, too. Ernestine can never do that.

Ernestine worries a lot. Her nephew died of cancer. Her father died of cancer. So did two brothers. Another brother is in the hospital. That brother, Ernestine, and her sister Bernadette are the last of the ten children.

"You worry too much. Worry is interest paid on trouble that never comes due. I think Sadie told me that," Emma says.

"I got up and did some crocheting," Ernestine says.

"You're always doing something. I'm such a lazy thing," says Emma.

"But you're smarter than me," Ernestine says. "You went to high school." Ernestine quit school after the eighth grade to work at the cork factory, where she met Ray.

"Look at that azalea," says Emma, nodding to a fuchsia bush bursting with tiny trumpetlike flowers. "I got a postcard from Shannon. She must have been in New York." They're both amazed at how their children and grandchildren travel.

That corner house, Ernestine says, used to be a store. Men shot craps behind it and women bought bean seeds for the garden there. Emma remembers Leo saying, as a boy, he bought bread wrapped in newspaper there. By the next day, it was hard as rock.

They miss the 9:05 bus so they have to take the 9:20, which is more crowded with neighbors going downtown to shop. Usually Emma and Ernestine sit in the same seat. But this morning they sit across the aisle from each other. No matter where they sit, they know the person next to them. "How ya doing, Erna?"

the woman next to her asks. Ernestine tells the woman she has a stiff leg.

Emma talks about the weather, how it's nice but a little cool so she grabbed a hat, any old hat, and it ended up to be Jeanne's, a little tan tam. They both love tams. "Jeanne won't mind," Emma says. Emma pulls the tam down to cover her ears. Some people wear them at a jazzy angle. She wants her ears warm.

The bus goes slowly down Lowrie Street, pulling over to let a car pass. A tavern sits across the street from the cemetery and has been there in some fashion since the days of horses and wagons. A worn metal ring the size of a grapefruit sat anchored to the curb. Ernestine's baby sister Bernadette loves to tell the story of the Memorial Day when her father went to that tavern after the parade and had a little too much and came home without his teeth.

"Sis," he whispered to her. Bernadette was about nine years old. "Come here." She did. He asked her if she knew where the tavern was and the alley next door. "I think I lost my teeth there," he told her. She found his teeth sitting in the gutter. When she brought them home, he slipped her a quarter. He was a good father, she says. He never missed a Monday at work and saved enough to buy the family a $750 player piano.

Emma and Ernestine get off the bus by the Troy Hill Pharmacy. Ernestine needs to drop off her prescription for arthritis. The man who owns the pharmacy, Chick Ambrass, just finished enlarging the store to make room for a video rental section. He also added a cooler for pop and a new display of greeting cards.

Ernestine waves two envelopes at him.

"Do you have a post office box here, Chuck?" She has always called him Chuck.

"No," he says.

"You need one," she tells him.

Emma admires the way Ernestine speaks her mind. When Ernestine was having gall bladder surgery a few years ago, the nurses were going to remove her wedding rings. She told them those rings had been on her finger since the day Ray slipped them on in 1930 and she wasn't about to take them off then. The rings stayed.

Outside the pharmacy Ernestine and Emma hitch arms and walk on the sidewalks. The streets are too busy to walk down their middles. Ernestine spots a dime and stoops to pick it up. Last week she found two pennies. A lot of people walk right over pennies. "I always say a hundred of them makes a dollar."

A blue plastic bucket filled with soapy water and rags has been left on the street behind a freshly washed car. "Someone should put that away," Ernestine says. She notices things that are out of place.

Emma is busy looking at the park. The park was the site of the Troy Hill Elementary School from the late 1800s to 1960. Then the city tore it down, which everyone here said was a mistake. All children who didn't want to go to Most Holy Name now had to leave Troy Hill. Sending children outside their neighborhood to school loosens ties to their community. They spend most of the day somewhere else. They don't meet and know their neighbors as they would if they walked to and from school.

The only consolation is that now the hill has a community park and an annual picnic there. Last year, Emma and Ernestine took home red and white helium balloons. Emma won a raffle prize: Lunch for two at Billy's restaurant on Lowrie Street. She plans to take Ernestine. Billy's has great crab cakes.

A sign posted along the edge of the park reads <u>POSITIVELY,</u> NO BALL PLAYING. Kids who want to play ball can go to the ball field a few blocks away, which used to be a cemetery. This park is more for rest than for play. A small gazebo stands in one corner. In another corner two metal stakes are planted several yards apart for pitching horseshoes. A flagpole with a plaque at its base rises in a patch of grass. On Memorial Day, the commander of the American Legion says a prayer there. Other than a single six-ounce plastic juice jug, the only trespassers in the neat park are a few dandelions.

Two blacktopped walks cross the park in a big X. Huge rocks, four feet long and two feet thick, border the walks. The rocks once lined the century-old reservoir, or water basin, that divided Troy Hill from Bohemian Hill. The city wanted to build a swimming pool at the site and began pulling out the rocks and hauling them away.

At the time, Mary Wohleber was president of the Troy Hill Citizens. Her motto, stripped across the top of the newsletter, was "If every man would sweep his doorstep, the whole world would be cleaner."

In that official capacity, as well as her unofficial capacity as preservationist, she wrote an indignant letter to the mayor.

The city, she wrote, had "wantonly destroyed a landmark in a community vitally aware of its historical and ethnic heritage.... For 130 years, that great stone wall has done its thing. Far longer than the one that will be erected in its place. This is progress?... Leave us something...."

The city gave her the rocks, which she had designated as historic landmarks.

"Mary just got back from wherever she was going," Emma tells Ernestine. Mary and Emma's daughter Jeanne taught at Most Holy Name together and have been good friends since. They take walks along the river and tour architectural landmarks together. Ernestine went to grade school with Mary's husband, Alan. "She was someplace far away." It was Bosnia. They can't keep track. All those names begin to sound alike.

"I can barely remember where I was last week." Ernestine laughs. Tonight Mary is giving a slide show and lecture on Allegheny City at the local branch of the Carnegie Library. Her next lecture, later this summer, is titled "Visit Merrie England with Mary."

Emma and Ernestine arrive at the Red Door.

Helen Lindenfelser, who lives farther down Lautner Street from Emma and Ernestine, began the Red Door more than fifteen years ago, when she was president of the Lutheran Church Women. The pastor approached her, saying he wanted an outreach program. Helen worked at Murphy's Five-and-Ten before getting married, and loved retail and sales. She suggested a thrift shop. The church basement was available. It was originally used for a youth group. But that group fizzled out, freeing up the space and the group's Ping-Pong table. Other folding tables were donated by a church that was demolished to make room for a freeway at the bottom of Troy Hill Road. Residents donated clothes, toys, and books. Helen could tell when someone died. The family dropped off bags of clothing.

Items sold for twenty-five or fifty cents. The first year, the Red Door raised four thousand dollars. Money went to a soup kitchen and an orphan's home. Helen ran the store for twelve years. By the time she left, the shop was making nine thousand dollars a year.

Tall and slender, now seventy-three, Helen wears blue jeans with a denim shirt embroidered with flowers, and a brown leather belt. Emma loves the way Helen dresses. She's so sharp and young. "You can get away with that, Helen. You have such a nice figure," Emma says. The five whimsical ferns in Emma's garden were a gift from Helen.

Helen gave up the store in 1995, the year her husband, Ralph, died. Helen loves telling the story of when they first met.

He was thirteen. She was fifteen. She was hanging her head out the window of her parent's house on Heckelman Street, which is just around the corner from where she lives now, when her cousin came over to show Helen his new bike. Ralph was tagging along on his two-wheeler and asked Helen if she wanted to take a ride. She hopped on Ralph's handlebars.

"So I'm having a good old time and we get to the end of Heckelman Street and this smart little kid says to me, '*Honey* and *Helen* start with the same letter.'

"I'm thinking, *Oh, give me a break.*

"Then, he tells me, 'When you put your head out that window'—now he's only thirteen—'I said to myself, that is the girl I'm going to marry.' He pursued me to no end. I wasn't interested. He was only a kid. I like tall blonds with blue eyes. Here is this little short fellow with dark hair and eyes. But that was the beginning of our love story."

They were married on a cold and rainy October 2, 1945, while Ralph was on furlough; ate a wonderful spaghetti dinner at Angelo's, a restaurant downtown; and spent their wedding night in the Fort Pitt Hotel. The room had cockroaches, but rooms were hard to come by during the war.

"It was a fleabag. Very unromantic, but that has absolutely nothing to do with almost fifty years of a wonderful, wonderful marriage," she says.

On a table next to her bed rests a white glass rose they bought at Busch Gardens one year. Next to it is a picture of them as a young couple. They are standing on a boat dock. Helen is looking up at the camera, wearing a white sleeveless dress. Her brown hair falls in curls to her shoulders. Her face is tan. Ralph wears a white T-shirt, the short sleeves stretching over his biceps. His dark hair is slicked back. It is the last thing Helen sees before she goes to bed and the first thing to greet her in the morning.

On a trip to celebrate their golden anniversary, they stopped at Lookout Mountain on the Tennessee border. After an early dinner they went back to their room and pulled out a deck of cards. Playing cards had become a nightly ritual after their daughter grew up and got married. Twice a week they also went out to dinner. One time to a fancy place. The other time to a hamburger joint. "They were just dumb little things, but doing them together is what made it special. I never wanted to leave Ralph, and now I'm glad I didn't, because that was our time together."

Helen was dealing. "He picked up three cards or so. All of a sudden he said, 'Oh, honey,' and he just toppled over. I thought I gave him a good hand and he's just being funny. I didn't know what the Sam Hill was going on."

Ralph was sweating. Helen yelled to him, "Are you OK? Are you OK?" He didn't answer. "Can you hear me?" No answer.

She ran out into the hallway, screaming for help. Members of a construction crew ran into the room. A nurse and preacher, both of whom were staying down the hall, followed.

The nurse took his pulse. Helen asked if he was OK. She remembers the nurse saying yes, but the look on her face was troubling. The ambulance took him to the hospital. Helen had no idea where the hospital was or how to get there. The preacher offered to show her the way.

After she arrived, the doctor came in and said he was sorry. There was nothing they could do for him. Ralph had had a heart attack.

"I was in shock. You know, I did not cry. To this day I really haven't. You see people going nuts on TV. Maybe it hasn't sunk in yet. I don't know. He always said he wanted to go first and he wanted to go fast. So he got everything he wanted." Her daughter is her best friend now.

After Ralph died Helen turned the thrift shop over to her friends at the church. She still comes by to help. Helen has a knack for making secondhands look appealing. Every shirt and pair of shorts and pants is folded neatly and stacked. None of the piles touch each other. Allow a little space between each stack, she instructed anyone helping her, and put the liveliest colors on top. "That makes it more appetizing," she says.

Nearly all the women on the hill have shopped at the Red Door. Margaret Fichter has run into Ernestine and Emma there. Margaret can still remember seeing Ernestine and Ray sitting on the bus together, going somewhere on a date. They were married on the same day as Margaret's brother.

Emma and Ernestine were among the first customers at the Red Door and remain among its most loyal. This morning the front door is propped open. They disengage arms. Emma starts down the first five steps, purse on one arm, holding on to the railing. Ernestine follows. They take it slowly. At the bottom a small sign is taped to a door with the warning THREE MORE STEPS.

By the time Ernestine reaches the last step, Emma is already inside, standing in front of a table. She picks up a pink-and-white-checked tablecloth that just came in that morning.

"Look at this, Erna. Oh, I love this," she holds it up as Ernestine approaches.

"That's nice," Ernestine answers.

"I don't need it. That is the trouble. I have a hundred table-cloths, but I don't have a pink tablecloth," Emma says. She pauses for a second. "Oh, I do have a pink one, but it's a fancy one with lace on it. I love this. And only fifty cents."

Emma brings the tablecloth over to the counter. The woman behind the counter tells her that the tablecloth just came in that morning. She and another woman volunteer every week. They total all the purchases on a small white slip of paper, with a pencil. The shop doesn't have a cash register. A calculator sits idle. They prefer adding themselves. "I'll hold on to this, Emma, until you're ready," the woman tells her.

Ernestine and Emma go their own ways, wandering through the long folding tables and card tables.

Ernestine finds a pair of socks and looks for stockings. Her stockings have runs in them. When she was working at Armstrong Cork, she turned her pay over to her mother, who gave her fifty cents for spending money.

"If we wanted silk stockings, we had to buy our own. Powder, too. I never bought lipstick because I never used it. Never smoked in my life and never used lipstick," Ernestine tells Emma.

"That is why you are such a good girl," Emma says.

"I'm old-fashioned," Ernestine says.

A woman comes downstairs to drop off several fancy dresses for little girls. Rows of tiny accordionlike pleats, called smocking, stretch across the top of one dress. A satin ribbon circles the waist. Ernestine rubs her fingers over the delicate smocking.

"My mother did this," she says.

Her mother made all the clothes for the ten children. Friends or relatives gave her mother old coats, and she would take apart every seam and reuse the material to make new coats for her own children. Her mother sewed the smocking by hand. Isn't that something?

It hits her as truly remarkable. All those kids and taking the time to make fancy smocking at the tops of their dresses. Her mother didn't have to do that. She wanted to make it special for her children.

"My mother was always crocheting, always knitting," she says. At home Ernestine has a little photo album covered in pink satin with the word *yesterday* embroidered on the cover. Her younger sister Bernadette made it for her. Inside is a picture of their mother, sitting on the couch, her ample lap filled with yarn. That is how Ernestine best remembers her. That black-and-white snapshot has became the defining and eclipsing memory.

Emma picks up a small pair of Hush Puppy shoes and brings them over to Ernestine. "For fifty cents, you can't go wrong," Emma tells Ernestine. Who will wear them isn't that important.

With all those great-grandchildren, they're bound to fit some-one, and if not now, in a few months.

"Hush Puppies is a good name. They'll last," Emma continues.

Emma buys for everyone. A friend of Jeanne's mentioned she was looking for a red coat. Emma spotted one and brought it home. She picks up three pairs of pants for Jeanne. If they don't fit, she can bring them down to Ernestine, for herself or one of her children or grandchildren. A plaque with three wild geese in midflight might be nice for her next-door neighbor. He fishes and might like this because it's outdoorsy.

Emma finds a flowered dress with shoulder pads. She disap-pears into the fitting room, then comes back out and reports to Ernestine. Ernestine has already paid for her things and sits on a folding chair with her bag.

"I hate these big shoulder pads, but I'm going to take it. I'll wear it with a jacket. As long as it's not too long," Emma says.

She doesn't want anything that needs hemming. That's too much trouble. Her sewing machine is broken, anyway. The foot fell off when she was trying to make some drapes for Christ-mas. Ernestine finished them for her. Emma likes telling people that story and always ends with, "Isn't that something?" She wants everyone to know how good a friend Ernestine is.

On her way to the counter to pay, she passes Helen. Helen picks up a pink tank top and begins folding it.

"Oh, look at that," says Emma.

"Check the size," says Ernestine. Ernestine thinks about things like size. And zippers. Ernestine slides them up and down a few times to make sure they don't stick. Only metal ones, too. She doesn't buy anything with synthetic zippers. They break.

"I don't worry about the size, Erna. I just look at it. I can squeeze into that. I'm small. I can wear it out in the garden," Emma says.

They wait at the bottom of the steps for a woman to make her way down. They know her. They pass each other every other week on these same steps. She asks how they are doing.

Ernestine says her knees are bad and she'd like to have them operated on, but everyone, she says, insists she's too old. "I'm not too old," she says. She mows her own lawn and washes attic windows. "I want to keep going."

At her granddaughter's wedding this winter, Ernestine danced the polka, the chicken, and the hokey pokey with her grandchildren and great-grandchildren. Her three grown daughters sat at a table at the edge of the dance floor, watching their mother, shaking their heads.

"We were like the eighty-seven-year-olds. We are content to enjoy and watch everybody else," her daughter Ruth Grabb says. "All the grandchildren and everybody were asking her to dance. She loves that. Dancing. The attention and the happy time."

The woman mentions a close relative of hers is sick and has just about had it with living.

Emma knows someone like that. "She says, 'I'm on my way out and I'm glad.' Not me. I'm not ready yet."

"Me, neither," says Ernestine.

They climb the steps, Emma first. Ernestine follows, holding the railing with one hand, her cane dangling from her other arm.

The bright midmorning sun blinds them for a few seconds. They put their hands up to shield their eyes. Across the street, a group of students from Most Holy Name play kickball in the empty parking lot. A woman with short brown hair, in navy blue pants and a white golf shirt, stands in the street, ready to retrieve errant balls.

"She's our principal," Ernestine says, nodding at her. "You wouldn't think that she was a nun. She doesn't look like a nun, does she?"

Or at least none of the nuns she had when she went to Most Holy Name. Sister Petronilla was the principal of the school. Nuns wore headdresses that seemed clamped to their foreheads, formless robes, and rosary beads, either at their waist or in their hands. Theirs arms didn't show. Their legs didn't show. If they had any hair, no one knew.

When Ernestine married, a relative who was a nun sewed two little cupid dolls on a Turkish towel as a wedding gift and had to leave it at the front gate because she wasn't allowed to deliver it in person. On the gift box stood a chubby little plastic couple, their hair, shoes, and clothes painted on. Ernestine keeps the two-inch-tall couple in the back of her china cabinet.

Just as Emma and Ernestine are about to walk to the bus stop, Ernestine's cousin asks if they want a ride. Her cousin stops at the Red Door occasionally and has driven the pair home several times. They help each other into the car. Ernestine lowers herself into the front seat of the little white Chevrolet, holding on to the dashboard. Emma stands behind her, holding Ernestine's bag until she gets in. Once Ernestine is settled, she hands it to her. Emma sits in the backseat.

Luckily, there are only two stop signs between the parking lot and their street. Her cousin's car runs fine as long as it keeps moving.

At the first stop sign, she pauses the car, looks both ways, and steps on the gas. At the second stop sign, she comes to a complete stop. The engine sputters. Emma starts to laugh. Ernestine starts to laugh. Her niece pumps the gas pedal and the car lurches forward.

"There we go," shouts Emma. The chugs and sputters don't bother them. It's like the little engine that could. They know it can. If the car stalls, they'll wait for it to start again. They aren't in any hurry.

CHAPTER SEVEN

Gypsy

EDNA MCKINNEY glances down at her wristwatch. She's always looking at the time. She has clocks all over her house. One on her table. Others on her dresser, bookcase, and TV, although the one on her TV lies facedown. Temperamental alarm clock. One day it ticks standing up. The next day it refuses to tick at all, unless it's lying down.

It's close to 11:30 and time to go. The Troy Hill 6A bus doesn't come until 12:07, but she likes to be prompt, or better yet, early. She doesn't drive, and if she wants to go anywhere off the hill, she has to catch a bus. Her senior citizen's bus pass, the OPT, entitles her to ride free from 9 to 4. Before or after then, the pass turns into a pumpkin. She doesn't know what OPT stands for. Old-people ticket, she muses. She is eighty— which sounds ancient, she says—but doesn't feel it.

If she misses the 12:07, she misses the connecting bus at the bottom of the hill, which takes her three times a week to the Sarah Heinz House recreation center for an hour of swimming in the indoor pool. That's her routine from early fall through late spring.

In the summer, she swims daily, walking down to the Cowley recreation center. All of the older ladies on Bohemian Hill, where Edna lives, went to Cowley as children and learned practical skills like sewing, and less practical ones like playing the harmonica, which Edna never mastered. They took dance. One-two-three-point. One-two-three-point.

Around Christmas the children performed for Mary Cowley, a tiny woman who started this recreation center and many others in the city. She sat in the front row, wearing a very big hat and looking pleased as the girls danced to "Glow Worm." Sometimes when Edna and her neighbors get together, they start talking about the sewing teacher who got mad if anyone ran out of red thread, and laugh as one woman does a perfect high-pitched imitation of the annoyed teacher. Mention "Glow Worm" and nearly all point their toes, tap their feet, and say together, "One-two-three-point."

Edna makes sure she has everything. Wallet for dollar bills. A purse for loose change. A package of six peanut-butter-and-cheese crackers in her pocket for an emergency lunch or snack. A little bar of soap, washcloth, shampoo, and one towel. When she gets out of the pool she scurries to the locker room, saving her one towel for her shower. She already checked the weather. No rain, so she breezes past the cardboard box holding a half dozen folding umbrellas. Closets, along with garages and yards, are extravagances on Troy Hill. Coats hang on racks behind doors. Any umbrella that can stand, does so in the corner. Edna's short umbrellas can't, so she lines them neatly in a box.

Before heading out, Edna glances in the little square mirror propped up on a chair. She pulls her white knitted cap down a little further to cover her ears. She bought the hat for fifty cents at a rummage sale at the Presbyterian church. Her oldest son, Art, called it her bag-lady hat. One time Art and his wife, Anna, were shopping. He saw a little old lady with a white hat and pointed to her. "Hey, look. That looks like Mom with her bag-lady hat on." Edna likes wearing it even more now. It's her joke with Art. "Every time I put it on, I think of Art saying, 'Oh, Mother, please, not that bag-lady hat again.'"

It keeps her warm this early spring day. The wind hides in ambush around corners. Walk down one street and a dried-up old leaf sits on the sidewalk like it was made of lead. Turn a corner and fairy leaves whirl like a dervish. A restored player piano flawlessly plays, "One Day at a Time" in the living room of one home. The hymn passes through a window, cracked open just an inch, and on to the sidewalk before being swept away by a gust.

Edna walks the quarter mile to the bus stop with purpose. Her shoulders are broad and straight, not hunched. Anyone glancing at her posture and march knows that she is not going to stop and chat. She has a place to go. Even her shoes are resolute, with wide, thick treads that disdain snow. Edna says those big white shoes and her long skinny legs make her look like Minnie Mouse. She likes to poke fun at herself. She would never do it to anyone else, though.

One time she was walking down the street and someone, who knows she is hard of hearing, yelled, "Hey, deafee." Edna didn't answer and the woman shouted louder, "Hey, deafee, didn't you hear me?" Edna was hurt and came home in tears. The woman who made the remark is large, and later one of Edna's friends asked, "Why didn't you turn around and make some comment about her size?"

"I can't," she told her friend. "I would never hurt anyone's feelings on purpose or try to get even. I'll just try to avoid her."

The bus shelter is by North Catholic High School, at the top of Troy Hill Road. She ducks inside. A few other people arrive. She knows them all. They know her and that she is going swimming. Six days out of seven, she is at this stop. When she runs out of clean clothes, she stays home to do laundry. Otherwise she's shopping, swimming, or off to a ball game, movie, or play. "If you want to get in touch with me, call early morning or in the evening. Otherwise the phone will ring off the hook," she tells friends.

Gypsy, her friend Marge calls her.

Marge isn't from Troy Hill. Edna met her years ago at another indoor community swimming pool that has since closed. Marge loves swimming, too. She gave her daughter directions. "When I die, have me cremated, throw the ashes in the river, along with a bathing suit." Marge is kindhearted. If she knows a friend is going through a hard time, she calls to say, "How are you?" Then, she listens and encourages. Lesser friends might avoid making those time-consuming and emotionally draining calls. Marge doesn't. She's tough. Not everyone knows how to take her. She likes to toss out verbal firecrackers and see who runs. Edna just laughs, knowing Marge is joking.

Marge waits for Edna in the beautiful marble-floored lobby of the Sarah Heinz House. Edna walks in. Marge looks up and asks, "Been at the bar all afternoon?"

They're like Mutt and Jeff. Edna is a string bean and Marge isn't. Marge is a year younger than Edna. Her daughter gave her a T-shirt with a pudgy, balding television star lying on a couch, wearing only boxers.

"I can't wear this," she told her daughter.

"Mom, you're the only one who *could* wear this," her daughter replied.

Marge wears it but keeps her sweater-vest buttoned over it.

Edna swims slowly, her head above the water, keeping her short gray hair and her ears dry. It is a smooth and practiced stroke, one lap and then another. She stops at one end and chats with others, lined up along the wall, about the water temperature and who is missing this week. Most of the weekly swimmers are retired men. Mary Wohleber comes down every once in a while. The other day Mary and Edna did chin-ups, hoisting themselves up on the diving board. Edna can't remember when she met Mary or how. Everyone knows Mary.

Then Edna continues. She is not there for anyone else. She is there for herself. "I jump in that water and all troubles go away," says Edna.

Marge stands in the shallow end, holding on to the wall doing exercises. Slowly, she extends one leg and lifts it up, and then back down. Up and down. Then, the other.

"She's a wonderful girl, a wonderful friend," says Edna of Marge.

Edna says she has a lot of acquaintances but few close friends. Mildred Mares was one of her closest and remains so, even though she moved. When they talk on the phone, they go on for an hour, jumping from meat loaf to grade school teachers to the Presbyterian church. Before hanging up, Edna tells her, "Mildred, you made my day. You made my week."

Edna cherishes her close friends and takes time to explain what makes them special. "Mildred never had to give me anything. She gave me her time. That was her gift. She was always there to listen," Edna says. "When I was happy, she was happy. When I bubbled, she bubbled."

Marge, too. Edna was going to Niagara Falls, and the bus was leaving the Uni-Mart parking lot at 7 A.M. Edna had to wake up by 5 A.M. The phone rang at 5 A.M. sharp.

"Gypsy, you awake?" It was Marge.

"Yeah," Edna replied.

"Good. G'bye." Marge hung up. That's a true friend, says Edna. Someone who wakes up to make sure you're awake.

After swimming, Edna and Marge go their own ways. Edna doesn't say good-bye. "See you whenever." That is her trademark sendoff because she isn't quite sure when she will see people next, unless she has her calendar with her.

Edna lives on Bohemian Hill and has for about fifty years. But she was born and raised on the other side of Troy Hill, a red-headed daughter of an Irishman named Lynch. Her mother's maiden name was Cernohorsky, which gave Edna legitimacy on Bohemian Hill. No one referred to her as Lynch or McKinney. She was Cernohorsky's girl, which was probably more accurate, anyway, since she spent so much time at her mother's childhood home with her grandparents.

Her mother died of a kidney disease when Edna was twelve. She remembers little of her, other than that she was sickly and always telling Edna to watch what she prayed for. "More tears are shed over answered prayers than those not answered."

"It's true," Edna says, "though you have to live long and say a lot of prayers to understand."

Edna's maternal grandmother, whom Edna called Bob, taught Edna most everything else. Use Black Cat polish to clean a black stove and Bon Ami to shine chrome. Add enough flour to grated potato, onion, and egg, until it feels right. That's the potato pancake recipe. The same vague impression applied to rolls, pies, and bread—enough flour, salt, nuts, and sugar until it feels, tastes, or looks right. Put a whole bay leaf, not minced, into jars of rice and barley to keep bugs out. Edna learned that from Bob long before she read it in *Hints from Heloise*.

As a schoolgirl in want or need of a quarter, she went to Bob. Bob put her to work, sweeping the yard or scrubbing the steps, and gave her twenty-five cents. As Bob grew older, Edna came over with her three young boys to wash her floors or do her laundry.

"Edna, I can't pay you," her grandmother would say.

"You don't owe me. I could never pay you back for what you gave me," Edna told her.

Bob made Edna, a skinny kid with a crooked smile, feel good and loved. Edna's two front teeth were off-center, so she looked like she had a smirk on her face, a Popeye grin. When Edna got dentures, the dentist asked if she wanted crooked dentures, too. "No," she told him, "make them the way they are supposed to be." She has a wonderful smile, not evolving or slow in coming. It explodes. Yet, she doesn't have crinkles in the corners of her eyes from years of laughing. Laughter has come relatively late in her life.

"Few of us ever knew Edna could talk and laugh so much," says Florence Klingman, who has spent her entire seventy-seven years on Brabec Street. When Edna first moved to Bohemian Hill, and for several years after, her new neighbors thought she was stern. "We thought she just didn't want to be bothered because she was from the other part of Troy Hill," says Florence. "We knew the wrong Edna."

Part of it is nature. Edna has always been a private person. "I'm friendly, but not outgoing," she says. "If you talk to me, I talk to you, but you can pass me on the street and that doesn't bother me."

She is rarely the first person in a conversation and is often not the center of it. She doesn't have to make people aware that she is there. Instead, she listens and then ventures forth, sticking to issues and not people, unless she has something good to say. Uncomfortable around gossip, she tries to change the subject. In offering advice, she does so almost self-consciously, not wanting to sound even slightly superior. "I probably sound like your grandmother, but . . ." And she goes on with a tip about making sure to finish prescription medicine, or a bit of wisdom about embracing your children's childhood while it is here.

She assumes people are honest and won't hurt her. Her son Art would tell her, "Mother, people aren't like that. You've got to watch your purse because someone will take it."

"That never enters my mind. I'm honest and I think you are," she says. "I've never gotten hurt by trusting. Yet, I think I have enough sense not to get mixed up with a con man."

Florence nods in agreement. "I know what you're saying, Edna. Like I can be trusted and I think everybody can be trusted," Florence says.

Edna has come to visit Florence to plan an upcoming trip to see Mildred Mares. Mildred told them over the phone to make sure they visit on Wednesday because the dining room has a nice buffet of fried chicken and lobster Newburg, but not the first Wednesday of the month because that is when the cleaning lady comes.

Florence splurged and bought fresh Danish from Guentert's, their favorite baker on East Ohio Street. Water boils on the stove for instant coffee. Outside it is dark and raining. Thunder cracks in the distance. "This is like spring," she says. It's been a strange year. Hardly any snow fell in the winter and spring was as hot as mid-July. Everything seemed a little off, not quite right. Like a too quiet child or a bald poodle.

Florence's kitchen is spotless. The stove sparkles, and so do the floor and walls. Florence is happiest cleaning. She sweeps her sidewalk and that of her neighbors, hangs her clothes outside even though she has a dryer. A little card sits on her table by her telephone, listing the golden rules for living.

"If you open it, close it; . . . if you borrow it, return it; if you value it, take care of it; . . . if it's none of your business, don't ask questions."

This year Florence took her first vacation, staying overnight in a hotel at Niagara Falls. She was with her sister-in-law Rose, who lives across the street, and Edna. All three stayed in one room. Edna slept on the floor and got up too early for everyone else. The three of them went for walks. Edna got lost. She often does, chasing some fact or interesting scene on the horizon.

Florence couldn't wait to get home.

"See, I'm different," says Edna.

"It's true," Florence says. "You were a bit more independent. You had to be. Your mom wasn't around."

Edna rarely misses a chance to go. Every year she buys season tickets to the Civic Light Opera and takes the bus by herself. Going alone doesn't make her feel friendless or lonely. Each show fascinates her. One has the most enjoyable dance; another is striking for its lavish set. Another delights her with its humor and song. "I enjoyed it immensely" is her standard review.

In the summer she loves to watch baseball.

On Tuesday afternoon a van takes a group of older adults to the baseball game. Edna has her OPT bus pass, a twenty-five-cent tip for the driver, a bag of pretzels, a can of soda, and extra straws in case anyone wants to share. She and a friend from the next street over sit by themselves. They enjoy each other's company. Both are quiet. Both love to read. Her friend brings a book and finishes it by the sixth inning.

The Pirates are playing the Colorado Rockies. It's Baseball Bingo Day. Fans receive a card and a yellow sheet of directions: If the Pirates catcher strikes out, it's I-17. If he steals a base, it's N-37, and a single is B-10. She gives away her bingo card. Edna doesn't play bingo. Even if she did, she wouldn't bother with this one. It's too confusing.

A few young boys walk by. The seats of their pants droop down to their knees. Their shirttails hang out. Thankfully, her three sons wore pants that fit, but they did leave their shirts out until she threatened them saying, "I'm going to sew some lace at the bottom of those shirts." After that they tucked their shirts in.

The stadium is one-third full. Edna and her friend pick a seat under the roof because the sky is clouding up. One midsummer game, Edna forgot a visor. The sun was blistering so she turned a paper bag into a hat. She sat there until an usher came up to her. "Excuse me. Would you like a seat in the shade?"

She said, "Thank you," took off her bag, and moved to a shady seat.

A vendor walks through the aisle, waving a huge inflatable black baseball bat. Behind Edna ten people stand in line at the concession, buying popcorn and twenty-ounce cups of Coke.

Down below, players warm up. Edna likes to watch the practice as much as, or even more than, the game when the ball, batter, and fielders all compete for attention. Now she can study individual players. She marvels at the precision of the pitcher repeatedly rifling the ball. In one corner an agile outfielder leaps into the air. Baseball is better than football or hockey, she thinks. In those sports, players seem to be clumped together, one uniformed mass crowding a ball or puck. In baseball the player hits by himself, catches by himself, steals bases by himself. He doesn't have to be part of a mob to shine. That's more her style.

A rather large young man sits in front of her. He is a regular. The usher calls him Big Guy.

"Hey, Big Guy. How are you doing?" the usher asks.

Big Guy nods his head up and down in response, and continues his chant. "*Let's go, Bucs. Let's go, Bucs. Let's go, Bucs.*" Bucs is short for Buccaneers, both nicknames for the Pirates. Throughout the game Big Guy offers his own play-by-play commentary. "Lousy swing." "Good pitch." "Lousy call." He pulls out a plastic juice bottle and empties the cherry juice into his mouth with one mighty squeeze.

A group of handicapped students pass in wheelchairs. Florence feels sad for everyone. Edna doesn't, but not because she isn't compassionate. "Look at those two boys. They have such a look of contentment and joy on their faces, like they're having the time of their lives," she says. Edna looks at what people have rather than what they don't.

By the sixth inning, the Pirates are ahead 5–0. A tiny sparrow flies between two metal girders in the ceiling above. Back and forth. Back and forth. Edna watches the bird.

Big Guy boos loudly. The right fielder had missed an easy pop-up. The crowd jeers.

She wonders, *Can the players hear that or can they block it out?* And if they can hear that, how do they concentrate? Resilience fascinates her.

She looks back at the sparrow. She wonders if it is building a nest.

Some people are ambushed by a new thought. A bit of information surprises them in an innocent conversation. Edna actively pursues new ideas. She is not obsessive or frantic about it, just constantly curious and amused.

On a van going to the mall, everyone plays bingo, except Edna. She looks out the window, wondering what happened to all the cows that used to pepper the hillsides. "It used to be that if you were anyplace in the country, there would be cows everywhere. Now it's a rarity to see a cow." All she sees are bulldozers. "What happened to all those cows and farmers?"

It got to be a joke. Anytime others spotted a cow, they'd say, "Hey, Ed, there's a cow," and chuckle.

Edna laughed, spun her head around, and said, "Where?" Then she watched until the next hillside eclipsed the cows, trying to absorb as many cows as she could before they were gone completely.

She went to the Andy Warhol Museum. Edna knew little of Warhol, other than he was from Pittsburgh, painted soup cans, and looked a little anemic. When the museum opened on the North Side in Pittsburgh, movie stars in strapless gowns stepped out of limousines, creating the closest thing to a Mardi Gras that Pittsburgh has ever seen. She wanted to see what all the hoopla was about.

"One wall had nothing but picture after picture of men's parts, and one with a bow on it," Edna tells Florence and Mildred Mares during the Wednesday afternoon visit to Mildred's retirement center. They have gone through the buffet line and are seated at a linen-covered table. All three prefer buffets, not because they can take as much as they want, but as little. They can't stand seeing food go to waste. When they were growing up, mothers would run after the horses with shovels and scoop up their "business," as they called it, to fertilize the garden. Edna dots her plate. A little breaded drumstick of chicken. A small pile of potatoes. Some lettuce. A roll. Nothing touches. They're all little islands, not one landmass.

"Well," Edna continues, "you don't know whether to laugh, cry, run, sit. Thank heavens there weren't any other people there. I think I would have crawled on my hands and knees out the door. I was so embarrassed. And then one complete wall of

Marilyn Monroe, just photographs, big. Jacqueline Kennedy, the same thing. I don't know what they raved about."

"I only thought he was famous for the can of soup," Florence says.

"Oh, there are a lot of cans down there," Edna says. "And then there was wallpaper with a cow's head. But it isn't even a complete head. It's like a strip with half of the head cut off."

"Oh my," Mildred says.

"There were a bunch of cartons piled up. I didn't know if it was a delivery or a display. They were just helter-skelter," Edna says.

"It looks like I didn't miss anything," Mildred says.

"Well," says Edna, "I'm glad I went for one simple reason. Now I'm satisfied."

Once the weather warms up, Edna spends the morning or late afternoons in her backyard, gardening. Putting her hands in the dirt and turning over dark rich soil is relaxing for her, like swimming.

When her older sister Helen, who was Mildred's classmate, was dying of cancer, Edna visited her and did her best to be bright and cheery. She came home filled with grief. The only thing that provided a degree of peace was working in the garden. She tries to explain to a friend.

"Just dig a hole. You don't know what you are going to turn up. All of a sudden you see these little worms going. Every once in a while a snake might come up, one of those garter snakes. They scare the living daylights out of you. But things are coming alive. It's just a good feeling."

On this overcast afternoon, Edna looks at the view. On a distant hillside, rows of tall narrow houses look gray and washed out, as if someone wetted a paintbrush and dragged it down a watercolor scene. To Edna, it is beautiful.

"You can see clear up to Mount Troy. Look at that. I love it here," she says. "This is my garden. This whole hillside. It is a jungle," she says, with pride, not reproach. Tangled trees fight each other for every inch of clearing. Leaning left and right, front and back, the unruly band of them fall all over one another like a band of drunken sailors.

In the middle is a wild rosebush. The prettiest red roses appear after the first few days of eighty-degree weather. By early July, it stops blooming.

Her lot is only 22 feet wide, but it is 117 feet deep. She points to the fence running wobbly between her yard and the one next door. "It's as crooked as a dog's hind legs," she says. She and her husband, Lou, built it when they first moved here. He carried the cement. Edna carried the two-by-fours. Once when Edna was trying to climb back up the steep hillside, she started to slide. Lou grabbed a rake and propped her up until she got her footing.

Lou built tiers into the back of the hillside and gardened every one of them. "We swear, when Lou would go down there, he would cuss at those plants until they got so scared, they grew," she says.

She dare not even venture down below now. Her son Art ordered her to stay away. She can imagine him now, watching her as she eyes the hillside and talks proudly of the tiers and fence, worrying that she might be tempted to explore. "For heaven's sake, Mother, don't go down that hill," she hears him saying. She laughs at his worry, always watching out for his gypsy mother. One summer Edna, Art, and his family went to the Atlantic Ocean on vacation. Edna got lost and some kind soul with a golf cart drove her back. Art saw her rounding the corner. "Oh jeez," he said to Anna. "Here comes Mom on a golf cart."

Four pairs of gloves hang from a clothesline under her porch. She bought them at the Red Door for twenty-five cents apiece and told the ladies she is always on the lookout for gloves. Months later, at a memorial service at the Lutheran church, one of them came up behind Edna and handed her two pairs of gloves. "You can pay next time," the woman whispered to her. Edna has passed Emma and Ernestine at the thrift shop many times. Emma's daughter Joan and her own son Jim were in the same class at Allegheny High School.

Edna's work gloves are an odd bunch. Two sets of men's leather gloves and two pairs of ladies' long evening gloves, one pink and the other peach. She likes the evening gloves for the garden. They protect her whole arm from poison ivy. Edna isn't particular. A glove is a glove. The old blade from an electric knife is, however, in careful hands, a weed whacker. She uses it to saw away thick brush to uncover a row of rocks that marks where the hillside drops off.

Last year she planted a special tomato plant. She thought she was going to get big juicy ones but got itty-bitty ones instead. Her cucumbers looked like miniblimps but tasted sweet, and her potatoes were no bigger than golf balls. "You never know what you're going to get," she says. After making potato salad, she buries onion peels, eggshells, and potato skins to enrich the soil. One time she dug a hole and dropped an old sprouting onion into the pocket of dirt. The next summer, she had an onion as big as a grapefruit. The wind picks up. She looks up. Leaves scatter.

When the sun begins to set, Edna turns to her house. She refers to it as the old green place with the dark green awning, next to the empty lot and that ratty-looking tree.

It's everything she says it is. Over the years rain deposited silt into the tiny grooves of the green siding, giving it a gray pall. The tree isn't so much ratty-looking as it is meager. Its trunk is no wider than a baseball bat, its branches the width of pencils, though not as sturdy.

"I don't have a beautiful home, but it's mine. Bought and paid for. I couldn't ask for anything else," she says.

Each room is orderly, even the laundry room. Lou painted the walls bright white, the pipes black, and the floor slate gray. "He was no jack-of-all-trades, but what he could do was perfect," Edna says, and stands back to admire her basement laundry room.

If you can't put it away, then throw it away. That's her motto. Edna hasn't made a checkerboard cake for years but walks right to her short green steel cabinet and pulls out a box labeled CHECKERBOARD CAKE. Inside are three metal cake pans with ringlike inserts that keep chocolate and white batter separate and produce the magical checkerboard effect. A handwritten note reads, "Too high for cake saver," reminding her not to put the tall finished cake under her metal cake cover. Edna's grandsons swear that all her cakes stood six inches tall.

Sometimes Edna gets in a baking mood and whips up two cakes. German chocolate with coconut pecan icing and raspberry with cream-cheese icing. If she's in a chocolate mood, she eats German chocolate cake and if not, the other. Maybe a little slice of both. It's a luxury, as is being able to spread herself throughout all five floors of her house. She fills each room with a purpose, if designated only by one item. The 1929 Singer sewing machine, which had belonged to her mother, sits on a table in one room, making that room the sewing room. Edna made all her clothes and the boys', too. Now, she cuts old tablecloths into small rectangles, hems the edges, and uses them as dish towels. Six bookcases packed with books make an adjoining room a library.

Walls are painted a solid color. Edna doesn't like prints or flowery wallpaper. Those big lusty blossoms seem like they will jump right out and suffocate you. Her kitchen is yellow. Her bedroom is peach. Her library is light green. She always liked that color. For her confirmation, she bought a pale green dress to wear onstage for her oral examination.

"Why are we baptized?" the minister asked her at the time.

"There are many reasons," she told him. She laughs now, wondering whether she ever elaborated.

Her couch, chair, and bed are covered in plain bedspreads. Bright orange for the bed and green for the couch and chair, though not her favorite pale green. They are green-without-an-adjective green, the color of healthy grass. A striped crocheted afghan lies across the back of her couch. Her younger sister Mary made it, using leftover scraps of orange, yellow, brown, green, white, and black. It's the only multicolored object in sight. Mary lives on Goettmann, which is the next street over, and is crippled with arthritis. Edna calls or visits her nearly every day. At the church strawberry festival, Edna won a raffle prize for Mary.

A few years ago a woman who had never been inside Edna's house came over. "Your place looks so sterile," the woman told her. Edna looked around. The woman was right. The walls were bare. Lou forbade nails in the walls. She didn't argue. When you live with something for fifty years, it just becomes part of the natural landscape. Edna knew her walls were empty. She just never knew they should be full.

Since then she has begun hanging a few pictures, but it is still a little awkward. With so much wall space and limited pictures, where do you begin? Put one eight-by-ten-inch photo on a blank wall and it looks like a huge lazy fly.

Above her couch hangs a long rectangular painting of four black-and-white Canadian geese flying over a lake. A small bronze-colored plate on the bottom of the frame is engraved FLYING HOME BY WESTAL. Edna has no idea who Westal is or was. A battery-operated clock was there before but broke. The stalled clock never bothered Edna, but Art took it down. There was a hole in the wall, so he found the painting to cover it up.

High school graduation pictures of her three boys, Art, Jack, and Jim, hang above her bed. Their faces look soft in the black-and-white photos, their lips tinted magenta and their eyes, the appropriate shade of blue, brown, or green. They are handsome boys, each one of them—their wavy hair, strong jaws, easy smiles.

Just before graduation Edna's boys each handed her a huge gown. "'Mom, iron this,' they said. I thought, *Holy cow, this is like pressing an awning.*"

Propped up on the nightstand next to her bed is a small picture frame. Inside is one sentence. "There is a special place in heaven for the mother of three boys." One of her grandsons had given it to her.

By 8:30 it's black outside. It always seems darker on this Bohemian end of Troy Hill. Once Bohemian Hill had a butcher shop and a handful of corner stores, which were the downstairs or front rooms of people's houses. Florence's mother, Julie, sold milk, bread, and lunch meat. There was one bar, which was closed on Sunday, and two private clubs, which weren't. They would be lit up at night. All are gone.

The first floor of Edna's house is dark. Edna is reading upstairs in her bedroom, sitting in an upholstered chair, her feet propped up on her footrest.

The TV is on a few feet away. She ignores it until the news or weather appears, or the Pittsburgh Pirates hit a home run. She doesn't bother with her hearing aid at home. It's annoying. Nothing sounds natural. The refrigerator roars like a hurricane or a waterfall. Everything echoes. She feels like she's living in a tunnel. She needs to hear the telephone and her alarm clock, and she can hear both without that thing in her ear.

Webster's Unabridged Dictionary sits open to the letter *C* on top of the bookshelf. "I have my nose in that book all the time. If I don't understand something, I go and look it up," she says.

A box of Kleenex, a pen, small squares of white paper, and a Marsh Wheeling cigar box sit on the table next to her reading chair. When she reads a line she likes, she writes it down and stashes it in the cigar box. Lou always had a cigar. She has an entire photo album dedicated to him. In just about every picture, he's got a fat cigar in his mouth or hand. If you don't see one, chances are someone told Lou to ditch the cigar. Instead of throwing it away, he just put his hands behind his back.

"See if I can remember the exact words," she says of one passage from a book about TV newscasters. "'Gossip may be a filthy marketplace with bogus goods, but that never stopped anyone from browsing there to see what they could pick up cheap.'"

In grade school, if she was assigned to read two books, she read four. Her father came down the hall, saw the crack of light under her closed door, and yelled, "Get that light out. You won't be able to get up for school." So Edna put a rug by her door so her father couldn't see the strip of light.

Her son Art was a big bedtime reader, too. Edna stood at the foot of the stairs and shouted, "You better get that light out." He wondered how she knew the light was on without coming upstairs. All she had to do was look out front. His bedroom light reflected in the windows of the house across the street. She didn't tell him. It's good for mothers to amaze their children.

As a mother and wife Edna had little time to read. Now she can't get enough, like a kid going through a growth spurt who eats a bowl of cereal, eggs, and pancakes, and an hour later is poking through the refrigerator. The phrase "I read somewhere" crops up in nearly every conversation. "I read somewhere that camels spit twenty feet." "I read somewhere that cucumbers take sixty days to go from blossom to fruit."

Edna reads best-sellers, classic literature, and history. She gives any book a chance and perseveres through most, although she couldn't get past the first chapter of *Silence of the Lambs* because it was so horrific. She loved a book about unforgettable women in the twentieth century, the variety and richness of their lives.

Volumes of condensed *Reader's Digest* books stand next to Edgar Allan Poe, which borders *Aesop's Fables*. She just bought two more Mary Higgins Clark books. A smaller bookshelf is packed with her sons' childhood books. *Tom Sawyer, The Mystery of the Silver Spider,* and a set of the Golden Book encyclopedias. Her grandsons read them when they were younger. If any great-grandchildren come her way, she will sit with them and read the story about Clifford, a big red dog who dresses up as a ghost for Halloween.

"I buy books and then trade them. Some are just pleasant. No big story, just enjoyable reading. Then I get into the real deep ones. I love to read. I'm reading all the time. They say you're alone but not lonely if you can read a book."

After she is done with each book, Edna writes a sound-bite-length analysis inside the front cover. A simple EM, her initials, is good. Her initials plus the first part of her last name, EMCK, is better. EM with a circle around it means she didn't like it. EM with a circle and X means she couldn't get through it.

"*Final Diagnosis.* That's about an autopsy. Oh, and this one is weird. It's about Vietnam. Somebody came back a psycho." Edna darts from one subject to another like a frantic goldfish. Here. No there. She doesn't dawdle with *uhmm*s, *likes,* or *you know*s but talks with the precision of a barber who trims bangs again and again and again. Clip, clip, clip.

She literally could not put down a Stephen King book about a woman accused of a murder and recounting her past to a sheriff. She'd walk up the steps reading it and forget completely why she went upstairs. But she gave up on another one of his books after fifty pages. People were just killing each other for no reason.

She buys books at thrift shops. Goodwill charges seventy-five cents a book. Even with the Goodwill 10 percent senior citizen discount on Tuesdays, she gets a better deal at the Saint Vincent de Paul store. Ten books for a dollar. She and the clerk regularly exchange favorites. Nearly everywhere she goes, Edna carts a blue plastic bag of books to trade with someone. Mysteries are exchanged with the lady down the street, romances with the lady at the store, bloody murders with a woman in town. She lent Mary Wohleber a book about Indians.

That is another reason Edna loves books. She can walk into a crowded room, and if someone is engrossed in a novel, she will gravitate toward that person. She figures the two of them will share a common interest and love. You can't get in trouble discussing a book. It's innocent. It's not rumor or gossip.

Nearly every Sunday, after church, she and Ellen Husak swap books. They write each other little notes. "They live happily ever after but it takes them a long time to get there," or, "There's swearing, but stick with it." Ellen's husband, Alois, jokes with Edna when he sees her walking toward them with her grocery bag filled with books. "Gee, I forgot my library card," he says. Mr. Husak lent Edna a fascinating book exploring the notion of creation.

Edna is immersed in a happily-ever-after Harlequin romance called *Father's Day*. She needed a lift after reading *The Divine Secrets of the Ya-Ya Sisterhood*. That book troubled her, the way the daughter was estranged from her mother, who drank a lot and ended up in an institution. In Edna's eyes, the daughter blamed her mother for things that never happened, or at least never happened to the degree or in the way the daughter remembered.

"It's a matter of perspective," Edna says. Show four people one picture and each is struck by something different. Is the glass half empty or half full? Her stepmother used to say it was half full of emptiness. Edna has always tried to see the good and positive. She tried to teach her sons the same thing.

"You know, you read something and you think, I've never thought of that. You are never done learning, never, even when you're a little old lady. The older you get, the more you know how little you know."

The other day she was listening to the weather report. The weatherman said it was fifty-six in Pittsburgh and fifty-seven in CAK.

"I didn't know any CAK. I looked at the map and I couldn't find it. I got two sets of encyclopedias. I got a great big dictionary. I have all these books and I'm hunting. I figured it out. CAK is Canton and Akron together." She has a mind for detail and numbers. To this day she remembers her sons' serial numbers from the army. They enlisted in the 1950s. Art's number is ER13540138 and Jack's number is RA15484083.

When she was forty, she thought about going back to school to become a practical nurse. Her sons said, "Mom, you're too old to go to school." Lou told her, "This is where you belong."

"You don't hear that today. I should have gone back, anyway. I just accepted that I was just too old. So I let it go. Forty today isn't old."

In fact, her good friend Mildred once said people become more astute when they hit forty. It's a part of growing up, Mildred says. "As a rule I don't think you really begin to appreciate things around you and what has happened before you, until you reach forty."

That's when life begins. "You can tell fashion and everything else to go to the devil, wear what you want, and do what you please," says Mildred.

Nobody hits a magical age and says, "OK, time to fall apart. Enough being young, I'm going to act and feel old, sit down, put my feet up, and close my eyes and wait until it's time to go. Maybe do a little crocheting here or there. A TV show, something to pass the time. Look out the window, see the sun come up and go down, and wait. Count another spring, another tulip, and another daffodil, watch another storm from the window, another snowfall." The body grows older but the spirit remains ageless.

Edna can't believe she is eighty. "I know I'm old. But eighty seems ancient," Edna tells Florence Klingman one afternoon. Florence is seventy-seven. "Just figure you have twenty more years. That's what I'm going to do when I'm eighty," Florence tells her.

With all of her reading, Edna often comes across articles about another ailment or disease. How an aching head and stomach or arm can mean something terrible. She closes the book and shrugs. "If I got it, I got it, and if I'm going to get it, I'm going to get it," she says, less out of indifference than faith.

Edna figures she'll be around as long as she has work to do, whether that's being a friend, a grandmother, mother-in-law, gardener, reader, churchgoer. "As long as you are here, there's some work you are to do that is not completed. When the work is completed, God will say 'OK, Ed, let's go. Time's up. That's enough.'"

Her hair, once red, is now gray. She doesn't bother dying it. "If I dyed my hair now, it wouldn't match my complexion. When God gives you gray hair, He gives you a complexion to match," she says. In all things, she accepts. Gray hair, she figures, is His will.

"Different people will ask me, 'How old are you?'" Edna says. "I don't know why, but I think when you get old you kind of hesitate. I always say, 'I have to think.' I know darn well how old I am. If I say 'How old do you think I am?' people always say ten years less. If I look eighty, they say, 'You look about seventy.' I know they're lying, but it still makes you feel good."

Her health has been good. She did have a little scare last fall. She was at an aerobics class and felt a little dizzy. She sat down in a chair. The teacher came over and asked, "How do you feel?"

"Oh, I'm OK," Edna answered. She looked at her watch. It was 10:50. Class would be over in ten minutes. No sooner had the teacher turned around than Edna rolled off her chair and fell to the ground. She had a black eye and a bump on her head, and spent the next four days at the hospital.

She doesn't know what happened. Neither do the doctors, apparently. It was just one of those spells. A lot of women up here have one of those mysterious spells. Sitting one minute. Falling the next. In the hospital for a few days. They have dizzy pills, as Emma Hildenbrand calls them, tucked in a drawer somewhere.

Edna went to the doctor and he suggested cutting back some

blood pressure medicine to see if dosage was the problem. She looked at him. "Oh, so that means if I don't drop dead in the street then you will know it was good to cut the medicine back."

Next time she went to the doctor, she wrote a list of questions and brought them with her. The doctor was getting up to leave. "Wait a minute. Don't you leave, yet. I haven't asked my questions," Edna told him. He looked at her and sat down quietly.

Edna relayed the conversation later to her daughter-in-law Anna. "You didn't, Mom," Anna said to her.

"You know I did," Edna said.

Anna never knows what Edna will say or do. They went shopping to get Edna a new stove. The salesman said it would be delivered Monday or Tuesday. Edna stopped him.

"Wait until I check my calendar," she said. She opened her purse and pulled out a little calendar. Monday and Tuesday were full. So were Wednesday and Thursday.

"Sorry, how about Friday?" she asked him.

The salesman looked blankly at Anna. "Do you have one of those calendars?"

"No," she said.

"Neither do I. We must be doing something wrong."

After shopping, Edna and Anna stopped for a buffet lunch at a steak house. They walked by the cinema. *The Odd Couple* was showing. They looked at each other. "What the heck," said Edna. They got a good seat and laughed until their eyes watered. Edna would see anything with Jack Lemmon and Walter Matthau. After the movie, it was late. Anna told Edna to spend the night.

They pulled out Anna's worn Scrabble game. Anna took the first five games and then Edna cleaned up. They play for keeps.

"Hey, that's no word."

"Look it up. See for yourself."

"Where's the dictionary?"

They were up to almost 3 a.m.

Edna and Anna were always close, but in different ways and for different purposes. Their relationship evolved as they did. In the beginning Anna was the little girl down the street playing with Edna's sons. Then she was Art's girlfriend. When Art was a teenager and had a hernia operation, Edna brought his bed downstairs. He hung out the first-floor window to talk to Anna. Then she became Art's wife and, later, Jim's and Dana's mother.

Edna was the mother, the mother-in-law, and then the grandma.

When Anna asked her advice, Edna responded with caution. "This is what I did. That doesn't make it right or mean it will work for you." Edna wasn't afraid of giving the wrong advice. Everyone is different. What works for one family, one child, one parent, won't necessarily work for another in another time and household. Her grandmother did the same for her. Listening and never being domineering.

Edna has lived long enough to know decisions in life are rarely all right or all wrong. You simply do your best. "You can't be afraid. You've got to stand up, do what you think is right," she says. If it was a mistake, accept it, learn from it, and go on. That's her philosophy.

Now Edna and Anna are best friends. Anna is twenty years younger. The women Anna works with say, 'My goodness, you and your mother-in-law are so close.'"

Edna and Anna talk at least every other day, sometimes daily, sometimes twice a day. The other night Anna was watching an amusing movie on television about a big dog named Beethoven and had to call Edna to make sure she had it on. They sat on the phone watching the movie together and laughing.

Anna had a Monday off. She called Edna. "You free to go to the zoo?" Anna asked.

"I'm ready," Edna told her.

They wanted to see the Komodo dragons. Edna couldn't understand the big fuss. They look like big lizards. At the dolphin tanks Edna stood close because she wanted to catch a glimpse of the dolphins' teeth. She wondered whether dolphins had big or small teeth. A dolphin passed, opened its mouth, and spit water out, all over Edna. She looked at Anna. "Dolphins have small teeth," Edna informed her.

As they approached the camels, she told Anna to stay away. "They can spit twenty feet. I read that somewhere." Giraffes have purple tongues, which protects them from sunburn. She read that somewhere, too.

At a reptile show, the trainer said a snake died and that his mate was dying of a broken heart.

"Where's a snake's heart?" asked Edna. She was curious. Does it have a long skinny one? Or a little one? Is it at the front or the back or dead center?

The man looked at her.

"Lady, no one ever asked me that. I have no idea," he told her.

Edna shrugged.

CHAPTER EIGHT

Anna's Inspiration

I WAS MAD AT HIM again today. I was hollering, Why did you leave me like this?" Edna was on the telephone, talking to Anna. "You know how you get sometimes?"

"Yeah. I do that, too," says Anna.

"I know he is up there saying, 'Mom, you shouldn't say those things. Mom, keep your mouth shut,'" says Edna. She told Art the same things, millions of times. He was so much like her. They both spoke their minds. "People would probably think I'm crazy talking to him."

"Don't feel bad. I do the same thing," says Anna. "It's natural for anybody."

Edna knows it's natural to get mad at someone for dying, as silly as it might seem. For some reason, you can't help but feel a loved one could have hung on and continued living if he or she had really wanted to. She's read about it.

"It's one of the stages. First you deny it. It didn't happen. Then you start blaming people—the doctors or someone.

"Then you get to the point that you're mad. That's the stage I'm going through now. I finally have come to the realization that he's gone. It's done and I'm mad. Art's gone and we have to go on. He left me and Anna in the lurch, and he is sitting up there."

Edna McKinney.

Art, her oldest son, had always watched out for everyone, especially Edna. Even when he was a child, all she had to do was say, "Art, run down to the bakery," or, "Art, run to the butcher." And Art was there and back in a flash. Art picked up his little brothers when they tripped, wiped their eyes or their runny noses. When he was in kindergarten, the teacher told Edna, "That boy is like a little old man the way he hovers over the other children."

He knew her so well. She was tough with everyone and determinedly independent, but with Art she could ask for help and be needy. She didn't have to always be strong.

"Mom," he told her, "you give everybody the impression that you are as tough as nails, but you are jelly inside like the rest of us."

"It's true," she says. "I guess I'm a little bit of each—happy and sad—inside. Nobody can be perfectly strong all the time. But I feel this way: If you don't stand up and take life, then life is going to knock you down. Every once in a while, I get in the dumps. And I have to get out of the house."

That's one reason she is on the go all the time. It gets too quiet. Her three sons have all died. Her youngest, Jim, died first, when he was eighteen. Her middle son, Jack, when he was thirty-seven. Art died when he was fifty-seven. Five months later, her husband, Lou, died. He was eighty-two. She is alone now.

Edna got a job at Armstrong Cork Company, the same place Ernestine Hepp worked, when she was a teenager. Edna's aunt Nellie Lynch worked there. Sack Alley Nell, they called her because she worked alone in a narrow little room, taking slabs of cork tree bark out of burlap sacks. It was a filthy job.

Edna wanted nothing to do with that and worked in the gasket department, where she met her husband, Lou. She wasn't quite sixteen and lied on the application about her age. One look and they would have known. She was a skinny little thing. "My dad said to me, 'You lied, so you do what you want. If you want to go in, go. And if you are afraid to go, you don't have to go.' Well, I was bullheaded enough to go, and they didn't do anything."

Lou was six years older and grew up on the North Side of Pittsburgh. He was Irish like Edna. His mother died too, when he was young. He had wavy black hair and deep blue eyes and wore soft felt hats and a topcoat. He was particular about the way he dressed. Edna's red hair draped down over one eye, like the movie actress Veronica Lake. Veronica Lake had an image, tough yet vulnerable. That was Edna.

Two years later they decided to get married. Edna's father said she was too young. Stubborn, she said she wasn't. So she and Lou ran away to Wellsburg, West Virginia, and found a minister, who pronounced them man and wife in his living room.

After the wedding each fell into the prescribed role. Edna waited on Lou. If he wanted sausage, she made sausage. Dinner had to be ready at 4 P.M. sharp. He was a good provider. He spent his whole career at Armstrong Cork. In 1948 the company sent him to a weeklong management school in Hershey, Pennsylvania. She was proud of him. He didn't finish high school, yet he was being sent to classes to be an assistant foreman. The company took a class picture. She points him out, the one in the overcoat and fedora and the best-dressed man in the group.

Edna worked for five months after they married, and then quit because she was pregnant. On her last day she went downtown to pick up her paycheck. She wanted to go out in style and had worn her long coat with a fur collar and her fanciest hat, a white pillbox that sat squarely on her bright red hair. A photographer standing on the sidewalk snapped Edna's picture. There she is, one foot thrust out below her long coat as if posing midrunway. She looks cool, pleased with herself and with life. This is what she wanted. Married, about to start a family. She never thought twice about quitting her job.

"My husband said, 'You're supposed to stay home.' And I did."

Her three sons were born a year apart. Art was born in 1937, Jack in 1938, and Jim in 1939.

When they were little, people up and down Brabec Street said, "Here come the McKinney boys." Not, "Here comes Art," or, "Here comes Jack," or, "Here comes Jim," but "Here come the McKinney boys." They were an ensemble. Never put Jack and Art on the same side of a basketball team, because they couldn't be beat. Tossing each other the ball, all the way down

The McKinney family.

the court, until they reached the hoop. One last pass. Jack to Art. Up and in. If Jim couldn't play, he'd cheer.

It was a hectic but normal house. Happy confusion, Edna calls it. Every day was consumed with cooking, cleaning, washing. Socks were darned; shirts, pants, and jackets made at her kitchen table.

Her ever hungry three boys and their friends would run up the steps, asking, "Did you bake anything?"

"Not today, but if you go buy a twenty-five-pound bag of flour, I will." Off they went, and twenty minutes later they'd be coming up the steps whistling and lugging a bag of flour on their shoulders. "Everybody came in, and you fed half of the neighborhood. But I enjoyed it." As the boys got older, she timed her trips to the A&P grocery store to coincide with the afternoon school-dismissal bell. The salesclerk asked Edna how she was going to bring eight bags of groceries home. Just about then her boys came through the door with a bunch of their friends. The boys grabbed the bags and carried them home.

Her photo album is divided into three sections, one for each boy.

Jim was long-legged, thin, and redheaded—all like Edna. He had his mother's crooked jaw. Not square below his nose, but just slightly off-center. Where his dimples came from, Edna has no idea, although she claims responsibility for the freckles and his Irish temper. Actually, the temper was from both Edna and her husband. "Two Irishmen, like two cats in a sack," she says.

When Jim was about four years old, Edna noticed something was wrong.

"See, he doesn't look right," she says. She is looking at a picture of a little boy, big eyed, standing outside, in front of a fence. He's dressed in white pants and shirt, and fancy two-tone shoes. His aunt was getting married that day, and he was the ring bearer. He does look a little uncomfortable, but any boy would if scrubbed and put into white clothes and ordered to stay out of the dirt, grass, and street. The soft fleshy tissue around his eyes might be a little swollen. That could be from lack of sleep. To anyone else, he looks normal.

But Edna knew his rosy face was growing pale and thin. He was always winded and couldn't keep up with the other kids. His limbs ached, and he was beginning to pass blood through his urine.

Her greatest fear was that Jim had Bright's disease. Sometimes called nephritis, it involves the deterioration of the tissues of the kidney. Her mother, her grandmother, her uncle, and her little brother Arthur died of it. Arthur died in 1936, right around the big Saint Patrick's Day flood. The Allegheny and Monongahela Rivers, swollen with ice and rain, spilled their banks, burying all but the tops of railroad cars and filling the first floors of downtown department stores. The flood caused forty-eight million dollars' worth of damage and blackened the city. Everyone was without power.

At that time, people laid out the dead in their own homes. Someone in her family contacted the electric company, which managed to provide Edna's house with electricity. The other homes remained dark, except for the flickers of candles moving from room to room. People passing Edna's house or looking up on the hill might have seen her front windows lit up and mistakenly envied her family.

Edna took Jim to the doctor in 1944. The doctor confirmed her fear that Jim had Bright's disease and put him on medication. Over the next few years he seemed to grow more tired and pale.

She took him to another doctor in 1948. That year sticks with her. It was a watershed—not that she recognized it as such at the time. Only later, with a panoramic shot of the years, could she pull out those moments that compressed time into one big Before and one big After.

The doctor examined Jim. He looked at Edna and said, "You have a mighty sick little boy.'" The gravity in the doctor's voice stung her. She knew Jim was sick, but something in the doctor's tone and face made her realize how severe it was. He told Edna to take Jim home, put him to bed immediately, and keep him there. Jim was in bed from that March through September. As devastated as she was, she was also relieved in a way. The doctor had confirmed what she sensed. Maybe Jim would get better because someone knew how sick he was. In September he returned to school, stronger, wearing jeans and flannel shirts like everyone else.

Jim was a quiet child. Who knows whether that was his nature or whether being sick made him subdued. It was probably a little of both. His hearing and vision weakened to the point where he needed glasses and a hearing aid. Edna had not known he was hard of hearing. With three young boys in the house, noise and yelling are part of the territory.

"We probably screamed at one another naturally. If a child doesn't hear, you tend to speak a little bit louder. You think he is not paying attention. I used to think he had a hole that went straight from one ear to the other."

His big brothers, Art and Jack, protected Jim and made sure no one teased him. When they played baseball, Jim was the pitcher. That way he could see the ball coming. He really wasn't supposed to play ball, but Edna knew she couldn't stop him from being a boy. And she knew Art would watch out for him.

In school, though, Jim wasn't allowed to participate in gym class or organized sports. He couldn't even go swimming, because he might catch a cold. If he had to go to the dentist, he needed a doctor's approval. At one point Edna was paying bills to five different doctors or hospitals. Every week she took five dollars to one of the doctors. The next week, she took five dollars to the next doctor on the list. And so on.

Lou handed his paycheck over to Edna. He'd say, "This is what you have to work with . . . I don't care what you do with it, but don't cry to me when it's all gone. If you want something, you will save your money, and if you can't save your money, then you don't want it bad enough."

Jim had to find his own place in life and it tended to be more on the subdued fringe of the circle rather than in its raucous middle. Instead of being a jock, he was a school crossing guard in eighth grade and received an eight-by-ten-inch Safety Patrol certificate from the Pittsburgh Better Traffic Committee.

Edna keeps the certificate tucked in the back of his grade school yearbook, in a cardboard box lined with plastic. With it are a half dozen yearbooks from Allegheny High School, where her three boys graduated, and dozens of *Wahoo*s, the school magazine. The box is heavy, thirty pounds, maybe, but she keeps them together. She doesn't want them to get dusty, torn, or separated. She carefully unfolds the plastic wrap and lifts them out gingerly, one by one.

She is not outwardly sentimental, but the care with which she preserves these, along with all of her sons' papers, awards, and letters, says much. "To me, this is a treasure. No way would I ever give them up. This is mostly all I've got," she says.

In one yearbook Art is honored for winning a swimming relay. Another mentions that Jack won a rope-climbing contest in a gym class exhibition of strength and physical fitness. In another a photograph captures a bunch of kids walking down some steps. Her Jim is by the railing. He is not identified. He is one of many. A good-looking kid with freckles, dimples, and dark hair, wearing jeans, like everyone else. It's just a glimpse of him. No great moment or day of note.

He was the classic nice kid, not flashy or full of himself. All the little boys in the neighborhood followed Jim because he played ball and was kind to them. "There goes the Pied Piper," Anna and Art would say when Jim walked down the street, a half dozen pint-size admirers in tow.

Scrawled in pen on the inside of his yearbook, his friends wrote, "To Jimmy, a sweet boy with a personality to match," and, "To Jim, one of the sweetest boys I have had the pleasure of meeting." "Keep your swell personality and you will succeed." "Remember me as I will remember you." "To A real swell guy whom I have known since grade school."

Edna goes to a cabinet in her kitchen. She opens the top drawer and pulls out a solid metal ashtray as wide as a softball, and as smooth as paper. Lou used it for his cigars. Jim made it in shop class. He also made two jewelry boxes, a candy dish, and a little hammer for the 1958 West Pennsylvania Industrial Arts Fair. Edna keeps old coins in one of the jewelry boxes.

The entire shop class received certificates of merit from the Ford Motor Company during an assembly in school. All the boys, except Jim, sat onstage in their suits. Their parents were in the audience. Jim told Edna when he got home that he didn't know there was going to be a big assembly or that he was supposed to get dressed up, and that she was invited. She suspects something was said in class and he simply didn't hear it. He hated his big clunky hearing aid and ditched it when he could.

"He wasn't too concerned, but I wanted my kid up there," says Edna. Jim was allowed to be involved in so few things. It would have been nice for him to have that one moment of public recognition and honor. She and the other parents would have applauded him.

By his senior year he stood six feet tall and weighed 150 pounds. Other than being pale, no one would suspect he was sick. He was built like a stalk of broccoli, his broad chest expanding exponentially from a narrow waist.

Still, he was weak. He never would have made it through his

last year of high school if it weren't for two neighborhood boys. One dropped him off at school in the morning and another brought him home. He was losing more and more blood. At his high school graduation he was sitting up on the stage and his nose started bleeding. Edna watched him. He didn't have a handkerchief. The boy next to Jim reached in his pocket and gave him one. The soloist played "The Challenge" on the trumpet.

The senior prom was Friday, June 13, Edna and Lou's wedding anniversary. Jim didn't have a date, so the teachers fixed him up with another dateless classmate.

He wore a white tux and a black bow tie and bought his date a huge wrist corsage that adorned her entire forearm. A friend rented a white Cadillac and picked them up. When it pulled up to their house, Jim shouted, "Mom, you got to come and look."

He didn't get home until 3 A.M. The next morning a group of boys banged on the front door to pick him up for a post-prom picnic at a lake. He spent the day horseback riding and came home laughing about how he was running after the horse, holding the reins, and trying to avoid stepping in anything the horse left behind.

The Monday after his prom, Jim was in the hospital. His body had only one third of the blood it needed. Eighteen of his classmates signed up to donate blood. One of the boys was black. Edna will never forget him. She opens Jim's yearbook, looking for the boy. There he is. His name is Cash. Like Jim he was described as quiet.

The other kids told Cash he wouldn't be able to give blood because he was black. "Well, today everyone knows that blood is blood," says Edna. "At that time, they thought because he was black they wouldn't want his blood."

Once Jim was stabilized, the doctors sent him home. Let him eat what he wants. If he craves ham, give it to him. Seconds, too, if he's hungry. Up until then, Jim couldn't eat much protein. When the doctor said that, Edna knew it was the beginning of the end. She would just have to watch. In early August Jim was admitted to the hospital. He slipped into a coma. On August 10, 1958, he died. He was eighteen. He would have been nineteen in October.

The same black boy came up to the funeral home. When he walked in, people looked at him. There were no blacks in the funeral home, or on all of Troy Hill for that matter. Edna told Art to go over and make him feel welcome. "He stayed there the whole time. He said, 'I don't care what anyone says to me. Jim was my friend,'" she says. "You remember those things. It will be forty years."

The only other thing Edna remembers about that night was being at home and someone telling her that she was sensible to take off high heels and put on bedroom slippers. The rest is lost to her. It's a black hole. There's probably some physiological reason for that, she figures. The nervous system or brain or some gland senses stress and triggers a reaction that causes the memory or the mind to shut down and take a rest until the body can regroup. It makes sense. But it's still God pulling those strings, she says.

"I honestly believe that you get to a certain point, God says, 'That's enough. I better give her a little bit of rest.' Your mind will go blank. No matter how much you try, you cannot get that part back in your life. It's gone," says Edna.

The funeral director said he never saw such a crowd for such a young man. They came in school buses.

A friend asked Edna after Jim died, "Don't you wish that would have happened to someone else?"

"I would never wish such a thing on somebody else. I've cried my tears and I have no regrets. If you dwelt on all the sad things, it would make you bitter and sour to the world."

Then she laughs. "In fact, when Jim died, they came and got a suit. I said 'But it's got grass stains on the pants.' And the undertaker says, 'It makes no difference. Nobody is going to see his pants.' So he was buried in a pair of pants with grass stains on them! Heaven only knows how he got them. Oh, when I think of some of those things . . ."

Once Jim asked his mother for money to go to the drive-in. Edna looked outside.

"Jim, it's pouring down rain."

Jim rolled his eyes. "Mom, who goes to the drive-in to watch the movie?"

"He told me things the others didn't. Maybe because I babied him because he was sick. My Jim was happy to the very end," Edna says.

She remembers the happy times now, time having healed some of the pain. But in the days and months that followed his death, she was devastated. She refused to leave the house.

Lou gently encouraged her. "Why don't you go out and do some shopping?" he would say.

She wouldn't go. "I was afraid somebody would ask me a question and I would cry in the street. That was for months. I was afraid somebody would talk to me."

At one point someone suggested to Edna that it was her fault that Jim died. Her side of the family had kidney problems, so she must have had a bad gene and given it to him, the person said. She's been fighting that goblin since. "That bothers me," she says. She recently read an article in the local paper about a boy with a rare degenerative disorder and circled the sentence mentioning the boy acquired the disease from a rare gene in *both* parents. "See," she says. "You need *both* parents."

Seventeen years later, in 1975, her middle child, Jack, died. He was thirty-seven years old. By then, she says, she was a little smarter and tougher. She went out, but if she saw anyone coming, she crossed the street so she wouldn't have to talk and possibly break down. If anyone pursued her, Edna gave them an excuse that she had planned in advance.

"'I have to go to the bathroom.' Everyone probably thought, *There is something the matter with her.* But that's the only way you get away."

Edna's daughter-in-law, Anna, remembers how different the two funerals were. "With Jim it was something that you knew was inevitable because of his illness. We had no control over it. You accepted it because he was sick.

"But with Jack you thought, Oh, if only he did this, or, If he would have let somebody get through to him. It was senseless. It didn't have to be. That's what was so hard. Why didn't he listen? He could still be here. That is how it was to me."

"It's true," says Edna. Of her three sons, Jack was the one with the most promise and brilliance. She tried to get through to him, but she couldn't.

She and Jack were both middle children, she of five and he of three. In nearly all of his pictures, Jack is grinning. He was much more of a grinner than a smiler. Grins have mischief. Jack had mischief. "He was full of the Old Mick," she says. "An Irishman all the way through, with the gift of gab." He was forever talking his way into and out of things. "He was a handful."

Learning came easy to him. His high school teachers challenged him to games of chess during free periods. His advisers urged him to take advanced courses, but he wasn't interested in doing anything beyond requirements. One of his teachers, well aware of his intelligence, told Edna, "I can only grade him for what he shows. Not what he knows." If he felt like going to basketball practice, he went. When his school buddies were late, Jack sneaked down and opened the locked school doors and got in trouble for defying the school's authority.

The only authority he liked was his own. But when he used it, he could whip his peers into model behavior. One time the Sunday-school teacher pulled Edna aside. He said Jack went into class, told everyone to sit down and start working on their lessons because he had baseball practice and didn't want to be late. They did. "The minister said, 'I wish he had to go someplace all the time, because he got them settled down and doing what they were supposed to do,'" Edna says. "He was a born leader." That's what was so maddening. He had such potential and could do anything he set his mind to.

The year Jack graduated from high school, 1956, was a feel-good time. The Depression and both wars were history. The world and country seemed flush. "Every day doors to new opportunities are before us," his senior yearbook proclaimed. "The door to a still-higher education, the door to employment best suited us, the door to matrimony for some, and the door to military training for others. All these, no matter which we choose, will be a door to success, because we have become intelligent persons possessing strong character and greater knowledge."

Jack chose the military, a seemingly odd choice for someone so defiant. But Art had done the same, and it was a ticket off Troy Hill. Jack enlisted the September after he graduated.

"Anything to get off the hill," says Edna. She was worried about him. "I said 'Jack, I'm not going along to talk you out of trouble. You get in it, you are going to have to get out of it.'"

He did well. Skilled in typing and shorthand, he landed a position as private secretary to a general stationed in France. When the general boarded a plane, so did Jack, pen and paper in hand.

He wrote home often. "Mom, I am sitting here with my feet up on the desk, waiting for the general to come back." She could imagine him writing that, grinning and pleased with himself. How could she not be pleased, too? Such an important post for her son. He traveled to Italy on leave.

Every once in a while Jack wrote her a poem in shorthand. She wrote back, teasing him. "Hey, you're not the only one who knows shorthand. I know exactly what you wrote." It was both a fun written banter, and something they alone shared. Art and Jim didn't do that. She could read it to Lou, but it wasn't meant for him. She wrote Jack and reminded him that the first Sunday in October was World Communion Day and that on that day, he could receive Communion at any Protestant church—French ones, too. As long as he was going to church, she thought he would be OK. She doesn't know if he did.

Jack was in France when the Red Cross tracked him down with word that his little brother Jim was dying. He grabbed a bag of dirty clothes, put on someone else's pants, and boarded a cargo plane home. When he arrived in New York, there was a snag with his flight to Pittsburgh, so he boarded a bus home. By the time he arrived, Jim had already died. Anna was at the house, waiting for him. Art, Edna, and Lou were at the funeral home. He didn't bother changing his rumpled dirty clothes. He just ran over. Art later took him home to get some clean clothes.

No one can say what impact Jim's death had on him. They were quiet people. They kept their emotions to themselves. Jack was home for a month before he had to report back to service. When he finally came home for good, thirteen months later, he was drinking heavily.

"I think Jim's death had a lot to do with it, because they all were real close," says Anna, Art's wife.

Maybe that was it, says Edna. And maybe it was the army. "You could go on Friday and you didn't have to report until Monday. No one knew if they were lying in a ditch someplace, drunk. They didn't care, as long as you reported Monday morning. I think a lot of them kids just busted loose."

One night, not too long after Jack came home from the service, Edna and Lou got a call from the emergency room. Jack was in a terrible auto accident. He wasn't driving. He never learned how to drive. At least he had enough sense to know alcohol and driving don't mix. Jack was in the front seat when the car came around the corner of Troy Hill Road by North Catholic and hit a utility pole.

Jack went through the windshield forward and then back again. The force landed him in the backseat. The priests from North Catholic rushed out and tied his head up with a handkerchief. Assuming he was going to die, they gave him last rites.

The doctors at the hospital thought the driver would have to be held for vehicular homicide.

"They told us his eye was gone and his jugular vein was cut. He was cut from his forehead to his chin. It took 250 stitches and he lived. They did a beautiful job on his face," says Edna.

It was nothing short of a miracle, she says. She praised the doctors and thanked them. They saved his life, his eye. They stitched together a face shorn and nearly split in two, having traveled twice through a jagged windshield. Privately she hoped that the brush with death would wake him up. But it didn't. He got out of the hospital and went back to the bar where they had been that night. The guys—his friends—had taken bets on how many stitches he would have.

Jack couldn't hold a job, even good ones. He worked for the post office, which promised respectable benefits and job security. He got fired because he didn't show up for work. Another time, he worked at the bottom of the hill in a juice factory and came home every day for lunch. Edna ate with him. It was nice having his company. When he got tired, he quit. His dad got him a job as a timekeeper in a packing plant on Herrs Island. That lasted about a month.

Every time he lost a job, Edna would try to talk to him, but it was so frustrating. She told him that she had tried to give him a solid foundation, like a builder would a house. "I got you to the top, that house is finished, you graduated from high school. You had a good solid foundation. And if you kick that foundation out, the whole house is going to come down."

He looked at her and said, "So?"

Another time she was so mad, she banged the table and a

piece of wood fell off. She must have sworn, because Jack turned around and said, "Mother, swearing doesn't become you."

At the time, alcoholism wasn't as widely considered a disease or a genetic weakness preying upon people with addictive personalities.

"They just considered it not being strong enough to stand up and take life. I don't know if it's true," says Edna. "It makes a mother feel better when she knows it's a disease, not just lack of willpower. I'd like to think it's a disease."

Her big brother Pinky thought she was foolish paying Jack's hospital and doctor bills, making him breakfast, lunch, and dinner. "Hey, Ed, why don't you kick him out?" he would ask her.

"I did. Regularly, once a week. I'd say, 'Don't come back.' And he would walk down the steps and wave, saying, 'Bye, Mother. Bye, Mother.' A half hour later he would come back in again." She took him back and never gave up hope.

"No matter how old they are, they are still your kids. You try to straighten them out. You get to the point where you can't, but you still try. You pick them out of the gutter regardless of how far they go. You pick them up. You never give up. You have to have hope."

Yet, she felt powerless, not knowing what to say or do and feeling as if she had said and done it all; appealing with love, anger, and forgiveness; trying to help him and to get him to help himself. He tried to quit every couple of days but went right back to it again.

"I think they get to the point where they almost can't." Her voice has lost its clip. It's tired and quiet. "The body," she says, and then pauses. "How would I say it? It's like you have to eat food. They have to have alcohol. Oh, he thought he could quit when he wanted to. Well, I don't think you can. You have to have help. But Jack was more like me, very independent, and he didn't want any help because he thought was able to do it himself. What did he tell me? 'I'm no alcoholic, I'm a chronic drunk. I'm not too far gone and I can stop if I want.'"

She would tell him to go ahead and stop. "I said a lot of things. Believe me, I said a lot of things, but it didn't do any good."

Finally, his body just broke down. "He went to a doctor toward the end. They put him on a special diet and everything. Well, after a while, everything is more or less worn-out. God only gives you so many parts and you have to take care of them. You don't get any more.

"My son died an alcoholic. Is it my fault? Should I have done this? Or maybe I did that wrong? I can't bring him back. I couldn't change him. I don't live all those days over, because they are gone. Maybe I've got the wrong outlook, I don't know."

It's strange. She has a thin stack of milky white school papers. All are Jack's. She doesn't have any from Jim or Art. Either the other boys didn't bring them home or, for some reason, they weren't saved.

At the top of one, he wrote, "John McKinney, Grade 3, June 17, 1947." He had graduated from pencil to ink, that grown-up world without erasers. He is practicing cursive writing, the capital and small *A* and *I*. The round, looping letters are slanted at the proper angle. "It is what we think and what we do that make us what we are," he wrote.

In fifth grade his teacher gave them a quote from a man named Albert Hubbard and told them to copy it. The words seem overgrown for eleven-year-olds, swamping them like a father's raincoat, the sleeves hanging to the knees.

"Genius is only the power of making repeated efforts. The line between failure and success is so fine that we are often on the line and do not know it," he wrote.

Edna stares at the sentence for a few minutes. "That was my Jack. He was at that line," she says. She quietly puts the paper back into the stack.

Art was the most popular of the boys, more outgoing than Jim but less cocky than Jack. He was handsome, his dark hair slicked back on the sides and cresting in an inch-high wave on top. His junior year he was on the high school championship swimming team and was starting forward for the basketball team his senior year.

Anna lived at the other end of Brabec Street. Her older brother owned a store, and when Art was about thirteen, he asked her brothers if he could sweep and take out empty bottles to earn a few dollars. Later they taught him how to wait on customers.

All the kids on Brabec Street loafed together, playing ball and swimming at Cowley. There was no need to leave their end of the hill. No one could really afford excursions. Anna and her brothers and sisters shared one bicycle that her mother won at a raffle at a movie theater on Troy Hill. To this day, at the age of sixty, Anna says her four best friends are from Troy Hill. They moved to other parts of the city but regularly get together and keep in touch. She thinks it's because all of their families were poor. They didn't have distractions. They had one another. "I'll be yours until the board walks," they wrote in her yearbook.

She and Art married in the Troy Hill Presbyterian Church right after graduation from Allegheny High School. Edna cooked a nice dinner. Two weeks later Art went into the service. Anna went with him. After his stint they moved back to Troy Hill, living next door to Edna and Lou. After Jim, the oldest of Edna's two grandsons, was born Anna and Art bought a house and moved to a suburb. But every Sunday they came back to Edna's house. Edna cooked a big supper of roast, potatoes, vegetables, and baked a special cake. One time it might be four tiers and another time, the remarkable black-and-white checked one.

After supper Anna and Art washed the dishes and Edna took her grandsons for an adventure. Sometimes they walked across the Sixteenth Street Bridge to peek in department store windows. At times they would be gone for two hours. Edna let the boys decide. Left, right, up the hill, or down. They'd pick berries on Nanny Goat Way, a path worn decades earlier by goats.

Before leaving the house Edna told Art and Anna, "Be sure to look out the back window in ten minutes." Then she and the boys walked to a clearing on a nearby hill. When they got there she told them, "OK, now look over to Grandma's house and your parents will wave. See them? There they are. Wave. Smile."

Art and Anna could see their frantic little waves. Maybe not the smiles, or even their faces. It didn't matter. It was part of the moment, the routine. Smile. Wave. It made them feel happy and made those Sunday evenings precious.

"We would stand there, my husband and I, and wave," says Anna. "And now when my kids get talking about that, they will go on and on forever about Grandma and her walks and her cakes."

Edna took the boys to see an opera and a ballet. "Just go one time with me, and if you don't like it, tell me. But I want to show you a little bit of everything," she told them.

She was so proud of Art and Anna's tight-knit family. Art started his own business and the boys worked for him. Art told his two sons that family came first. "You don't know how I miss my brothers," he would tell them. "So if you don't do anything else, always remember you are brothers. Stick together."

"That was very important to him, to have my boys care about each other," Anna says.

Lou retired from Armstrong Cork in May 1972, after forty-three years. Edna has the company announcement in a scrapbook. It refers to him as Perry, a nickname some friends gave him because he went to Perry High School for a few days before dropping out to get a job.

"Perry, Louis D. McKinney, a mat and sheet slicer in the sheet department will be going on early retirement as of May 1, 1972, after completing forty-three years of service at the Pittsburgh plant. Lou became an employee of Armstrong Cork when he was only sixteen years old, as a catcher, splitting in the gasket operations in 1928." Lou was so good he could pick up a slab of cork, smell it, and tell whether it should be used for insulation or bottles. "We certainly wish Lou and his wife, Edna, all the happiness and luck in the world during his future years of retirement. E. A. Wighim, Plant Manager."

Lou had no problems adjusting to retirement. He had his two grandsons to enjoy and his backyard. Uncle Lou's Hillside Farm, the neighbors called it.

He terraced out back, creating tiers with railroad ties and bringing order and purpose to an otherwise worthless piece of sloping land. Every summer a colorful waterfall blossomed. Red tomatoes spilled into green cabbage, which cascaded to purple eggplant, to red roses. He tried strawberries but the birds ate them. If tomatoes weren't perfectly round or unblemished, he threw them away. It was as much art as sustenance. He spent his waking hours nine months out of the year perfecting his garden. Anna and Art took home baskets full of vegetables.

That's how Edna knew something was wrong. One day out of the blue, Lou announced to the neighbor, "I'm not going back to the garden." It was the strangest thing. It would be as if Edna said to the same neighbor, "I'm not going back into the kitchen," and walked away to let everyone fend for themselves at breakfast, lunch, and dinner. Tomatoes, eggplants, flowers, you're on your own now, Lou was saying. Weed thyself. Water thyself.

At the time, it was odd, but not enough to cause alarm. Maybe he just got tired of it and needs a break, Edna thought. Doesn't everyone?

Her son Art threw them a surprise fiftieth wedding anniversary party. Art made some excuse about going out to dinner, to get them all dressed up. They walked into the basement of Most Holy Name Church and everyone yelled, "Surprise." There were refreshments and a disc jockey. Lou was in the middle of the room spinning, dancing, and jumping. Art leaned over and whispered to Edna, "Mom, he's acting weird." But they just figured he was excited.

Then Lou started asking innocent but unsettling questions. Where is the silverware? The silverware rested, as it had for the last fifty years, in the same kitchen drawer. No one had moved it. And yet he genuinely had no clue where it was. He's just getting forgetful, Edna thought.

One day a neighbor found him going through her mailbox. Not taking the mail, just looking at it. The local bank called. He had gone to the first teller and said he wanted to buy a six-pack of beer. The teller said we don't sell beer. He went to the next teller's window with the same request. He walked into the kitchen of a house where he used to get a haircut, sat down in a chair, and said, "I want a haircut." The family living there finally convinced him to leave.

It was embarrassing. Edna had guarded her life and privacy, but with Lou nosing through people's mailboxes, it felt like the drapes had been pulled open.

She felt more alone than ever. She didn't want to talk to anyone about it. What would she say? "Lou put his socks in the freezer"? "Lou locked me out on the porch and I had to beg to get in"? They would be incredulous. She could hardly believe it and she was living it.

He got into her makeup. When he heard her coming up the steps, he jumped into bed and pulled the covers over his head. A grown man acting like a two-year-old. She didn't know what was wrong with him. She just thought that maybe he was senile. That's what they thought then. You get old and you get senile. She didn't know anything about Alzheimer's.

"I thought somebody sat me out in the middle of the desert all alone. To me it was the most terrible thing in the world, till I found out it's very common. I thought no one was going through this but me," she says.

Once, she came upstairs and found him wearing her slacks

and a pullover sweater. He outweighed her by eighty-five pounds. She had to coax him like a baby. "Put your hands up." Removing the clothes was like pulling off his skin. And after she got them off, she thought, Where am I going to hide my clothes?

It got to the point where she couldn't leave the house or sleep soundly because she was afraid Lou might slip out without her hearing him. "Morning, noon, and night. You can't rest. It's like when you have a new baby and you are afraid for it. You jump up at night. Is he sleeping? You creep through the house so you don't wake him. I got up at five-thirty to do my laundry so it was done before he got up. I had to get a special lock on my door so he wouldn't escape. It was constant worry."

She stopped going swimming. Marge was the only one who called. "Oh boy, what did he do now?" she asked. He poured milk when there was no glass. He threw his dentures away. Edna looked through all her cupboards and both freezers. She even moved the stove thinking the dentures might be under there.

Marge listened and then told Edna, "You better take care of Edna because no one else is going to. Get on with your life. You're sitting on the bottom. You can't go any lower. You got to stand up and take it, because you're not going to get any special favors," Marge had told her.

"It was just what I needed. You could talk to her and tell her anything and not worry about it going any further," Edna says.

Edna didn't like to bother Art. He and Anna had their own small business and two sons. "When it first started out I think she thought she could handle it," Anna says. "But we could see the toll it was taking. She was really uptight, always concerned about him being OK, and making sure nothing would happen to him."

Whenever she did need help, Art was there. Once she called from the emergency room of Allegheny General Hospital. Lou had wandered away and medics had picked him up. He was on a gurney when she arrived. She didn't know if he had been in an accident or had suffered a heart attack. She was so shaken she couldn't even dial Art's number, so a nurse did.

"All I said was, 'Art, I'm down at Allegheny General.' And he said, 'Mom, I'm on my way.'"

After Lou locked himself in the bathroom, Art drove over and took the doors off the hinges. He did all the house repairs. Art encouraged her to tell her neighbors. "This is no disgrace. Don't keep it a secret. Tell everybody. Tell the firemen, the policemen, so if anyone sees him where he's not supposed to be, they can bring him home or contact you to come and get him."

Edna coached kids up and down the street. "If you see Mr. McKinney wandering outside, try to bring him home. Say, 'Let's go home.' If you have to take his hand, take his hand. And if he won't come home with you, run down and tell me."

Art addressed the intangible things as well, trying to make her laugh and defuse her anxiety. As Lou got progressively worse, he didn't talk much. He would simply yell over and over, *"Hey, Ed; Hey, Ed; Hey, Ed."*

Edna had looked at Art. "If he hollers 'Hey, Ed' to me one more time, I'm going to bop him.' And Art said to me, 'Mom, it's your new name. Hey Ed.'" She broke up.

"He'd be running around in his underwear. Then he would put his slippers on the wrong feet," she says, and laughs at the thought. "You can't help but laugh now, because it looked so funny. Oh, it's easy when you are looking back, because it's all gone. I'll admit it. I lost my temper. I remember saying I could have thrown him up against the wall and hoped he would stick forever. It's not like a kid, where you can say, 'Go sit.'"

Edna single-handedly cared for Lou for ten years at home. As Lou grew progressively more unpredictable and demanding, Edna grew weaker and more tired. She lost twenty-five pounds. Her face was long and drawn. Her arms were thin. Art feared he would lose his mother first.

"My god, she had to be that wide," says Anna, holding her hands about ten inches apart.

Art and Anna had a friend whose daughter was a nurse. The daughter started coming a few hours a week to give Edna a break. Edna ran down the street to Mildred Mares's house and just exploded with conversation. Mildred sat and listened and was happy that Edna was able to have some time for herself. They didn't talk about Lou. They swapped recipes and talked about grade school teachers and the church. Edna felt alive after that little break.

But having a nurse a few hours a week wasn't enough. Finally Art said to her, "Mom, look at yourself. You can't tell me that you can't look in that mirror and see what is happening to you." She knew he was right.

Art checked out several nursing homes and personal-care homes and took Edna to see them. They finally settled on Sky Vue Terrace. It was on the bus route and Edna could visit Lou daily.

Art handled everything. The insurance, the medical forms,

the doctors. When Lou went into the nursing home, Edna was handed a list of things he needed. A certain number and type of undershirts, pj's, sweatpants, and shirts, all bearing his name. She and Art stood at the kitchen table, each with black markers, writing PERRY MCKINNEY, PERRY MCKINNEY, PERRY MCKINNEY on the waistband of his pants, on his T-shirts and underwear. They even wrote his name on the ears of a six-inch tall, stuffed yellow Easter bunny. They ran out of ear before they ran out of letters so they put PERRY on one ear and MCKINNEY on the other. When Edna gave it to Lou, he sat there and tried to twist the ears off. She rescued the bunny, ears intact. At Easter she hangs it like an ornament from the top of a cabinet in her living room.

Daily, Edna rode the bus to see Lou. She took him out for walks, bundling him up in hat, gloves, scarf, and blanket during the winter and pushing him around the building in his wheelchair. When it was raining she asked him, "Do you want me to get my umbrella?" He nodded yes and out they went. He loved being outside. When it came time to come in, he dragged his feet.

In the summer they sat on the bench and ate a little snack. Art and Anna joined them at times.

For hours she sat at his side, paging through family photo albums. He turned the page. She asked, "Who is that?" He stared at her. Whether he knew or not, he never said. She brought bags of crayons, markers, and paper, anything to stimulate his mind. He never wrote recognizable words. Maybe a letter. Usually he just scribbled. Once she bought a stuffed penguin. It became his best buddy.

Art developed diabetes and had bypass surgery when he was in his fifties. He quit smoking, went in for regular checkups. He continued to run his business and work around the house. He loved being outside, just like his mother.

On weekends he spent half the day mowing, weeding, and trimming the lawn. Anna watched from the window, worried he might get overheated.

"Why do you stay out in the sun for so long?" Anna asked.

"Because I enjoy doing it. I'm not going to sit in a chair and worry about what I shouldn't be doing, or about having a heart attack, because then I'm wasting the rest of my life, too. I can't do that," he told her.

Soon after Lou went into the nursing home, Art, Anna, and the boys were going to the Atlantic Ocean for a vacation. Art insisted Edna come along. She was worried. Lou had only been at Sky Vue for a few months.

"Mom, you need a break. He'll be OK," he told her.

He and Anna joked about getting Edna a police whistle to wear around her neck, knowing she would roam. She did and couldn't find her way back. That's when someone brought her back on the golf cart.

That fall, Art got together to play volleyball with a group of friends from church. One afternoon they were standing around choosing sides. Suddenly, without any warning, Art collapsed. He was rushed to the hospital but it was too late. Art died of a massive heart attack. He was fifty-seven years old.

Anna and her sons went to the hospital. When she arrived, she called her brothers and sisters, who came to be with her. She couldn't call Edna. She had to tell her in person. Her two sons went with her.

"Going to her house with my boys to tell her was the hardest thing I ever did in my life," Anna says. "That was the only time I ever saw her fall apart. She said, 'I just can't take any more.'"

And yet, in the days, the weeks, the months, and few years since, Edna's resilience and faith have been a source of strength and inspiration for Anna.

"I think she was able to deal with it because it happened two times before. Not that it makes any one death easier, but I think she was stronger because of it," Anna says.

Then, too, she suspects Edna was tough for their sake. "Maybe she wasn't as strong as she seemed, but she did it for me and for my two boys. That would be like her," Anna says.

"Don't worry about me. I'm fine. Worry about them," Edna would tell Anna.

Edna went to Sky Vue to tell Lou. He didn't cry. He took a piece of paper and a green felt marker and began drawing. He did that a lot—doodling and sometimes making one letter, maybe an *R*, or an *O*. It was random. Nothing made sense. When he had to sign his name to a form to get into Sky Vue, he wrote a line of *R*s.

Lou made some marks on the paper. When he stopped, Edna looked. In capital letters, he had written, "ARTART." He had retraced each letter several times, slowly and deliberately, with particular effort. He didn't say anything, but she knew he had grasped what she said. "I guess he probably understood for that moment, and then it was gone," she says.

Edna keeps the paper folded up in a little square inside her wallet, tucked behind her senior citizen's bus pass. She looks at it and almost apologizes for keeping a three-year-old piece of paper with only six capital letters. "I guess I should throw it away. I carry this wallet all the time," she says.

Edna sometimes wonders if Art knew he was going to die, if his body and soul were sending signals that he kept to himself because he didn't want Edna or Anna to worry. He was so anxious about getting his father in a nursing home and getting Edna all squared away, taking care of the legal work. Lou went into the nursing home in July and Art died on November 19.

"I honestly feel there's something that pushes you, like *I must get it done*. And then when it's done and you're free, you feel, *Well, that's it. I did my part*."

Lou continued to deteriorate to the point where he was curled up in a ball, not responding to anyone.

In April, five months after Art died, Lou died. He was eighty-two. A nun came into the room to try to comfort Edna. Anna was there and remembers Edna telling the nun, "Please, I know what you are trying to do and I appreciate it. But don't feel sorry for me. I don't want pity."

Edna says it was the most peaceful death she had ever seen. She was sitting at his side. He was curled up in a fetal position and had been for weeks. Then he straightened out, put his arms down, shut his eyes, and quit breathing. It wasn't violent. He didn't fight those last few minutes.

Lou was finally safe. He wouldn't get hurt and he wasn't going to suffer any more. For the last ten years, she had worried about him, that he might run out of the house, lock himself out, or eat something that would make him sick.

"They say a child is taken into heaven without hesitation. When my husband left this world, he was nothing but a child.

Whatever he did wrong, it's gone. Maybe I shouldn't feel that way, but I honestly do. A lot of people would think that's weird. It's a good weird."

She stops and shrugs. "Maybe I just want God to make sure He takes Lou up there."

Edna has reconciled her life—though not materially well off, and filled with setbacks and tragedy—as well lived. She did her best with the hand dealt to her, being there always for Lou and loving each of her sons deeply.

At times, looking at a picture or paper overwhelms her with a sense of loss and loneliness. She acknowledges those feelings, and then turns the page. She refuses to spend the rest of her life locked in sorrow. Instead, she cherishes what she did have. Her eighteen years with Jim. Doctors said it was a miracle that he made it those last three years. Jack survived that nightmarish accident. Art was alive to help with Lou. And she and Lou had fifty years together before he got sick.

Then, too, she has her health. Her daughter-in-law, her grandsons, her friends, her church, her home, the ability to come and go, her jungle out back, her vision and books. As she grows older, the desire to learn and do something positive becomes more intense.

One of Edna's favorite words is *enjoy*. It is almost a command. Life is too short not to. "What life you have left, enjoy. Because you cannot go back and do this over again," she says.

It would seem such a simple mandate. But it's not. Often people are so engaged in what is just around the corner that the present is little more than a bridge to something else. Either that, or the current moment is consumed by and with the past.

Few things delight Edna more than stories about her grandsons. She can't brag enough about those two boys. They are good workers, good husbands. They shovel the neighbor's walk, as did her own sons. They bought beautiful houses and nice cars. She doesn't begrudge them that indulgence. "I give them credit. Why should they wait like we did?" she asks. One grandson drove over on his new motorcycle wearing his helmet. "He looked like a man from outer space," Edna says.

Her grandson Jim got a promotion. "You would have thought he got to be President of the United States or something," says Anna, describing how Edna said to her, " 'Just think, they are young kids and they are already bosses.' She was so happy and she said to them, 'Oh, your dad would be so proud.' "

One brother helped the other remodel a kitchen. They made new cabinets, installed a white ceramic floor and a black marble countertop. When they were done, they celebrated Anna's birthday there. Edna was amazed and later told a friend how professional it looked.

"She just makes the kids feel so good because she always praises them, you know. She just enjoys every little thing. That is what is so amazing about her," says Anna.

Art was a lot like his mother, Anna says. She's only come to realize that since he died and as she and Edna have become such close friends. It's not just the physical resemblance or quirks. Neither of them could tolerate dirty dishes in the sink, especially if they weren't stacked. Dirty dishes were bad enough. Disheveled dirty dishes were just too much.

It was more in the way they lived their lives. "He always would say, 'Well, don't look on the bad side, look at it this way. It could be worse than it is.' And that is exactly how she is," says

Anna. Maybe that shouldn't be so surprising. But sometimes it's hard to imagine an adult as anything but independent and self-made rather than a person shaped by his or her parents.

Anna doesn't quite know or understand how Edna can be so upbeat after losing all three sons and a husband. Anna has a hard time managing one loss. "God only gives you as much as you can handle," Edna tells Anna.

Well, Anna says sometimes she has a hard time accepting it. "Why would God do this to me? I'm not a bad person. I know you are not supposed to say that, but I get upset, because I think it wasn't fair what happened to me." Let alone to Edna. Anna gets angry for her. "She has been this good person all her life. Why does she deserve all this? I can't imagine Him wanting to make somebody like her suffer. She has had so much, and yet she is so faithful and such a believer. Why would He want her to go through that? Then I look at her. And I see how much faith she has. I think if she can keep going and have the attitude that she has, I can't possibly be sitting here feeling sorry for myself. She is a big inspiration."

Every Sunday Edna walks to Troy Hill Presbyterian Church for a 9:30 service. The first row is empty. Florence Klingman and the Husaks sit in the second pew. Edna sits behind them. Everyone sits on the right-hand side of the church. Years ago that was the men's side. Women filled the pews on the left. When the numbers dropped off, the women decided among themselves to join the men, even though women outnumbered them. That way, at least the handful of people who are there, are there together.

Service lasts for less than an hour. Edna prays quietly, follows the program, listens to the Reverend Heidrich preach and read from the Bible. She recites the Lord's Prayer, sits, stands. She doesn't sing the hymns because she doesn't trust her hearing aid. She's afraid she will belt out with gusto a song meant to be dolce. After services she exchanges books with Mrs. Husak, visits with her neighbors for a bit, and walks home.

In the process of engaging in that simple weekly routine, Edna finds solace. There's a feeling that she is never completely alone. It's not so much a certain religion or church. She is Protestant because her father was. If he was Catholic, she would have been Catholic, she says.

"I don't push religion on anybody. That's my private affair. I believe what I believe. But if I don't go to church, my week is not complete. I'm not going because I think God is going to give me something. I go to get strength to get through the coming week. God's been good to me. I've got my health."

After Lou died Edna felt for the first time that she no longer had to be vigilant. "I always felt like I was carrying a keg of dynamite, ready to explode, first with the boys sick and then my husband. After he was gone, I felt a big load off my shoulders," she says.

It's not that she has forgotten. The boys' pictures hang above her bed like a shrine, always smiling for and at her. "When someone close dies, they are always there with you," she says. Art seems to stand at her side, protecting and counseling her. "My Art used to say 'Mom, you have to laugh every day.'" She does now. One time she was wearing something that reminded her grandsons of Granny Clampett on the *Beverly Hillbillies.* So she played it to the hilt, putting on big boots, a hairnet, an apron, glasses, and a Granny pout. They took her picture. Anna never knew she was so funny. Edna was so consumed with caring for others that her own vitality, intelligence, and humor were often muted.

In the garden Edna tells the flowers they better grow straight and strong. "Lou's up there watching you, and if you don't grow, he is going to be mad." He took care of every little plant. Among them she feels his presence. It's comforting.

She's waiting for the hydrangea to bloom one of its many shades of purple. Her son Jim brought it home as a Mother's Day present in 1958, three months before he died. By the fence is a lilac tree. Lou planted it but it nearly died. Trying to bring it back to life, she had her grandsons cut it back to a small bush. When she did, the neighbors thought she was nuts. It hadn't blossomed since, but this year she had hope.

Now, a few weeks later, two clusters of lilacs sit on the top of Edna's lilac bush, blooming for the first time in years.

"Those two are just a beginning. Probably next year there will be more. It's good and healthy and thick."

CHAPTER NINE

Pillars of the Community

CECILIA GUEHL NEVER went to the Cowley recreation center, or pointed to "Glow Worm" as a child, but she is going there this evening to give a talk to Troy Hill Brownie Troop 1436 about growing up on Troy Hill. So, today she prepares, as she does in all things, with diligence and professionalism.

She jots down her own thoughts. She mentions the talk to her best friend, Thelma Wurdock, after mass that morning. Thelma tells her to remember the man who delivered vegetables by cart.

Cecilia talks with her older sister, Loretta, and adds a few more notes. What name, building, or date one can't recall, the other will. Loretta has an exceptionally keen memory. She remembers the name of the girl who was her fellow butterfly when they were in first grade. They both wore white. The eighth-grade girls were the queen butterflies, which made them more important. They got to wear pink, blue, and yellow. Then, too, Loretta remembers the name of the woman who at daybreak went rapping on the doors of the H. J. Heinz Company workers, alerting them that trains loaded with tomatoes had arrived and to hurry in and make ketchup. Virginia Wilhelm did that.

But of the two of them, Cecilia is more comfortable in front of a crowd. She was a secretary to the chief executive officer at Heinz, which meant dealing daily with powerful people. It demanded poise and presence. Secretaries handled pretty much everything then, drafting letters for the CEO to sign and screening calls diplomatically. She hung up on only one pesky caller, and that was with her boss's blessing. Cecilia served on the National Council of Catholic Women, attended annual conventions, and met Mother Teresa. Cecilia went up to Mother Teresa and asked to take her picture, which sits in a gold frame on her piano. Loretta has always been one of the more quiet members of the family. Brilliant, but quiet.

After checking with Loretta, Cecilia goes upstairs to her IBM electric typewriter, types her notes, and staples them together. Cecilia is a perfectionist, especially when it comes to committing anything to paper. In all her letters, the date is where it belongs. Top right-hand side, just below the return address. The margins are set at 1.5 inches. The text is perfectly centered. The spelling is flawless.

While Cecilia takes care of correspondence, Loretta manages household accounts, monitors investments, and prepares tax returns. Loretta helped draft complex contracts at Twentieth Century Fox for forty-one years. She left that job—after their oldest brother, Francis, died—to take over the finances for the family funeral home business.

They were never ladies of the house but, rather, single working women who shared the same world, identity, and daily routine. Leaving home in the morning, they returned in time for dinner, which their mother had ready when they walked through the door. They traveled the world and were on a four-week tour of Europe when the Catholic Church began implementing its new decree that all masses be said in a country's native tongue. French, Italian, and German were all Greek to them. They couldn't tell an *Our Father* from a *Glory Be*.

Even in dress they complement, rather than duplicate, each other. If one wears a flowered skirt and plain blouse, the other wears the opposite: plain skirt, flowered blouse. Loretta wears earth tones—brown, beige, and burnt orange. Cecilia prefers royal blues and roses. Her businesslike blouses have little bows that tie at the neck.

The brownie troop meets in a back room of the recreation center, which is less than a half mile from the Guehl home. Cecilia drives. Loretta goes as backup and for support.

The door stands open. Voices come from a small office crowded with three big men in jeans and baseball caps. One man leans back in a folding chair, his tennis shoes propped up on a metal desk. The Brownies, he says, are in the back room, which is on the other side of the gym, where a full-court basketball game is in progress. Stay close to the wall so you don't get hit, he advises.

The Brownies just finished making bunnies out of empty tuna fish cans. First the cans were spray-painted white. The girls then glued on two pink paper ears, a nose, and a mouth for the face and added pipe cleaners for whiskers. The cans were initially supposed to be jack-o'-lanterns but the troop never got around to making them in October. So now they are Easter bunnies to be filled with candy and given out to anyone receiving Meals on Wheels. A white paper banner is taped on the wall. WELCOME TO BROWNIE TROOP 1436.

Nine girls, ages six to eight and dressed in shorts, or overalls, and T-shirts, sit in a circle on metal folding chairs. Loretta, age eighty-seven and in a skirt and blouse, joins them, as do two Brownie leaders—one of whom is Margaret Fichter's niece—and a grandmother, who heard that Cecilia was going to speak and thought she might enjoy the reminiscence.

Cecilia stands in the front of the circle, next to the American flag, holding her typed notes and a travel-size pack of Kleenex. She begins.

"When I was young, about your age, girls pushed baby dolls in carriages. Radio and television had not been invented."

A girl whispers, "Wow." Cecilia looks up from her notes and smiles. She is pleased. They are quiet, attentive. No one is talking to her neighbor.

"Some people had Victrolas." Silence. She glances up. The girls stare vacantly at her.

"Does anyone," offers one of the Brownie leaders, "know what a record is?"

"It's a little flat thing that you put on a record player," answers one girl in overalls.

"A Victrola is like a record player," Cecilia explains. "Lucky families had a piano." Her family was lucky. Their piano sits in their living room. She learned to play as a young girl. The Guehls were fortunate in many ways. They were among the first in their neighborhood to buy an electric washing machine, in 1917, the year Cecilia was born. In the early 1920s the Guehls bought a car, and in the late '20s, an electric refrigerator.

"There were no supermarkets," she continues. She enunciates and talks loudly to be heard over the screeching of tennis shoes stopping midrun and the banging of errant balls slamming into the wall. "Food was sold in little stores at the corners of streets. Bread was sold in a bakery, and fruit and vegetables, by a man with a cart."

"And there were no plastic bags for groceries. Women carried food home in baskets." Even if they could get a ride, those independent, hardy German women might not take it. Years ago a group of businessmen met in the boardroom of the brewery at the bottom of Troy Hill Road to demand better streetcar service. When the last speaker was done, the streetcar superintendent rose from his seat and said he could run streetcars every five minutes up and down the hill and the Germans would continue to walk. "If you gentlemen will just look out the window, you will see what I mean," he said. Outside, a dozen housewives carrying heavy market baskets walked past a waiting streetcar and trudged up Troy Hill Road.

"You bought as much as you could carry," Cecilia continues. Most people didn't have electric refrigerators. They had iceboxes, which, she explains, were cabinets of wood lined with white porcelain.

Every other day, the iceman came with twenty-five pounds of ice.

A little girl raises her hand. "Was the iceman strong?" she asks softly, her eyes bigger than her voice.

"Ohhhhh, yes," says Cecilia gravely. "He had great big

blocks of ice and big tongs, and he would cut the ice block and sling it over his shoulder like this." Cecilia heaves her arms over her shoulder, as if hoisting a big sack.

Loretta adds, "On Saturdays he would come around and collect his money."

Cecilia resumes. "There were two movie theaters on Troy Hill." The girls exchange looks. *Incredible.* Movie theaters to them are huge buildings in malls that stretch a half a city block with a dozen screens and vast candy counters. Where would one movie theater—let alone two—go up here on the hill?

"They were across the street from each other on Lowrie. The Colonial had cowboy movies and The Lowrie had high-class movies," Cecilia says. One theater had a bowling alley in the basement. The films were silent. Pianists, including their aunt Matilda, had cue sheets to tell them when to speed up for the chase scenes. Between reels, signs flashed on the screen asking ladies to remove big hats and everyone to watch their manners. DON'T SPIT ON THE FLOOR—REMEMBER THE JOHNS-TOWN FLOOD? one sign read, referring to the infamous—at least locally—flood in Johnstown, Pennsylvania.

"Ice cream cost five cents, and you could also get a huge candy bar for a nickel."

A hand shoots up. "Did they have Nintendo?"

"We didn't even dream of anything like that," says Cecilia. No, they had games like Parcheesi, tiddlywinks, and pick-up sticks.

"We used to make scooters out of old wood boxes," Loretta adds.

"Which we called Pushies," Cecilia continues the thought almost uninterrupted.

"And we would put roller skates underneath as the wheels," Loretta completes the sentence.

One girl volunteers that her dad has Parcheesi. "Well, you tell your daddy you met a lady who played that game," Cecilia tells her. The girl beams.

"Did they have softball and soccer for girls?"

Those were boy sports. "We didn't mix with boys," Cecilia says. Everyone knew his or her place. Girls behaved like young ladies. Pink was their color. Boys were boys and belonged to blue. Girls who played ball were tomboys. There were no tomboys in the Guehl house.

Cecilia wraps up her presentation with a neat summary. "This century has seen the invention of many things—automobiles, refrigeration, washers, dryers—that have made life much more enjoyable." It is a way of letting them know they have much to be grateful for.

"Any questions?"

There are several. Most deal with what it was like to live in that white house with the big front porch shaded by a green-and-white-striped awning. Not tall, narrow, or huddled with others, it stands unto itself, a wide and rambling anomaly. A small widow's walk tops one tower, lined with a wrought iron fence. A giant elm tree shades the corner of a generous lawn. Buckeye trees used to grow in the yard. Kids threw just about anything up in the branches, trying to dislodge the shiny mahogany-colored nuts, which they hollowed out for rings and pipes. Once, Cecilia's father was in the front yard and a roller skate fell from a branch and nearly knocked him on the head. That's it, he said. No more buckeye trees.

A small plaque hangs on the outside wall, declaring the

home a historic landmark. Their friend Mary Wohleber took care of that. Their mothers worked together on the Toy Mission, gathering gifts for children during the Depression. Mary's daughter, Sarah, played as a child with Cecilia's nephew Frank. That is often the case on Troy Hill. When someone says, "We know each other's families," it means, Our mothers were friends, we are friends, and our children, too, play together. Cherished ties are passed down.

Aside from being one of the oldest, biggest, and most distinctive houses on Troy Hill, it's a funeral home. That is what interests the Brownies. John Guehl Sr., the women's father, operated a funeral parlor in the downstairs for much of their lives. Although another man runs the business now, the Brownies know the two Guehl sisters still live on the second and third floors.

"What was it like to live in a funeral home?" a girl asks.

"It was an experience. You had to keep as quiet as possible," Cecilia responds.

"Did you go to the funerals?" another child asks.

"Only if was a real good friend or relation," she answers.

"Were you scared?" asks another.

"You got used to it," she finishes.

One of the Brownie leaders, trying to broaden the line of questions, asks Cecilia about her career. She was at H. J. Heinz for thirty years.

"As what?" a child asks.

"A secretary," Cecilia says, adding that she was secretary to the chief executive officer, the man who essentially ran the company. "I told him what to do and he did it." She, Loretta, the two troop leaders, and the grandmother laugh.

"When you were little, did you go to camp with the Sarah Heinz House?" someone asks. The three-story-tall brick and marble recreation center, where Edna swims, sits across the highway at the bottom of Troy Hill Road. It was built in 1913, as a memorial and tribute to Henry Heinz's wife, to offer classes and camp to local children. Many children went and continue to go to summer camp sponsored by Heinz House.

"Yes," Cecilia answers. She went to camp.

"Did you skinny-dip?" someone asks.

"No. We wore bathing suits. It was a different world," Cecilia says diplomatically, neither condemning nor condoning theirs, but clearly distinguishing it.

"Did you have to grow up and learn to be a housewife?" asks a girl in braids.

Cecilia pauses. She never was a housewife, literally or figuratively. She worked. First her mother, then eventually her older sister Dorothy, kept house. "Well," she tells them, "I watched out for a smaller brother and sister, and later a nephew and two nieces, who grew up with us." She isn't a grandma, she explains, but is old enough to be one. She is an aunt, ten times over, and has great-grandnephews.

"Were you allowed to wear pants?"

"No one even tried," she says. As children they played in dresses. As young women they went to work in dresses. They came home and ate in dresses, and washed the dishes wearing dresses. When women began wearing pants, she and her sisters continued wearing dresses, or skirts and blouses. To this day neither of the sisters has worn pants. Nor did their mother, their other sisters, or their niece who grew up there, until she moved to California in 1970.

"On the hottest days of summer, you wore white gloves and a hat to work," says Cecilia. After work they carefully placed the hats back in their sturdy hatboxes.

Cecilia asks if anyone has white gloves.

Two girls raise their hands. Cecilia informs them that she no longer has hers. She wouldn't abandon dresses. Gloves, though, gladly. "I threw mine away. When girls stopped wearing them to work, I decided I didn't need to save those sons of a gun."

One of the troop leaders asks Cecilia how the hill has changed. For one thing, families aren't as big. She was one of seven children, four of whom have died, leaving herself, Loretta, and their brother John Jr., a retired doctor, who married and left Troy Hill in the late 1940s for Mount Lebanon, an established Pittsburgh suburb. Seven was considered a good-size family but not large, like thirteen children, or huge, like the family with sixteen children.

More than seven thousand people once lived on Troy Hill. The population is now less than half, and older. The Christian Mothers are grandmothers. Daughters have lives these women never imagined, speaking Mandarin Chinese and earning Ph.Ds. A fourteen-year-old visits her grandmother and requests "old people food," which she goes on to explain is meat, mashed potatoes, gravy, and a vegetable, what "old people" considered a timeless well-rounded meal. They always knew their neighbors' parents and grandparents, but that is changing as the older ones die and newcomers arrive. It is not as self-contained as it used to be. They must drive off the hill to grocery shop.

Then, too, the air is cleaner now. At one time the air was so dirty, she could barely see the sidewalk in front of her. "If you wore a white slip, by the time you got home it was black around the bottom. But on the other hand, people were working." People here always make that important distinction, especially given the painful decline in the steel industry in the years since. A slip edged in soot was a small price to pay for fathers and brothers earning a good wage. No one in her family worked in the steel mills, but neighbors did.

"How old are you?" a girl asks.

"Well," she says, "I've already told you, indirectly. Remember, at one point," she says, guiding and challenging them, too, "that I said I lived in that house for seventy-one years. And later I said I was ten years old when we moved in?"

"Eighty-one," volunteers one girl.

"I'm ancient," Cecilia says, and smiles.

The troop leader stands and thanks Cecilia and Loretta for coming. The girls clap.

After her presentation, Cecilia sits on a chair next to Loretta. It went well. Cecilia is pleased. The girls asked a lot of questions. That is a sign that they were interested. She has been to enough meetings to know when people are or aren't listening.

She has always enjoyed children. Their sister Dorothy Spreng came home in the 1940s with her three children. The oldest, Ann, was in second grade, Lynne was in first grade, and Frank, nicknamed Skipper, was a baby. Cecilia took Lynne to see *Swan Lake* for her twelfth birthday. When Ann needed to use the word *candle* in a sentence, Cecilia and Loretta always had a suggestion. Frank learned to walk holding on to Cecilia's finger. She was in charge of baby-sitting him when Dorothy was at Christian Mothers' meetings. Frank grew so attached to his aunt that he ran out of the house crying when she went off to work. "It was nice to have a little kid like you," Cecilia says of her nephew and nieces. She brought them discarded and out-dated forms from work. They used to play office on the back porch, and during tax season, Frank lugged his little briefcase to the table and pretended to fill out forms. Frank now has a Ph.D. in economics and is a university professor.

"What do we do when we have guests?" the troop leader asks.

"*Guests first!*" the girls shout in practiced response.

A girl hands Cecilia and Loretta a round white cookie on a perky Easter napkin covered with pink and blue eggs and a big-toothed bunny, and a half cup of Pepsi.

"There is this boy in my class. He is as tall as you," the girl informs Cecilia.

"*Is* he?" Cecilia answers, sounding amazed. Cecilia stands barely five feet. Loretta is about the same. Either could be taller on any given day, depending on the size of their heels. Cecilia keeps a thin pillow on the driver's seat, so she is comfortable and to give her a little more height.

As the sisters eat their cookies, the girls line the tuna bunnies with shredded green Easter grass and hard candy. When Cecilia and Loretta have finished, they gather their purses and coats.

The troop leader hands them each a sandwich bag of but-terscotch disks and peppermint drops. "Go out the back door," she suggests, "to avoid the basketball game."

It is dark and getting cooler. The sisters walk slowly down a ramp, testing the ground in front of them to make sure it doesn't drop off. Loretta stops and looks out. "Cece, see how nice it looks over here. Look out that way."

From where they stand they can see down the Allegheny

River. Two bridges cut across the river. Directly below them the lights of the J. S. McCormick Company reflect in the still water like so many stars that have fallen from the sky and come to land neatly in a row. In the distance the golden onion dome of an orthodox church hovers like a tethered balloon in the evening light. It is still. The sound of traffic below is dull, leaving the moment uninterrupted.

"You can see more lights from here than from our kitchen window," says Cecilia.

They both stand on the curb, staring at the city below, ignoring for now the cool night air and breeze. After eight decades of living up here and eight decades' worth of nighttime skies and lights below, the view on a clear night remains something to savor. They love this hill.

"Well?" says Cecilia. Their silver Oldsmobile is parked across the street. She and Loretta look to make sure no headlights are coming around the bend in the road, before leaving the sidewalk. A ball bounces. Three teenagers shoot baskets in a circle of light on an outdoor court next to the recreation center.

A few blocks away, in Bohemian Hill, Florence Klingman walks briskly down the middle of the dark street, with a small white plastic pail. Tomorrow is trash day and she had gone to the Presbyterian Church to empty the wastebaskets. There isn't much. She passes Edna McKinney's house. The upstairs lights are on. Edna is reading.

Back at the Guehl home white lace curtains hang drawn in the windows. Years ago women kept their curtains, or shutters if they had them, closed six days a week so the sun didn't fade the

Dorothy in her wedding dress.

carpets or sofas. On Sundays, in honor of the Lord's Day, the curtains were opened and the sun was welcomed.

Inside, china cabinets filled with hand-painted plates and figurines line the hallways. The large wood dining-room table is covered with a tablecloth and fresh flowers. Their father replaced the plaster ceilings downstairs with rich wood panels and converted the brass chandeliers from gas to electric. Rugs are Oriental. Everything is tasteful.

Dorothy kept the house and everything in it spotless and in perfect working order. "We work at it. We hate dirty houses. I'd move into one room tomorrow if I couldn't keep the house clean," Dorothy once said. She knew the best plumbers and electricians. If the curtains weren't hanging in proper folds, she called Norma Weir, Ernestine Hepp's niece—the one with the beautiful yard and holiday displays—for a new set.

The sisters take pride in the house. The sign out front reads, ROBERT HUGHES FUNERAL HOME, but those who have lived here for any length of time know it as the Guehls'. Nearly all of Troy Hill has passed through their front door and rested on their couches and chairs, either paying respects to a neighbor or relative who has died, or as dinner guests. As children, they had learned to play quietly in the attic with one of the seven Guehl children, and a generation later, with Dorothy's three.

The reputation of the house and the Guehl name are thus entwined. Both deserve to be upheld. In a way, the community relies on the home to make a good showing. It stands sentinel at the top of Troy Hill Road, bidding welcome and good day. If someone drove up and saw a shabby-looking house, the whole neighborhood might be dismissed as equally worn. First impressions are important. The Guehl house, painted bright white with green trim, is a pleasant greeting.

The most recent glossy book about landmark Pittsburgh architecture included a photograph of the Guehl home. The wood siding of the house is intricately carved in little round scallops that resemble fish scales. A home improvement sales rep called the Guehls recently, pitching aluminum siding. Cecilia politely but firmly said they were not interested. If they installed new siding, this house would lose its historic value so fast it wouldn't be funny, Cecilia knew.

Troy Hill never had rich or poor sections.

Across the street from the Guehls lived an attorney. A doctor lived a few doors down, and next to him, James Botzer, the pharmacist who smoked good cigars and would drive six hours to Philadelphia with his wife, Helen, simply to try out a new restaurant. They and a few others—like the head of the savings and loan, and the jeweler—belonged to a small and distinguished circle of men who wore suits to work each day.

In between and all around lived the sausage maker, the mill hand, the truck driver, and the printer. Their paths and interests crossed on the street, at the Knights of Saint George meetings, choir picnics, or card parties. They worshiped and picnicked as a group. Their children played together. Ernestine Hepp's younger sister Bernadette remembers spending an afternoon at the Guehls with the youngest, Mary Margaret, playing with dolls dressed in fancy velvet clothes. Tiny bottles of sweet-smelling cologne sat regally on dressers. "It sure was special, because in our house, we didn't have cologne like Cody Number Five or Lady Esther perfume." Her father drove a truck for Armstrong Cork. The big thrill was when he brought it home, loaded the kids up, and dropped them off at school, to the awe and envy of their classmates.

Sarah Wohleber Lucas, Mary's daughter, valued that diversity and, having moved, sees the impact of its absence. "As we've grown up and moved out of the cities into suburbs, we've lost the mix, and when we do so, we tend to judge people by their financial level. I think it isolates us more," she says. "People today wouldn't think of living in a community that did not reflect their position."

Here, all are neighbors. Some are more fortunate, educated, and successful. Others less so, but those differences didn't define them or frame friendships. In fact, more significant than the contrasts is the commonness of their experiences. Essentially, all are trying to make a living, raise a family, and do some good with their lives. Everyone faced loss and disappointment. It was how people and households dealt with those struggles that mattered. Character, not wealth, determined worth.

They were aware, almost intuitively, of the needs of the community and one another, and responded according to ability and strength. Not everyone is suited to be the hill's champion, but Mary Wohleber is. Ernestine Hepp makes chicken soup, and Margaret Fichter delivers baskets and Communion to shut-ins. Emma Hildenbrand shares tomatoes, and Edna McKinney, her favorite books.

The Guehls had more, were expected to give more, and did so. When the new convent was being built, John and Anna bought pedestals and statues, a large donation that merited particular mention in the church's sixtieth anniversary publication.

By all measures John Guehl was a local success story. Son of German immigrants, with just a sixth-grade education, he ran a successful business and supported seven children, one unmarried sister, and three grandchildren.

He and a few other fortunate men pooled their money to establish the Workingman's Savings and Loan, which helped many neighbors buy their first homes. At one time he was president and his oldest son, Francis, vice president. Conservative and well run, the savings and loan survived the Depression and still exists, although now as a bank. One of his granddaughters is secretary. Then, too, John Guehl served on the local board of trade, offering advice to fellow shop owners and discussing ways to improve the community.

The baker, butcher, jeweler, and shoe repairman lived on the hill. They knew what their customers bought and on which days, knew the colors of their houses, and the names of their children.

The Guehls had a somewhat different relationship with the community. In a way it was more personal. Over the years, they would be in touch with nearly every household on the hill, helping them during the most vulnerable and painful moments of their lives. Their neighbors trusted the Guehls to offer support, know what to say, or when to say nothing at all, and to show compassion, if even in small ways. There always seemed to be a funeral in the holiday season. Not wanting to seem insensitive, the Guehl family muted its own celebration. The tree was off in the corner, away from the window. They didn't outline their rooftop or front door with strings of festive lights.

The business required a certain propriety and honor, not just of John Guehl but of his entire family as well. His wife, Anna, a warm and generous woman, came downstairs when there was a funeral. "Before you leave, come up for some coffee and sweet rolls," she would say. Her own parents had died of pneumonia within two weeks of each other when she was a teenager. She watched out for two younger siblings and ran the household while her older brothers went to work. An experience like that can make a person tough or sensitive. She was both.

She wanted everyone to feel welcome in her home. Whoever was working for her husband that day—parking cars or bringing umbrellas out to visitors in the pouring rain—was asked to stay for lunch or dinner. Even without guests, she was preparing up to thirty-five servings a day just for her own household. A few more never mattered. Cousins, nephews, neighbors, and priests would stop in, and when they did, she would say, "Throw another cup of water in the soup," and then set another place at the table.

"On any given day it was like the Last Supper," says John Jr.'s wife, Fern. "Nine people might drop in for lunch."

With a crowd to serve and entertain, the Guehls never had to run over to neighbors' houses or to even linger on the front porch. Their home was their social life. People came to them.

"It seems like everyone gathered here," says Cecilia. A blind cousin spent days there in the summer. He would sit on the front porch and listen closely to footsteps coming up the walk. "Loretta, is that you?" he asked when she arrived home from work.

Like her husband, Anna was aware of her family's good fortune and sensed a responsibility to serve the community in whatever way she could. The Christian Mothers relied on her organizational skills. Once, the group was hosting a party and needed to make and serve hundreds of sandwiches. "Somebody said, 'Wait until Mrs. Guehl comes.' My mother arrived and got an assembly line going to put the sandwiches together," says Loretta.

Still, with seven children and, later, three grandchildren, and a large house that always had to be ready for company, she couldn't often be absent. So she pursued charity from her home, through small daily deeds.

She kept tabs on her neighbors, especially the older ones, making a list of people who were sick or alone. After making fresh cookies or soup, she sent one of her daughters or, later, her granddaughters over with a plate or pot. It cheered them to know someone was thinking of them.

"In her day, I suppose grandmother was a social activist within the community," says Ann Spreng Meyer, Dorothy's oldest daughter. "She didn't go to the hospital and volunteer three days, but she kept track of all the little old widow ladies and unmarried friends."

At Anna's funeral, neighbors and friends approached her children, telling them of a kindness their mother had done. Many times her children were unaware of the specific act or the impact that her daily charity—to them routine—had made.

"She was always supporting somebody, going out and buying a kid an outfit," says her son John Jr. Anna knew how many of the children at the orphanage across the street didn't have First Communion dresses and made sure each got one.

The Guehl household was different from the rest of the hill in many ways. Politics, for one. Democrats reigned on the hill. Among them was neighbor Andrew "Huck" Fenrich, a powerful politician who helped others find jobs. Joe Fichter turned to him, after Reymer's closed, and got a job as groundskeeper with the sanitation department. Huck's grandson had no problem collecting one hundred signatures for a petition to name after his grandfather a new playground with slides, a swing set, and plastic horses on springs. People signed the petition and then spent the next ten minutes on the doorstep relaying a story of how Huck had helped a family member.

The Guehls were staunch Republicans although, Francis, the oldest of the seven children, confided to his nephew Frank Spreng that he did vote for John F. Kennedy, but only to demonstrate the power of the Catholic vote. "He didn't think Kennedy would win, anyway," Franks says.

Anna was the lone Democrat. She didn't care how the rest of the household voted. She would not be swayed. "My mother always knew what went on in the world and politics and had her own ideas about who should get elected," says Cecilia. "She was pretty... *hep* is the word."

Even neighborhood children, who knew little of politics, sensed instinctively that this house was unique. They would run in and out of each other's houses, forgetting to wipe their muddy or dirty shoes. Not here. "I would stop and think, *Wait a minute. I can't go in. I have dirt on me. I have mud on me,*" says Carole Brueckner, who lived at the end of their block and played with Dorothy's son Frank. If the kids were outside yelling, at least one adult would look out the window and tell them to quiet down.

That was the other thing. The house was filled with adults. First there were the parents, John and Anna, then John's sister Rosalia, the resident seamstress who took hemlines up and down according to current fashion, grated potatoes, and made noodles. After rolling noodles she draped them over chairs, tables, and counters until they dried.

Then, there were the four adult unmarried children. The oldest, Francis, and three unmarried sisters, Loretta, Cecilia, and Mary Margaret. Mary Margaret, the youngest, was known throughout Troy Hill as Tootie, which seems to have come from Loretta, who was in charge of singing to her as a baby. Her favorite song at the time was about a woman named Titina.

> *I'm looking for Titina, Titina, my Titina,*
> *I've searched from Palestina to London and Peru.*
> *I'll die without Titina. I can't eat my farina.*
> *I don't want Rose or Lena, Titina I want you.*

At some point in the singing, Titina was shortened to Tootie. And it was at that point, Mary Margaret became Tootie.

Fern Guehl, John Jr.'s wife, will never forget meeting the family for the first time. She was astonished. "I couldn't imagine all these women not having boyfriends and getting married and going off to their own homes," says Fern.

She tried to get Tootie, who was about her age, to start writing to the lonely soldier boys. Everyone needs a pen pal. Consider it a patriotic duty, one small part and effort to help our soldiers fight World War II. Tootie said it was a nice idea. Fern has no idea whether she ever wrote a letter.

Young women were supposed to get married and have children. That's what she—and just about everyone—thought. The hill's biggest and most active club for adult women was the Christian Mothers. Single women couldn't join. Marriage seemed the only conceivable and acceptable path, other than the convent, of course. Barring those two options, the assumption was that women had little choice but to be miserable, lonely old maids.

The Guehls defied that notion, emphatically and resolutely. "There were no old maids in our house," says Lynne Spreng,

Dorothy's daughter. "There were three working women. Three career ladies, although you didn't use that word in those days. They were working women."

In that respect, they were a contradiction. The family upheld convention and propriety. Rebellion wouldn't occur to them. Yet, here they were, going against the grain, and doing so without a hint of apology or the thought of shrinking back into some timid existence hoping no one would notice that they weren't following suit. The rest of society and the world could do and think what it pleased. They had enough self-esteem and self-worth to go their own way. They also had the resources. Some women at the time felt they needed a husband "to keep them." That was not the case in the Guehl house. Anna made it very clear to her children that they could always stay home and be provided for. Breakfast, lunch, and dinner, and a clean bed awaited them.

All three of the sisters worked in high-profile jobs. They didn't work in broom factories or wait tables or ring cash registers at the five-and-ten. They weren't making pickles or sweeping floors. They sat behind desks. It took Cecilia a year to find a job after she graduated from high school, and once she got it, she prized it. It was something she was trained for. In school she was noted as an efficient stenographer.

"You had a job, and that was the most important thing in your life," Cecilia says.

At one point Fern asked Cecilia point-blank, "Don't you want to get married?"

"I don't have to do that," she recalls Cecilia saying. There's nothing wrong with not getting married, and in fact, there are a few things right about it. If she wanted to travel to California or New York, or go out and buy a fur coat, she could do so without asking someone's permission.

"What about children?" Fern asked.

"Well, I have yours," Cecilia responded. Actually, it turned out to be Dorothy's children.

"I never regretted not getting married," Cecilia says.

Cecilia could say with pride that she worked for Heinz. Many people on the hill and throughout the city worked there and considered it a benevolent employer. The biography of founder Henry Heinz is titled *The Good Provider* largely because of his enlightened treatment of women, who received weekly mani-

Cecilia Guehl and Mr. Heinz.

cures if they worked with food, could take classes in cooking and millinery and attend monthly concerts.

Cecilia began in the stenographer's pool and from there was assigned as secretary to the assistant controller. He was promoted several times and was ultimately named chief executive officer. With each promotion, he took Cecilia along. She was surrounded by powerful, intelligent, and highly regarded executives. A descendant of Henry Heinz had an office just down the hall. She traveled on the company plane and was privy to undisclosed plans. But she was trustworthy. She knew from the family funeral business the importance of being discreet. By nature, too, she is prudent. The fact that her boss thought enough of Cecilia to bring her along with his every promotion provided a measure of reward. She knew she was valued. She retired with a generous pension and a silver tea service.

Loretta never joined the union because she was considered management, serving as the manager's secretary. And Tootie, another financial whiz, ended up as head of salaried payroll at then-huge Pittsburgh Coke and Chemical. Brilliant with numbers, she also loved Shakespeare and could recite passages and lines from memory. She and one of her nieces had season tickets to the local Shakespeare theater.

The Guehls had a nice comfortable life. Everyone knew his or her routine, when to sit down for breakfast, and what time dinner would be served. Holidays were like a well-orchestrated dance. One year's Christmas, Easter, Memorial Day, and Thanksgiving resembled the last and the next. Members of the family could come and go as they pleased and did so regularly, accompanying one another to symphonies, plays, the theater, and museums.

Children in the neighborhood called the sisters Miss Guehl, not Aunt Loretta or Aunt Cecilia as they would other grown women on the street. These ladies would never utter earthy, improper, or even unkind words. They were genteel. Opinionated, but genteel. Knowing how to be both requires class.

"They were all fine, very nice, very pleasant, and definitely a cut above. You can tell just as soon as you start talking to them. There's a grace and a charm there that you don't find all the time. Even today you just don't find it, and they had it," says Sarah Wohleber Lucas. "They would come to church and they'd have these little mink stoles on."

Even Dorothy's younger children acted and dressed differently from their friends. Their great-aunt Rosalia made both girls lovely fur hats with velvet crowns. The ladies of the house thought they were charming. The girls, though, hated them and sobbed Sunday after Sunday until Anna took them to Barney Michael's department store and bought knit hats with pompoms so they could be like their friends. "It did not match the other children and we wanted to be the same as the other children," says Lynne.

Once Ann and Lynne decided to go sledding after school without first coming home to tell anyone or changing out of their matching cream-colored corduroy jumpers. Their mother, Dorothy, went searching for the girls, found them muddy and red-cheeked, and sent them to bed without their supper. As their mother went down the front steps, Anna, their grandmother—who in their eyes was the household's ultimate and feared boss—came up to their room with a box of cereal, two bowls, milk, and the order not to mention a word of it to their mother. Lynne will never forget that kindness—or her sister, Ann, asking, "Where's the sugar?"

Other than that one transgression, they were model. "You wouldn't want anyone to say John Guehl's granddaughters were misbehaving," says Ann Spreng Meyer. "We all pretty much did our own public relations for the family and the business. We learned how to be nice and not very argumentative, and not to discuss religion or politics. We didn't always agree, but we would nod and say OK."

That's how it was with all the Guehls. They wouldn't argue or disagree in public. Discussions were kept for the kitchen table. Thelma Wurdock recalls being there for lunch. John Sr. was discussing politics. Anna pointed a finger at him and said, "Now, John, I think that is enough." He left it at that. He always called her Little One.

Dorothy was more outgoing than her sisters. She knew most everyone, and those she didn't, she would talk to, anyway. Among her close friends was a bishop who became a cardinal in Rome. She wrote him a letter to ask if he could arrange an audience with the Pope. He did. She and her daughter Lynne had nice seats up front in a huge auditorium. Dorothy turned around and saw a few African American priests sitting in the row behind them.

"Where are you from?" she asked them.

"Tanzania," they replied.

"Do you know Father Joe Noppinger?" she continued. Father Joe is a white priest from Baltimore who had been at the Guehls home several times for dinner. Dorothy knew he taught in Tanzania.

"Father Joe? He's our teacher," they replied. Lynne's jaw dropped. Her mother fished through her purse and pulled out a small green Heinz pickle pin and handed it to them. "Give this to Father Joe," she told them. "He'll know who you saw."

Dorothy was president of Christian Mothers for years and worked closely with Margaret Fichter, another longtime president. When the Troy Hill Citizens was being formed, Mary Wohleber recruited her, knowing the Guehl family name would offer credibility and Dorothy's energy would provide momentum. The pastor, too, called on Dorothy, to organize and run a committee to keep tabs on tuition payments. If Dorothy couldn't do something, she would find another who could.

That's where Cecilia came in. The citizens group didn't have an office or a staff. Dorothy compiled a rough newsletter. After work Cecilia polished the wording and typed it up. She labored at it, insisting on the professionalism that she was used to at Heinz but without the same resources. She didn't get paid or seek recognition. She simply went upstairs to the third floor and typed.

Same with the tuition-overseeing group. When parents fell behind, Dorothy alerted Cecilia, who sent a letter gently reminding them to pay up. "Really, my sister Dorothy was on that committee. I just did all their typing," says Cecilia.

Soon, it didn't matter if Dorothy was involved or not. Officers of church and community groups brought their correspondence to Cecilia, asking her to make sure it was correct, the grammar and wording proper, the spelling accurate. "Would you mind?" Pinky Botzer McGlothlin would ask. And Cecilia never did.

"I always called Cece my secretary," says Pinky, who was head of the Troy Hill Citizens. "Cece, I would say, I need a letter sent to this one and that one, and she would have them done for me." Pinky went to school with Cecilia's niece Ann. Her own mother, Helen Botzer, went to school with Cecilia's older brother, Francis. Loretta and Cecilia have rings from the jewelry store that Pinky's grandfather owned at the bottom of Troy Hill Road.

"Cece didn't go around and tell everybody. She just did it. There are no airs. But, see, that is the old school. When she takes something on, she doesn't leave it up to anybody else. She just does it, and all the proper way. That's my friend Cece," says Pinky.

Every year the church publishes an annual year-in-review. Cecilia compiled that booklet for years. She combed church bulletins and announcements, culling important dates. After, she wrote a concise, thoughtful history.

One year she didn't do it. A fellow parishioner stopped her outside of church. By the way, he asked, did you do this year's year-in-review?

No, she responded. He could tell. It was nice to know people appreciated and recognized her work. She always prided herself in being thorough.

Mary Wohleber knew that Cecilia had the best typing skills on the hill and asked her to serve as secretary of the Saint Anthony Chapel Committee in 1972. Cecilia gladly accepted the position and has served loyally for thirty-six years. Chapel broadened Cecilia's circle of friends and involvement in the community. People got to know her better.

One day the members of the chapel committee assembled to hand wash the stations of the cross. Carole Brueckner was up on the ladder. Cecilia was down below, wringing rags and handing them up to the washers. Carole was nervous. It was her first time cleaning the stations.

"I was really afraid that I was going to grab on to something and break it. I almost felt like doing this was sacrilegious. Then, I mentioned something to Cece about being scared and she said 'Aw, c'mon. It's just like washing a dirty kid's face. Don't worry about it,'" says Carole.

Cecilia has a wonderful sense of humor. One of her favorite stories is about the time she got into trouble with Sister Annunciata.

Cecilia and Dorothy were enlisted by the Most Holy Name nuns to go to the Good Shepherd Home every Saturday to pick up the Communion wafers baked by the cloistered nuns and carry them back to the church. One day Dorothy couldn't make it, so Cecilia went by herself.

She gathered the boxes and stacked them carefully, one on top of the other. She was on her way out when the heavy door smacked her from behind. Boxes of hosts flew into the air and fell to the ground, spilling the white paper-thin circles all over the sidewalk and in the dirt. They weren't consecrated yet, but it didn't matter. Cecilia felt doomed. She scrambled after them frantically before anyone could see her. "I scooped them up, dirt and all, and threw them into the box," says Cecilia, hoping and praying that no one would notice. Sister Annunciata cornered her later and demanded to know what had happened. "That door got me," Cecilia meekly told her.

The good nuns also did laundry, mainly the white detachable starched collars that all the men wore. Molly Fichter had to take some of the family laundry to the nuns when her mother, Margaret, was sick. The nuns did their best. But they weren't familiar with washing colored clothing. The laundry came back bleached and several sizes smaller.

A few years back Cecilia was honored with the North Side Leadership Conference Award. The group didn't cite one landmark contribution, because there wasn't one. Rather, it mentioned years of service, typing various letters, minutes, and correspondence for church and community organizations.

In doing so the group recognized that such sustained and quiet dedication and loyalty, though often unrecognized, are as vital as running the show. Four hundred people attended the Thirteenth Annual Awards Dinner at a Greek Orthodox church. Music and dancing followed. The State House of Representatives passed a resolution congratulating her.

"Of course, I had to go up and receive it. I felt a little self-conscious," she says.

And a few months later, at the summer Troy Hill festival, she was introduced and cheered. "I didn't think I did that much," she says. It is something she knows how to do and does well, so why not? She freely proffers her skills. It doesn't matter who asks. She wouldn't slough off the Brownies because they are little girls or answer only the pastor because he is the pastor. She didn't gauge her giving on the status of the petitioner.

That is the way she was raised. Ideals and codes of honor have always been important to the Guehls, and are not treated lightly or abandoned easily.

This year a Troy Hill couple received the leadership award. The husband owns a beauty shop on the hill. His wife is a school crossing guard. Both dress up as clowns and entertain school and church youth groups.

Cecilia and Loretta's oldest sister, Rosella, married and moved to Canton, Ohio. Their younger sister, Tootie, died in a tragic auto accident in 1981. She and Cecilia, their niece Ann, and Ann's daughter had just left a concert hall together after an evening symphony performance downtown when an eighty-three-year-old woman lost control of her car and rammed into them. Tootie was killed instantly.

"I don't remember all the circumstances. I think I tried to block it out of my mind to the best of my ability," says Cecilia. Tootie had just retired the week before, at the age of fifty-six. She and Cecilia planned that summer to travel to Germany to see a Passion play that is staged once every ten years there.

"The only thing I have to say is that it was a terrible thing for the woman who was driving, too," says Loretta.

That left Cecilia, Dorothy, and Loretta at home. They were always close. When Dorothy first moved back home, the grown sisters shared one room and two double beds. A handy sink sat in the corner. At night they washed out their stockings and gloves and hung them by the mantel to dry. Dorothy could keep an eye and ear on her two daughters, who shared a little room in the back of the sisters' room. If the two little girls were up talking too late, Dorothy fired a slipper into their bedroom, aiming low and usually hitting Lynne's bed.

Dorothy ran the house and the social calendar, figuring out who was coming to dinner, what to serve, where everyone would sit, and what dishes would be used. Loretta cooked and kept the books. Cecilia was the household correspondent and dishwasher.

They were a triumvirate. Dorothy's grandchildren sent letters to the house addressed, "G'Ma and the A's," as in grandma and the aunts. "We sound like a rock group," Dorothy once told her daughter. They kept in close touch with all the nephews and nieces. Dorothy once shipped a ham bone to her nephew, part of a practical joke between the two of them. They remained fiercely independent, in large part because they felt physically and emotionally safe on the hill. They know most of the neighbors, and their neighbors' parents and grandparents. Dorothy often walked to evening meetings. One time Ann asked whether that was a good idea.

"What if some kid harasses you?" she asked.

"They wouldn't dare," Dorothy replied. "I know practically every kid on this hill. Even if I don't know them, I'll just look at them and say, 'Don't you dare, or I'm going to tell your mother.'"

In a community this size and so contained, old and young are neighbors. They occupy one set of streets. Their lives may not be entwined, but at least they cross, frequently. During one sermon the priest told the story of how a young man approached an older woman after evening mass. "Where do you live?" he asked. The woman told him. He offered to walk her home, saying it's too dark to walk home alone.

Kids do hang out in the cemetery, smoking and drinking,

and drag race on backstreets. And at one point this year, a Troy Hill boy broke into the church and took some things. A few weeks later he wrote a letter of apology that was published in the church bulletin.

In the winter of 1995, Dorothy was getting weaker. She had been sick for more than a year but, like her mother, never wanted to go to the doctor. Anna would say, "Oh, I'm much improved," when the girls would urge her to see a doctor.

"Mom, one day you're going to die of improvements," their brother Francis told her. When she did finally make an appointment, Francis instructed her, "Now, Mom, make sure you tell the doctor what is wrong."

"He's the doctor. Let him find out," she replied.

Dorothy had gone to a Christmas party at Pinky Botzer Mc-Glothlin's house, and Christmas services at Most Holy Name. But by February 1996, she was in the hospital. That winter was particularly icy and cold. Her sisters needed to be with her, but the thought of driving was too much. "We were so unnerved we didn't even want to drive. And it was such bad weather," says Cecilia. Pinky and her sister Eileen Schullek, who grew up on the hill but has since moved away, offered to take turns driving them to the hospital and back.

"These people are younger than we are," says Cecilia of Pinky and Eileen. "We sort of grew up with their parents. They would do anything for you."

Dorothy died just before Fastnacht. The morning of that day, Margaret Fichter arrived at their side door with a bag filled with a dozen doughnuts.

Every day, at least once a day, Cecilia works in her third-floor office. On one afternoon she might be typing the minutes from the latest chapel committee meeting or sending out sixty-eight invitations to chapel volunteers for an annual thank-you dinner at Billy's.

Recently the city magazine published a small but rather flip description of the chapel. The chapel, it said, was a mix of ornate Victorian splendor with a dash of George Romero, a film producer most well-known for the horror film *Night of the Living Dead*. It describes the statues in the chapel, saying martyred saints, whose throats were slashed, had "some rather messy throat surgery."

Cecilia refused to let the remark go by unchallenged. She rifled off a letter to the editor. The writer's "flippant write-up indicates that he is no critic of religious art."

Another afternoon, she sends a letter to her former employer, Heinz, asking the company to donate surplus to Most Holy Name's Saint Vincent de Paul Society for needy families. She types memos to herself about what needs to be done around the house, and she dutifully records births, weddings, and transfers in the family tree and address list. A copy of the updated family tree is then sent to a niece interested in geneaology.

"We call it the home office," Cecilia says. "We know where all the nieces and nephews, and grandnieces and grandnephews are. If anybody needs Rebecca's address, we have it. Maria just moved from Indianapolis to Fort Wayne. We can provide her address."

Cecilia carefully reads local newspapers and magazines

from beginning to end, clipping relevant stories and dispatching them accordingly. Anything about Heinz, she sends to her niece Ann, even though Ann quit working there in 1963. A five-day series of articles on the demise of a Pittsburgh institution, Westinghouse Electric Corporation, went to Ann's husband, Tom Meyer, who once worked for the company. The couple now lives in Maryland.

A nephew in Canton, Ohio, gets tool-related stories. All mentions about construction of new local buildings or renovations of old are mailed to a grandnephew in Atlanta. "I'm trying to lure him back to Pittsburgh," Cecilia says. At the end of the day the newspaper is in pieces. She sends obituaries of people they knew, in case they want to send condolences.

Part of it is a sense of duty, being the matriarch, or at least the corresponding one, and living in the homestead. The other part is devotion to her family. She cherished being daughter, sister, aunt, and now great-great-aunt. Family can be exasperating at times, and many who leave do so willingly. But in the end, family is what they have.

After relatives receive one of Cecilia's letters, they respond with notes and news, which she in turns spreads, letting everyone know that the kids in Denver are doing well in school.

"We have not lost track of one another because of Cecilia," says Lynne Spreng, who lives in a nearby suburb and visits her aunts Cecilia and Loretta at least once a week and talks to them almost daily.

Lynne's sister and brother, Ann Spreng Meyer and Frank Spreng, live out of state but come into town several times a year to visit Cecilia and Loretta.

Frank usually comes during tax season. While he was there in March, Thelma stopped by with her taxes. She had a question about capital gains. Frank helped her. He always called her Aunt Thelma because she was over at the house so much.

Just as Thelma was leaving, Mary Wohleber dropped by. She was leaving the next day for Bosnia and wanted to let the Guehl sisters know where she was going and when she would be back. Frank and Mary's daughter, Sarah, were classmates.

After Mary left, Frank helped Loretta with her taxes. She asked him if she had correctly calculated the original discount interest on some bonds. He listened. She had. Then they had a great debate about whether she could expense or depreciate a roofing improvement. "Now, how many eighty-seven-year-olds could enter into a serious discussion on expensing repairs? It's an extraordinary thing. Even when she has a question, it is simply that she hasn't known the appropriate rules to follow. She is always on the right track."

Frank says, "Loretta and Cecilia remind me of my own children, two generations later." One of his daughters is an accountant. The other is a lawyer. "It is really a circumstance of where they were living and the time they were living in. They were born in an era before they were supposed to do those things."

Neither Cecilia nor Loretta betray any sign of regret. That's just the way things were. "If we would have had the opportunity to go to college, we would have. But we didn't," says Cecilia. Their lives were no less full. When she was seventy-nine, Cecilia flew to the West Coast and took a cruise up to Alaska. She got a kick out of the T-shirts. ALASKA, WHERE MEN ARE MEN AND WOMEN WIN THE IDITAROD.

Since Dorothy died a few years ago, Cecilia and Loretta have done their best to assume her duties. Loretta decides what to serve. "Cece never complains. Whatever I make, she eats. I suggest something for lunch, and she says, 'That's fine.' "

Cecilia washes the dishes and does all the driving. If the Federal Reserve Bank downtown has a special bond offering, Cecilia drives, drops Loretta off in front of the bank, and circles around until Loretta is finished. Cecilia answers all phone calls. They never had an answering machine. Too rude. Anytime Dorothy dialed and got a machine, she would mutter and then shout, "*You there? You there?*"

Their home remains the gathering place at holidays, although the crowd is smaller. Frank and his daughter spent a few days with them around New Year's Day. Another nephew from Ohio came with his wife and children for dinner. Thelma was over for Christmas dinner, as were Lynne and Cecilia's great-niece, Beth Ann, and Beth Ann's two sons.

Cecilia takes the coats and retrieves them, answers the door and shows guests out. Then she does the dishes. When the great-grandnephews come, Cecilia reads them a book. "She has got to be the favorite aunt because she reads," says Loretta. "But then one of the little kids will say, 'Aunt Loretta, your meat is real good.' "

The other day, which was not any special occasion, they had a crowd for lunch. The funeral director came with his son. The cleaning lady was there. Ann and her husband were in town.

"All of a sudden we had six people for lunch," says Cecilia. "If we weren't there, they wouldn't get anything to eat. So we just sort of stay around."

Cecilia will look out the window, see another car outside, and set another place. Loretta will throw another cup of water in the soup.

CHAPTER TEN

Fast Friends

THE DOUBLE BACK DOORS of Saint Anthony Chapel swing open and those who attended the morning mass and novena come slowly down the four steps. A few continue walking across the street to the parking lot or down the sidewalk to their homes.

A core lingers. Then, as they have week after week, year after year, they break into five or six little circles of friends. On the steps or sidewalk, they exchange pleasantries, note the blushing leaves on the tree, and relay recent illnesses and recoveries. Over time they have shared the momentous—births, promotions, and weddings—and the mundane, weeding tips and flu remedies. Whether deliberate or not, the unscheduled but well-practiced and anticipated fellowship has nurtured ties and friendships.

Thelma Wurdock stands off to the right side of the steps, waiting for her best friend of seventy-five years, Cecilia Guehl, who emerges moments later with her sister Loretta. The sisters stop by one group. Cecilia hands one woman a white envelope containing the freshly typed minutes of the Monday night chapel meeting. One of the ladies tells Cecilia she hasn't been feeling well.

"The problem is, I can't breathe," the woman says.

Cecilia looks at her and says with a straight face. "Not breathing? That is a problem," she says. They both laugh.

The Guehls begin walking toward Thelma. "Guess I'll just have to mail these," she says, waving the other half dozen envelopes.

Thelma reports that her poison ivy is almost gone. She doesn't know where she got it. If she's outside and the wind blows a certain way, the next day she comes down with a rash. Doctors used to give her a shot every March, April, and May just to ward off the rash. She wishes they still did.

"Remember, Sebastian gave it to me once," she says. Sebastian is one of the two local stray cats who live somewhere on this block. Thelma lives in the house on the corner. She and her mother moved there twenty-five years ago, when their first house was torn down to build the church parking lot. Her mother was eighty-two. Thelma is almost eighty-two now.

The other cat is Rocky. Rocky is sneaky. He watches on Tuesday mornings for the chapel doors to open, waits for everyone to come out, and then tries to slink in. Not about to let a scruffy cat in their chapel, Cecilia has to rush up the steps to close the door. Another time, one of those two cats nearly gave Cecilia a heart attack. He walked up alongside her and brushed against her leg. "I never saw him coming," she said.

Margaret Fichter scoots by and waves. They see each other every morning at mass, either here or at Most Holy Name.

Margaret noticed when Thelma was out for a while with a bad back and when Cecilia wasn't in her pew during a stretch of bitter cold weather, and inquired. Today Margaret continues on. She has a lot to do. She's baking a cake for tomorrow's Golden Agers' meeting and then going bowling this afternoon. Last night she and the Ladies of Charity had a meeting. The Guehls and Thelma don't go to Golden Agers or bowling and Cecilia jokes that any day they are going to need a Lady of Charity for themselves. The sisters prefer to stay home. Thelma says she isn't a joiner and never has been.

Thelma hands Loretta two empty round Tupperware containers. "The oxtail soup tasted like my mother made it," she tells Loretta. Whenever Loretta makes a special dish, she puts a serving or two in a little container and Cecilia drives it over. Chili, dumplings, sauerkraut, doughnuts for Fastnacht. During Lent, Loretta made a batch of fried-egg potato soup, which is potato soup without meat. At one point this year, Thelma was sick and in bed. She didn't want to get Meals on Wheels because the portions are too big. So the sisters became her unofficial meal service. Loretta cooked and Cecilia delivered. It made all three of them feel good.

Thelma is like Cecilia. She worked full-time, lived with her mother, and didn't cook. Dinner was waiting for Thelma up until her mother died, at the age of eighty-nine. Thelma was close to sixty then. The first day she returned to work after her mother's funeral, her brother stopped by with a meat loaf. "I know you don't know how to cook. You can live on this for a couple of days," he told her.

A woman and her sister stop by on their way to their car. They don't live on Troy Hill but attend Tuesday morning mass at the chapel. They belong to Saint Nicholas Church, which is just below Troy Hill. Thelma heard someone saying the church was going to be picked up, blue onion dome and all, and moved to widen the road below.

"What's new?" Cecilia asks the sisters.

They had taken their uncle in for a checkup. Doctors found cancer. He's eighty-nine.

"Aw, gee, he doesn't deserve it at that age," says Cecilia. No one deserves cancer. But he's lived that long. His poor body has probably been through enough.

"Any family?" Cecilia asks, meaning children.

He never married.

"Oh, like us old maids," Cecilia says, gesturing to herself, Thelma, and Loretta. They laugh.

The lady and her sister leave. The other groups have begun to break apart.

Cecilia, Loretta, and Thelma are the last to go, lingering awhile longer in the sunshine. They dress nicely with blouses and skirts freshly pressed. They wear stockings and pumps and their hair is set in soft waves. Loretta's hair is white. Cecilia's is more pepper than salt. Thelma's hair is chestnut brown with two white stylish curls above her forehead.

Cecilia tells Thelma that her nephew Frank and her niece Ann are coming in for a visit. They consider Thelma family, as she does them. Frank sends her bouquets and cards that read, "Aunt Thelma." A place was always set for Thelma at the Guehl dining room table for holiday meals. Thelma's mother, too, was included until she died. When the sisters weren't home on Thanksgiving one year, Loretta cooked a big turkey dinner with stuffing, gravy, and potatoes the following Saturday and had

Thelma over so they could continue that tradition. This Easter Thelma joined them and their niece Lynne for Loretta's special orange-glazed ham rolls. Loretta grinds the ham and pork herself. Orange marmalade is brushed on top for the glaze. The recipe specifies for six. But she makes it into ten smaller rolls, which worked out well this year because her great-niece and her family dropped in. So everyone had a little ham roll.

Seventy-five years ago, before the Guehls moved into their current home, they bought a house whose backyard met Thelma Wurdock's backyard at a gated fence. Cecilia and Thelma pushed their baby buggies side by side. They've been best friends ever since.

Cecilia Guehl and Thelma Wurdock as children.

Cecilia refused to go to first grade until Thelma, six months younger, was eligible. When they were in the second grade, Cecilia's aunt Rosalia made First Holy Communion dresses for both girls. Thelma's skirt was layered with ruffles. Cecilia's dress was embroidered. They wore white stockings, white patent leather shoes, and bows the size of dinner plates on their heads.

Thelma's mother snapped a picture of them standing on the sidewalk in front of a spiked wrought iron fence that once ringed the church. Each holds a candle in her right hand. They are smiling and squinting from the bright morning sun. Thelma is a little taller.

Thelma brought this picture and two more with her this morning. She is joining the Guehls for a light breakfast. Loretta is in the kitchen. Cecilia and Thelma relax in the living room. Dainty flowers rest on the wallpaper and in vases. Handsome grandfather and mantel clocks chime on the hour. A dish of fresh salted cashews sits on the coffee table for guests. Thelma nestles in the corner of the couch with a pillow behind her back. When she is there, that is Thelma's seat. She's had a bad back for years, and this is the most comfortable spot. Cecilia sits in a chair.

Cecilia's First Communion dress sat in her dresser drawer for seventy years. She recently gave it to her niece Johanna, who wanted to have it put in a special frame. Cecilia couldn't find her bow, so Thelma donated hers. That way Cecilia's niece could have

Cecilia and Thelma as working women.

the complete outfit. It's fitting, Thelma thinks, that something of hers and something of Cecilia's be kept together.

Thelma hands Cecilia another picture of the two of them, seventeen years later. Again they stand side by side, this time, though, in the Guehl's lovely front yard. They aren't holding anything. They are young working women, with dark hair in tight curls and dark glasses that look like butterfly wings. They worked in the same office at the time, rode to work and ate lunch together. After work they went to the movies.

Thelma is still taller. Her skirt is tapered. Thelma was stylish. Years ago she bought a sporty white Fiat with a sunroof. When she drove down the street, people would stop and look. "It was an eye-catcher, believe me," says Thelma. "I thought I was pretty snazzy."

Cecilia's dress doesn't taper. It was dotted Swiss with a modest flare. Her aunt Rosalia had made it.

Thelma asks Cecilia if she saw the morning paper with the full-page ad for spike heels. "Some of them are over a hundred dollars," says Thelma.

Cecilia wore pointy high heels when she first started to work at Heinz. Five days a week, she walked up and down Troy Hill Road in them.

Her mother, Anna, thought she was crazy. "How many years are you going to try walking up and down the hill in those heels?" she asked Cecilia.

"Until I die," Cecilia stubbornly told her.

"Yeah, we thought it was great when we got into high heels," says Thelma.

"I got past that stage," says Cecilia.

The next picture is taken more than fifty years later. This time they are sitting side by side on the couch in the Guehl living room. It is Christmas. They are in their late seventies. Thelma wears a sweater. Cecilia a blouse. Cecilia never wears sweaters. In the winter the sisters keep the heat turned high. They exchange gifts. If Thelma can't find a nice blouse, she

Cecilia and Thelma at Christmas.

buys Cecilia a bottle of Shalimar perfume. Cecilia buys Thelma
a magazine subscription or books.

Thelma looks at the three photographs. "See, we've been
together all those years and still are," she says.

Troy Hill is rich with friendships, and the friendships themselves
are rich in scope. Edna McKinney has her fellow readers and
swimmers, her friends from her street and church. She keeps in
touch with Mildred by phone. Edna remembers being a little girl
and walking her grandfather's watch to Florence Klingman's
home, where Florence's father repaired watches. Now, seventy
years later, they see each other every Sunday at the tiny Troy
Hill Presbyterian Church and serve on the church session. When
Edna bought a new stove, Florence came to see it.

One afternoon, sitting in the cool community room of their
church, Florence asks Edna what she thinks about the debate

regarding creation in the Bible and evolution. Florence respects Edna's opinion because Edna reads so much. Edna tells her about a book that explains creation, in which one of the seven days is really thousands of years. They probably wouldn't have talked like this before. Edna was so busy with her family. Now they have time for the luxury of introspective talk. There is no reason to hold back, nothing to hide or fear. Experience has a way of making people less beholden to ego. They didn't have big ones to begin with.

Emma Hildenbrand and Ernestine Hepp have been best friends for less than ten years, which in Troy Hill and among women of their generation is the blink of an eye. But they have managed in that relatively short time to develop devotion for and genuine enjoyment of one another. Emma doesn't play bingo just because Ernestine does. Ernestine doesn't forgo bingo just because Emma doesn't play. They don't have to share everything, every interest, but they do share time, and they shelter each other from loneliness. They care for each other. That is enough. When Emma was locked out of the house, she took great comfort knowing she could go to Ernestine's home.

Margaret Fichter has her friends from choir, her friends from bowling, her friends from the Ladies of Charity. They are all dear women, and they check up on her when she isn't at church or at practice one week. But she and Helen Steinmetz have something deeper, simply because they have spent so much time together. Joined in first grade by the common misery of runny noses, they shared classrooms for the next eight years. Their friendship continued after graduation, even though they began going their separate ways. Helen went to commercial school to learn typing and shorthand. Margaret wanted to, but had to get a job at Heinz peeling tomatoes. Still, she wasn't jealous that Helen had an opportunity denied her.

"We didn't know enough to be jealous. We just accepted one another and that was it," says Margaret. Margaret called Helen's mother Mom Steinmetz. "She loved to sing," Margaret recalls. "'In the Good Old Summertime,' that was one of her favorites."

On Margaret's wedding day Helen straightened out Margaret's veil and made sure it would trail neatly behind as she walked down the aisle. Margaret joined Christian Mothers. Helen couldn't. So they formed their own card club. Four of the original eight still play. Margaret rarely brought pictures of her children to the card party. That night was their time. They didn't try to impress each other by cleaning and cooking all day, either.

"We didn't care if you had dirt there," says Helen.

"No, just as long as we had something to eat," says Margaret.

"We never criticized anybody's home," says Helen.

"We were all in the same boat," says Margaret.

It is wonderful to have a close friend who knows and loves us *now*. These women are even more fortunate. They have known and cared for each other as long as they have known themselves. Their earliest memories are blurry split-second scenes of pushing doll buggies on the sidewalk alongside another little girl. That little girl, now grown, remains their confidante. Such shared time and experience provides a singular perspective. They know how far a friend has come and grown. Every step forward is more fully appreciated in light of every personal setback. Florence Klingman admires Edna's resilience and wishes she could laugh and enjoy life as deeply. They can see that being generous or diligent is not just a phase in their friend's life but a way of life. Thelma always knew Cecilia was a hard worker and is proud of the fact that she hasn't said, "I've had enough. I quit." Cecilia knows Thelma has a big heart. Once, when her manager had to cut one of two staff positions, Thelma volunteered to give up her job so the other woman, who had a physical disability, wouldn't lose hers. Thelma collects buckeyes off the street and keeps them in her pocket to give to neighborhood children. She doesn't want them running in front of cars and getting hurt.

For the most part, their circle of friends is limited to the neighborhood. Mary Wohleber is an exception. She continues to write letters to people she met years ago in England and Wales.

Loretta appears at the doorway. "Breakfast will be served in a couple of minutes," she says.

Cecilia and Thelma follow her out to the kitchen. In the middle of the table is a small flowerpot with four daffodils.

They are a gift from Emma Hildenbrand and her daughter Jeanne, who stopped by Saturday for a visit. Jeanne has been compiling her family history. She brought some old black-and-white photographs of her grandmother—Leo's mother—and Anna Guehl playing cards with a group of women. Jeanne wanted to know if the Guehls recognized the other ladies.

Emma comes along for company. She didn't know the Guehls well, and only through her husband's family. As a boy, Leo stopped by the Guehl house on his way to school to pick up Rosella, Cecilia and Loretta's oldest sister. Rosella was often late. So Anna would look out and tell Leo to go ahead or he would be tardy. His sister Margaret, or Sis Hildenbrand, was recorder of the Most Holy Name Drama Society when Francis Guehl was secretary. Both families went to all the performances. Emma has a picture of Leo's father and John Guehl Sr. standing in front of a barn at a church picnic.

"When they brought those daffodils, there were no flowers. They have just been popping out like mad," says Cecilia.

Hanging on the wall in the kitchen is a calendar with an enlarged photograph of Dorothy's two great-grandsons dressed in sharp black suits that look like little tuxedos. Cecilia had the calendar custom printed, along with twenty others. Every year the boys give calendars as Christmas gifts, but they rely on their great-great-aunt Cecilia to have them made. She and Loretta attend the boys' piano recitals and invite them to the Saint Anthony's festival and the annual church Harvest Festival. One of the boys won a big can of caramel popcorn and a two-liter bottle of pop. Before the Harvest Festival, they went to the polka mass. Just as Dorothy's children were like their own, so, too, are her grandchildren and great-grandchildren.

Cecilia pours the coffee. Loretta spoons out grapefruit and orange sections, and passes the sliced cinnamon bread. They begin discussing American history and Stonewall Jackson. Cecilia recently subscribed to a new magazine called *American History* and gave Thelma the first two issues. Thelma is a history buff. Her niece bought her a tome on the Civil War, describing every battle and general. These women are avid readers and always have been. By engaging one another with what they just learned, they keep their friendship alive and growing. When they were both working downtown, the bookmobile stopped regularly at their office. Thelma was always getting a new book or two. Mysteries, politics, or history. After Thelma retired, she went to the Carnegie Library every week.

"Our favorite thing is to sit around and talk," says Thelma. They don't bother with prologues. The background, setting, and mood are understood. Their lives are so braided that if one drops a sentence, the other can pick it up, whether it is about work or summer camp, the 1920s or the 1990s. It is not an interruption, just a completion, their sentence and thought so often in tandem. Whatever one has to say is both relevant and interesting to the other.

The same people figure prominently in their lives. Their mothers, Anna and Mary were best friends. Mary came over four days a week to help Anna clean the house. Thelma fondly remembers Cecilia's older sister Dorothy rushing over the day Thelma's baby brother, Warren, was born and, later, pushing him in a buggy—protectively, as if he were her own brother. On the anniversary of Dorothy's death, Thelma joins Loretta and Cecilia for mass and lunch. Over the years they have begun to break the past into similar eras. Not before or after wars, or by the decades, but before or after a brother or sister or mother died.

Thelma coughs. "Do you want a drink of water?" Cecilia asks. And without waiting for an answer she gets up. "I'll get you a glass of water." She returns a moment later with a tall glass of ice water.

She has always watched out for Thelma. When they were young girls attending classes at the Sarah Heinz House, they had to go onstage to perform. No one had time to rehearse or plan. Cecilia, at least, knew how to play the piano. Thelma didn't know what she was going to do. It was getting close to their turn. Cecilia took charge. She looked at Thelma. "I'll play the piano and you sing," Cecilia directed her. They went onstage. Cecilia sat down and began to play "Trees."

"She is sitting playing the piano and all the other girls are behind us and I'm struggling to sing, 'I think that I shall never see a poem as lovely as a tree,'" Thelma recalls.

"I forgot that," says Cecilia.

"I have never forgotten that," says Thelma.

Cecilia was more outgoing. In high school she was a school booster, although she doesn't remember boosting anything and thinks she joined because her homeroom teacher was the club moderator. "I guess everybody in 203 joined to stay on the good side of Miss Miller," she says.

Thelma thinks there's more to it than that. "She's willing to do anything she's asked to do on these committees. Anything they want typed, she does," Thelma says. "I'm a sit-back person."

"Well," says Cecilia, not wanting her friend left unacknowledged, "I'll tell you how many years you've been sitting an hour a week in a chapel. We started that in April of 1983, and you've been sitting for an hour ever since."

"No kidding? That long," says Thelma, with a grin. "No wonder my rear end is flat."

Cecilia's first job was answering phones and writing letters for Monogram Films, whose office was on "Film Row," then a section of a downtown boulevard occupied by United Artists and Twentieth Century Fox. Every neighborhood had a little theater with names like the Gem, the Happy Hour, and the While-Away, sometimes two, until there were six hundred in the western part of the state and their region. Getting the movies to the theaters was the work of Film Row.

When Monogram Films needed a third office girl, Cecilia suggested Thelma, who had yet to find a job. Thelma was hired.

Working was the next passage of their lives and they entered it sitting a desk away, thus creating a whole new dimension to their friendship. They went out to lunch together. Neither splintered off into another world, another existence as mother or wife. They were always just Cecilia and Thelma. As long as they had each other, they had no reason to feel like they were the only ones working and single. Their married friends could join the Christian Mothers. They couldn't, so they relied even more on doing things together.

Soon they were savants, not just of films but of stage. When a new play opened on Broadway, the two friends took a train to New York and stayed at a hotel across from Times Square. They saw *My Fair Lady* and *The Sound of Music*. At every show, Cecilia bought a program. She has kept them carefully stored on the third floor of the Guehl home.

"Remember all the Ethel Mermans," says Thelma.

"We always went to see anything Ethel Merman was in," says Cecilia. "If we didn't get to see them in New York, then we would go here."

About sixteen years ago, the Christian Mothers opened membership to single women. Cecilia and Thelma joined. They don't play bingo or attend monthly meetings. But every year, they attend the two Christian Mothers' annual dinners. One at Christmas and one for Mother's Day.

Just before the Christmas dinner, the brother of a woman who is mentally disabled calls the Guehls to see if Cecilia can take her. She can and does.

The woman sits between Cecilia and Thelma. Mary Wohleber joins the table. Cecilia tells her she received a box of seafood from a former Heinz executive, now in Florida. He sent two and a half pounds of shrimp and four containers of cocktail sauce, in dry ice. She and Loretta will serve it over the holidays. Mary just got back from Syria and is getting her house in order for the annual tree-decorating party. She is giving a talk on immigrants next month at the library. Last time, she had the audience in tears.

Emma Hildenbrand isn't a member of the Christian Mothers, but she and Jeanne like going to the special dinners. They pick up Ernestine Hepp, and the three of them sit with the pastor and his assistants. Emma loves the little favor, a ceramic sack with angels on the front and filled with chocolate kisses. She brings it home and places it on the mantel next to the china girl Sadie gave her.

Tonight's dinner choice is roast beef or pork, both served under a blanket of thick gravy, with small round boiled potatoes, and soft broccoli and cauliflower. The woman with Cecilia can't finish her roast beef and wants to take it home to her brother. Cecilia flags down a server, who returns with a piece of aluminum foil. She piles the leftover beef into a Styrofoam salad bowl and wraps the foil tightly over the top. When the winning raffle numbers are announced, Cecilia and Thelma check the woman's raffle tickets to see if she has won.

After, they sit back in their chairs and turn their attention to tonight's entertainment, Bernie Impersonator Extraordinaire.

Bernie wears a white linen jacket over a black T-shirt. He brought his own laugh track to get the audience going and fill the silence in case a joke falls flat. Thelma notices and leans across the table at one point and whispers, "I think that's canned."

The impersonator part consists of imitating several accents, like an Irish brogue in a joke about an Irish priest. Priest jokes, as long as they aren't disrespectful, go over well.

"A young girl walks into an Irish church. The priest introduces himself and asks the girl a little bit about herself. The girl tells him she is a gymnast and she works with a circus.

" 'Ye don't say?' the priest says. 'Can ye do a few cartwheels?'

"Just as she does a few cartwheels in the aisle of the church, two elderly women walk in.

" 'Oh, Lordie,' one whispers to the other. 'Look what father is giving out for penance.' "

The mother's day dinner, held the Friday before the actual holiday, is scheduled to begin at 6 P.M. If a friend is running late, they put a purse on a metal folding chair to save a nearby seat. Many of the women treated themselves today to a cut and perm at one of the two beauty shops on Troy Hill.

A pot of yellow mums sits in the center of every table. After dinner one of the club officers stops at each table with a brown paper bag filled with little squares of pink paper. One square is marked with an *X*. Whoever draws the *X*, takes the mums home. Everyone, though, leaves with a miniature white watering pail covered with yellow and red tulips.

After the ladies are seated, Father W. David Schorr, the pastor of Most Holy Name, says a prayer for all mothers and grandmothers. Most here are grandmothers. Once a year Father says a mass of healing for those who are sick, infirm, or suffering. Cecilia and Loretta went this year. The pews were filled with older women. "Father," Cecilia asked him, "did you ever know there were so many old ladies up here?" He certainly did. A few months ago, a ninety-three-year-old woman died. He had visited her a week earlier and she'd said her biggest worry was who would scrub the floors while she was in the hospital. He joked at her funeral that there should be a box of detergent in her casket so she could polish the pearly gates.

Servers in white shirts and blacks pants move swiftly through the folding tables, placing a Styrofoam plate on each purple place mat. Tonight's dinner is breaded chicken breast, the same little round potatoes, and a green bean and cream of mushroom soup casserole, which the women decide is better than the broccoli and cauliflower.

Just as the ladies are finishing dinner, the side doors open and two men wheel an amplifier onto a little wooden platform at the front of the room, next to the kitchen where the caterers are cleaning up. The tall and serious-looking man with a dark beard and long narrow face wears a brown suit and a tie that matches the silk handkerchief sticking out of his vest pocket. His partner, beefier and shorter, has slicked-back gray hair. He wears bifocals and a white shirt open at the collar.

"Think it's a magic act?" someone asks.

Grace Lutheran Church had a magic act at its last dinner, and everyone said it was great. It wouldn't be a comedy act. That would be too much like Bernie.

The president of the Christian Mothers' and Women's Guild approaches the microphone, welcomes the women, wishes them happy Mother's Day, and introduces the act. "Here to entertain you are Doctor and Jimmy." Taped behind her on the wall is the bingo menu. Hot dogs for sixty cents and pizza for a dollar.

Doctor, the tall thin one, stands at the microphone and explains that he is a clinical psychologist during the day, a singer at night. Jimmy sits next to him in front of a portable black keyboard. He is a professional musician, day and night.

Doctor holds the microphone in his right hand, cocks his head slightly, clicks the fingers on his left hand twice, and begins.

"It haaaaaad to be you . . . ," he croons. He has a beautiful, deep voice that resonates and sways easily and naturally like a weeping willow tree in the breeze. He, on the other hand, doesn't sway, or really even move that much. Every once in a while, he tilts his head and clicks his fingers. After every song, the women applaud politely and fold their hands. His next song, "Pennies from Heaven," is a little peppier, but he isn't.

One woman leans over to the woman sitting next to her. "He's got a lovely voice but he should do something . . . Just move a little," she whispers.

Her neighbor nods. They sit up and return to their smiles.

Finally Doctor suggests a sing-along medley. He begins with, "When you're smiling . . . ," then follows with, "I want a girl just like the girl who married dear old dad . . . ," and ends with, "Let me call you sweetheart...," He loosens up. The women start singing and swaying in their seats.

Margaret Fichter sits at another table, with her sister Cecilia Uhlig, tapping her feet. Her eyes are closed and her mouth is open and full of song.

What really gets them going, though, are the polkas. A table of six women in their late sixties or early seventies, at the far right of the room, begin doing a version of the chicken dance in their seats. Shoulders up, shoulders down. Arms flap, hands clap. Wiggle in your seat. Repeat. Doctor and Jimmy speed up. The women speed up, too. One woman can't keep up with the others and is flapping when they are clapping. Another wearing a corsage pinned to her dress is laughing so hard that she begins to turn red and rests her head on the table. Two of them lift their bifocals and use a Kleenex to dab the tears in their eyes.

Doctor closes with "When the Saints Go Marching In." The women at the chicken dance table are still laughing. Doctor and Jimmy pack up their amplifiers and keyboard and wheel them away at 7:50.

After they leave, the president announces that the raffle is about to begin. The ladies pull tickets from their purses and lay them out on the table in front of them.

Several generous local businesses have donated gifts for the raffle. Perfume, clocks, dinner for two, a lamp, an electric teakettle, a two-and-a-half-pound can of coffee. Cecilia wins a nice blanket. On her way back to her table, she stops to talk to a woman she hasn't seen in a while.

"How are you doing?" Cecilia asks.

"Fine except the osteoporosis," the woman replies. Her shoulders are rounded, not square.

"You know what the problem is?" Cecilia asks her.

The woman shakes her head no.

"We're getting old. And my father always said, 'It's hell to get old.'" Of course, he was ninety-three when he began saying that.

The morning of Mother's Day, two days later, the mothers gather again in the same hall after mass. This time, the fathers, sons, and grandfathers, who are members of Saint Anthony's Lyceum, cook and serve sausage, eggs, rolls, and coffee to all the women. The men's social group, formed in 1923 to succeed Saint Anthony's Literary, Dramatic, and Musical Society, once had a bowling league, baseball team, and a newspaper, called the *Lyceum Chatter*.

They began serving the breakfasts forty-five years ago. Carole Brueckner is there. Her husband is on the board of directors. She has a picture of her grandfather serving one of the first breakfasts. Margaret's husband, Joe, helped for years, too. Mothers get carnations. Little white vases with red carnations sit in the center of each table. Mary Wohleber just got back from a van trip to Utah. Mary grabs a partner and starts dancing as Bob Hamilton, an accordion player, starts to play "The Happy Wanderer."

The Guehl sisters don't come to the breakfast. They don't think it would be proper. It's one thing to go to the Mother's Day dinner because they are members of the Christian Mothers and pay their own way. This is free, a special treat for mothers. Thelma doesn't go, either.

This year the men served 181 women in twelve minutes, beating last year's record. Bob Hamilton begins playing "Edelweiss." The mothers and grandmothers link arms and sway. It looks like a mess hall at camp.

CHAPTER ELEVEN

Memorial Day

THE MEMORIAL DAY parade begins at 9:30 A.M. sharp, in front of North Catholic High School, across the street from the Guehl home. Rows of hand-carved wooden nameplates, each bearing the name of a North Catholic graduate who died in service, fill a grass plaza outside the front door of the school.

On either side of the nameplates, small American flags whip frantically in this morning's breeze. Above the school door hangs a banner, WELCOME TO TROY HILL, HOME OF NORTH CATHOLIC TROJANETTES. STATE CHAMPS IN 1980, 1983, 1984, 1988, 1993, 1994, AND 1995. At the corner of the school building, a metal plaque honors six gas company employees who died in an explosion while working on Lowrie Street on November 17, 1971.

Ed Smith, commander of American Legion Post 565, stands by the flagpole in front of the school. At his side, a young girl, no more than five, dressed in a blue cape and white dress, holds a bouquet of red, white, and blue flowers.

Smith says a prayer. At the rehearsed moment, the little girl stoops down and places the flowers at the base of the flagpole. As she does, Smith intones, "Although these flowers may wither and die, the memory of our departed comrades will live forever."

He raises his right hand in a salute. The rifle guard members raise their guns, point into the air, and fire. Once. Twice. Three times. The little girl, a member of the junior auxiliary of the ladies' auxiliary, covers her ears. Spent casings hit the asphalt with a ping and then roll. Two little boys and a girl watch carefully where the casings land. Out of fear, respect, or decorum, they wait until the parade proceeds to the next monument before grabbing the casings and shoving them into their jeans pockets.

The gunfire pierces the silence above the school and spreads across the hill, drawing out those not already sitting on their front steps alongside white plastic pots filled with pink geraniums. Small flags hang from mailboxes and line front walks like an all-American knee-high picket fence.

Cecilia and Loretta Guehl watch from their front porch. An aging white convertible leads the parade. The lone Gold Star mother sits in the front seat, waving. The car is followed by the Ringold Band, marching. The Ringold Band performs every year, although the piccolo player, who is now in his nineties and plays a solo during "Stars and Stripes Forever," is missing today.

Several color guards, four Little League teams, the Starlettes Dancing School, the Brownies, the Boy Scouts, two fire trucks, and two Humvees follow. The Humvees look like tall jeeps that got squashed. The older Little Leaguers ride two-wheelers with red, white, and blue crepe paper woven in the spokes of their wheels. The younger boys walk.

Pinky McGlothlin stands at the corner in front of the Guehls'. As each group rounds the bend, she claps and cheers. She shouts to the color guard members by name. "Hey, John." She waves up to the Guehls. They are like aunts to her. She called their mother, Anna, Grandma Guehl.

After the last of the two Humvees pass, the Guehls go back inside and upstairs.

The parade here, like most parades, is a tradition. It stops at five monuments for prayers and taps, before ending with services at Voegtly Cemetery on Lowrie Street. Some things change. Years ago twice as many Little League teams marched, and the American Legion had its own drum and bugle corps, with blue and white uniforms. Majorettes, wearing hats with plumed feathers and high white boots, led the parade.

Speakers change, too, depending on which politicians are in office and available. The veterans can usually count on Reverend Heidrich, the minister of Troy Hill Presbyterian Church. Reverend Heidrich was named after two uncles, Harry and Rollo—who both died during World War II—and has delivered a short speech at the cemetery every year for the last nine years. He used to walk the entire parade route, but his feet are bad now. He wears tennis shoes with his dark blue pants and black coat, and rides in one of the parade cars.

As the last fire engine, flags dangling from its long ladder, passes, those on their front steps or on the sidewalk rise and follow. The crowd doesn't evaporate in its wake. It picks up and accompanies the Little Leaguers and the dancers to their next stop, the little memorial park next to the American Legion building.

The color guard—five men carrying flags and rifles—walk rigidly down the center of the street, followed by a group of men in dark pants and white shirts. One lone tall sailor stands out. His suit is as white as powdered sugar and snug. His chiseled face is tan, and his mustache and hair gray. Others march. He swaggers, the old salt.

An older woman, with shoulder-length white hair and a white cotton sweater to match, comes to her front door, drying her hands on a dish towel. She opens the screen door and steps halfway out of her house, buttoning her sweater. She remains there, door open, until the last soldier has passed, and then retreats back into her home.

Tiny azalea bushes line the fence at the park. The wind has paused. The flag clings to the pole like static. A small monument at the base of the flag reads, DEDICATED TO THE GLORY OF A BRIGHT GOD IN MEMORY OF OUR MEN AND WOMEN WHO BY THEIR UNSELFISH PATRIOTISM HAVE ADVANCED THE AMERICAN IDEAL OF LIBERTY AND THE UNIVERSAL BROTHERHOOD OF MAN BY SERVING IN THE ARMED FORCES OF OUR COUNTRY. The smell of roast beef surrounds the little park. Next door the women's auxiliary is cooking a postparade dinner for members. The clatter of dishes fills the pause after the commander's prayer and then scatters with the round of gunfire.

The American Legion Hall and Veterans of Foreign War Post 7090 buildings once belonged to German ethnic groups, which disbanded during the war years because of strong anti-Kaiser and anti-Hitler sentiments. For much the same reason, sauerkraut became Liberty Slaw. The German Club of Pittsburgh, founded in 1905, changed its name to the Lincoln Club, in 1918.

While the solemn arm of the parade visits the monuments, the rest of the marchers idle in the street. A couple of Little Leaguers try to pull the crepe paper tails hanging from each other's baseball caps. A dancer in a purple leotard, her dark hair crowned with a flower wreath, stands with hers arms folded, looking pretty, but bored, behind the Starlettes Dancing School banner.

Two tuba players, each with their candy-apple-red jackets buttoned tightly over broad middles, face each other and talk. Above them, their tubas stare blankly at each other. The Ringold Band is an institution, both here and throughout the city. Membership consists of former or retired professional musicians or young talented amateurs who gladly perform in communities that have no band of their own. On Saint Patrick's Day and the Fourth of July they march in the big parade downtown. Most Monday nights they entertain residents of local nursing homes. Since the American Legion no longer has its own buglers, two of the band's players follow the color guard to each monument. They stand off at a distance. One plays taps first and the second one follows with a soulful echo.

Memorial Day was originally called Decoration Day. It was largely conceived by mothers, wives, and sisters who decorated the graves of loved ones who died in the Civil War. It was first celebrated in 1868, three years after the end of the Civil War.

Decorating graves remains a part of life for many of these women here, and not an unpleasant part. Their parents made a day out of it, packing picnics and bringing jugs of water, fresh flowers, and shovels to the cemetery. They trimmed the grass around the headstones and planted bulbs. After, they sat on long stone tombstones that resembled settees and relaxed while the children played in the grass. They always felt satisfied. Just as they would after a good spring cleaning at home. Everything looked nice, presentable, for Memorial Day visitors.

They still tend the graves several times a year. Fewer people do that today, leaving their care to professionals. Death and anything touching it are largely avoided. For these women, death was an accepted part of life, sad but hopeful, too. "Hello Central," they sang when they were younger. "Give me heaven, for my mother is there."

Over the years, the day has evolved into a three-day weekend and the unofficial beginning of summer. Memorial Day arrives and children can no longer concentrate on schoolwork. Tulips, daffodils, crocuses have already come and gone. The trees are full-fledged green, not just a gauzy overlay of it. It is no longer its own holiday. Its meaning has fallen largely from sight and awareness. Such nonchalance and indifference are both the price and blessing of living in peaceful times. Husbands, boyfriends, brothers, sons, and fathers aren't fighting and dying in war on this day. Many communities gave up Memorial Day parades because only the veterans groups seemed interested. There were fewer of them, too.

Here on Troy Hill people continue to pay tribute and to honor patriots. Even if no one in their own family died in wars, they knew neighbor boys who did. Maybe it was fifty years ago and they can't even recall the face. But those boys deserve to be remembered and to have a silent prayer offered in their name.

"During the war, everybody helped one another and would ask, 'Did you hear from this one?' 'Did you hear from that one?' That was happening all over the streets here," says Thelma Wurdock. The day the war was over, the man who sold vegetables in the cart went around offering free shots of whiskey.

It is their duty in a way to remember, and they aren't ashamed to act out of duty. To them it doesn't mean being slavishly chained to ritual or form. It's doing what is right. They don't feel burdened, but rather, uplifted by it, as they do by charity. Life only finds meaning when connected to something beyond themselves, they believe.

As far as they are concerned, people could stand a little more duty in their lives. Cecilia Guehl couldn't get over how few people voted in this last election. There wasn't much on the ballot, but it was still a voting day. "Didn't we fight a war over that?" she asked.

They line the streets this morning not because life has passed them by, but because this is where it is right now. This is the most important place for them to be. It's a beautiful day, besides. Rain had been pouring all week, but it let up today. They are glad to be out and see friends and neighbors.

Pinky walks down the sidewalk, following the parade. Her daughter and granddaughter are somewhere ahead. Pinky's uncle Al Smith had a shortwave radio in the third floor of their home. He was listening to it November 11, 1918, and heard that the armistice had been signed. He ran down the steps and told her grandparents. The great news would be hitting the streets and, being twenty-one years old, he wanted to be a part of the celebration. He put on his cap and went downtown. His cap blew off, and he caught pneumonia and died. That was as close to a war-related death as anyone in her family came.

She heard that story again and again. Her mother would say, "I have a story to tell," and the kids would say, "Mom, we already heard that."

"Well, sit down and hear it again," she would reply.

As much as they might moan, they sat down and heard the story again. Now Pinky is glad because the story it is not sketchy. It is firm. Many stories are lost because people don't think to ask about them or sit long enough to absorb them. It's a shame, Pinky believes, because they can provide so much richness and humor. Without them, there is little perspective of what shaped those before us.

Before her mother died, Pinky interviewed her on video, talking about the Irishman who rented a room in their house and ate a pound of oats every morning with a stick of butter sinking in the middle of the bowl. Her mother was dressed in her favorite red and white dress. None of her brothers or sisters knew Pinky had made the tape until the day of her mother's funeral. She invited them all back to see it. They laughed and cried. Her mother had been in the hospital weeks before Christmas. She said, "If I make it to Christmas, we'll have to throw a big party." She didn't, but their family had the party, anyway. They hold one every year in her honor. The Guehls are always invited.

Pinky considers herself lucky having shared a house with her grandparents and an unmarried aunt and uncle. They filled her with stories. They treated others with kindness. No gossip was allowed. "Always think ten times before saying anything unkind about another," she heard repeatedly.

Her grandmother would feed the hobos on Thanksgiving. They knocked at the front door. "Come around back and into the kitchen," she told them. She dished up plates as they sat at the table, until Pinky's father suggested they eat on the porch. Before they left, she packed a sandwich and a piece of pie. Pinky's family had tremendous faith. If Pinky needed any example of how to live her own life, she needed only to look at her mother and grandmother as they aged. Both were peaceful and content until the day they died.

Turning seventy or eighty was not a coda, Pinky saw, but another stage of life with its own setbacks and opportunities. Growth—intellectual, emotional, personal, or spiritual—continues. They didn't like the pains, but they didn't deny them, either, or surrender to them.

"We were so fortunate because we had all these older people to grow up with in this house, and, frankly, in the neighborhood. I always said to my kids, 'Don't just mingle with your own age, because elderly people can give you such an insight to life. They have experienced it,'" Pinky says.

Not only that, but they'll surprise you. One time, her parents heard screaming downstairs where her grandmother lived. It was about 1 A.M. Everyone was sleeping. Pinky's grandmother was yelling, "Don't you do that, you rotten thing." They came rushing downstairs and into her room. Grandma was standing in front of the television, yelling at a wrestler on television who was waling on her favorite heavy weight.

Pinky's grandmother also firmly believed in eating cake, ice cream, or pie before dinner. That way you would always have room for the good stuff.

Margaret Fichter and her oldest daughter, Joann Ibinson, walk down to the Troy Hill Monument with Joann's two grandchildren, Margaret's great-grandchildren. Margaret baked the baptism, First Communion, and wedding cakes for all of her grandchildren. When the great-grandchildren were born, though, she stepped back, so her own children could have that special relationship and tradition. "You are the grandma now," she would tell them. "That is your privilege. I had my grandchildren. I'm here if you need me. I have to step back and let you make that connection."

The children sit on the curb. Margaret and Joann stand behind them on the sidewalk. People stand with their hands behind their backs or in their pockets, or with their arms crossed. Though sixty-eight degrees, it's a little cloudy and cool.

They are waiting for the parade to arrive at the monument, which stands in the middle of the street, right at the Y where Ley Street meets Lowrie Street. It looks as if the asphalt opened a tiny crack and out sprouted a three-sided stone tower. Cars have knocked it down twice. Another time, it was taken down deliberately for the filming of the movie *Hoffa*.

At each round of rifle fire, Margaret's great-grandchildren cover their ears and look back at Margaret and Joann to make sure everything is all right. Joann marched in the parade when she was in the local dance school. They staged a Tom Thumb wedding once. Margaret made the costumes.

Margaret and Joe used to carry folding chairs and set them up on the sidewalk, to watch the parade. Once it passed, they folded the chairs up, then walked to the cemetery for the closing service. Joe brought his camera. After the final taps, all the kids in the parade went down to the Texaco gas station for hot dogs, chips, and pop provided for free by the local businesses. Later, at home, Margaret and Joe had a special holiday treat. Joe shaved ice for snow cones. Margaret brought up the homemade root beer. As her kids got older, they began calling it the Mayberry Parade, but they always brought their own kids. Now their grandkids come.

Margaret's niece Selma joins them on the sidewalk. "Where's your mom?" Margaret asks.

Selma points to the sidewalk across the street. Cecilia is there. The sisters exchange waves, smiles, and nods.

The parade proceeds, onlookers in tow, down the street to Voegtly Cemetery. A century ago it was at the bottom of Troy Hill Road, next to Voegtly Church. When the church was destroyed, the cemetery was moved up to this hilly expanse of grass.

It is filled with trees, probably half as old as the tombstones and monuments themselves. But the trees look older, gnarled and bent, while the stones stand upright and tall.

A wrought iron fence lines three sides of the cemetery. The fourth side drops off into a cliff and a busy boulevard down below. Trees and bushes on the hillside mute the sounds of traffic. Every once in a while a train whistle reaches the tombstones above.

Rows of stones and monuments face the cliff, their backs to Troy Hill's Lowrie Street. It's as if they are sitting patiently waiting for some grand show to begin, which does every morning. Just before dawn the sky above is midnight blue. A scull glides on the river below, the early-morning rowers dipping their oars into the still waters and lunging forward with each stroke. Across the river—beyond the market district, where long trucks deliver lettuce and bagel makers boil circles of dough, behind the hills that rise in tandem with Troy Hill as if they were one plain until the river cut through the middle—the distant horizon turns the color of a ripe apricot, trumpeting the sun's arrival.

When the sun reaches the hill, it shines right in the faces of the Reif family—Josephine, who died in 1963; her mother, Louisa, who died in 1924; and her father, Karl, who died in 1894. RUHE IN FRIEDEN, his tombstone reads; German for "Rest in peace." Two older monuments, carved in the shapes of trees, stand a little farther back from the cliff, to the right of the Reifs'. On each tree is a scroll; the messages have been erased by time, wind, and rain. They rest not only in peace but in anonymity.

The lawn is freshly mowed. New flags have been posted by each veteran's grave. The crowd that lined the sidewalks now stands in ragged rows among the monuments. Margaret stands beside Selma. Selma surveys the cemetery, the crowd, the band. "This is why I live here," she whispers to anyone and everyone around her.

Mary Wohleber stands twenty feet away with Pinky McGlothlin. Mary got Pinky involved years ago in Troy Hill

Citizens and the fights to save the fire station and the chapel. They would sit on the floor of the newly opened chapel gift shop with Cecilia Guehl and try to figure out what items would sell. Huge rosaries that were supposed to go like hotcakes barely moved.

Mary is dressed like a flag. Bright red pants, blue and white shirt. She's animated, hugging people. She wrote the 152-year history of this cemetery. She loves this cemetery and all old cemeteries, really. Last year, in celebration of National Library Week, she narrated a slide show called, "The Dearly Lamented of the Victorian Era."

Most of the audience was older. She had to be delicate because they had all buried loved ones. She wanted them to feel hopeful, not sad, and charmed them with her sensitivity. She amused them, too, quoting from an 1889 tombstone, "'Here lies our infant son. Now he never hollers. He graced us for fourteen days. And cost forty dollars.'"

She can't stand flat marble or stone markers in the ground, which are buried by grass clippings in the summer and brown curling leaves in the fall. Everyone should have a big tower. Better yet, one with angels. "We are all special and contribute, and people should know that we were here," she says.

Dozens of conversations pause when the Ringold Band stops at a small crest of the gravel road. On an adjacent hillside, the rifle squad stands at attention, each member with one hand resting on his rifle and the other hand placed on the small of his back.

Two young boys carrying the blue-and-gold banner reading RINGOLD BAND step aside, making room for the band director. He steps in front of the musicians and nods. This is the band's big moment. The director lifts his stick. The silence gives way to "Stars and Stripes Forever."

The anthem has been the group's trademark song since the 1950s. It played that popular piece for a band competition held in a local amusement park. The band hit the climaxes of the song with such passion and perfection, the judges threw their sheets up in the air, a sign that there was no need to even judge them. The band took home a first-place trophy.

Margaret searches for the ninety-year-old piccolo player. Years ago, he played the flute but went to the piccolo as he got older because that instrument is lighter. When it comes time for his solo, two girls step up for a duet. It takes two of them to do what he did. He was such a master. He finally retired.

All week people have been out to the graves here and in nearby cemeteries, planting new flowers and weeding.

Edna McKinney and her daughter-in-law, Anna, brought red geraniums to put on Art's grave. It was windy. When it's windy she chooses a low geranium or petunia because a tall lily would just blow over. The cemetery where Art is buried is right across the street from Saint Francis Hospital, where he was born. Edna looked at the hospital, then the cemetery, then Anna, and said, "Art didn't get too far did he?" They both laughed. It's the sort of thing that Art would say. The trip to the cemetery turned into a daylong outing. Anna's boys bought Edna a gift certificate to a bookstore. Edna carried her list of books and authors. Anna sat in the coffee shop and sipped cappuccino.

Margaret and Molly went to Saint Mary's Cemetery on Mount Troy, the next hill over, where Joe, Paul, and Dolly are buried. Molly stopped by the store beforehand and bought some Wrigley's gum to put on her uncle Paul's grave. Paul loved Wrigley's gum. They planted fresh flowers and weeded around the hostas.

Molly wore her father's green work shirt from the sanitation department. Often when family members die, their clothes and other belongings are given or stashed away. Out of sight, out of mind, and hopefully out of sorrow or loneliness, too. Margaret thinks that is silly. As if she should ever want to get over Joe. She wears his white sweatshirt with JOE in gold letters. A granddaughter made a matching one with MARGARET on it. They would wear them together.

On Christmas Eve Margaret led the family to the cemetery, continuing a Fichter tradition and assuming the role Joe played. The headlights of their car lit the path to the family plots. They arrived in time for the 6 P.M. ringing of the Angelus bells. Margaret recited the prayer and blessed the graves with holy water, making the sign of the cross and saying, "In the name of the Father, and of the Son, and of the Holy Spirit, amen." After, she led them in singing the Latin hymn "Let the Heavens and Earth Rejoice," in harmony. At home she blessed the tree and the crib. Joe used to do that every year. "That is my job now," she says. Each new task and accomplishment adds to her identity.

"I think she continually surprises herself," her daughter Cecilia says. "To us it always looked as though my mother could do anything herself. But she drew incredible strength and support from my dad's support of her. She did a lot of the things, but she knew he was there for her."

———

A small temporary stage is set up along the edge of the cemetery. Jean Geyer, one of Margaret's fellow choir members, walks up to the microphone and sings the "Star-spangled Banner." People place their hands over their hearts as she sings. After, Reverend Heidrich is introduced. He gives his speech, recalling his first Memorial Day parade. It was led by two veterans of the Spanish-American War. No one even remembers that war. He challenges all not to forget.

The lone Gold Star mother, Alice Smith, sits tall on a metal folding chair in the first row, with the councilman and the state representative. Both of the politicians wear suits and red-white-and-blue ties. A blue cap sits neatly on Alice's blond curls. She wears a bright yellow dress and black shoes. Her husband carries the American flag for one of the color guards. He sits on stage, too, but in a back row.

Their son, Frederick, was killed in Vietnam, and she has graciously agreed each year to participate in the parade. Her son's best friend has the honor of driving her in his aging white convertible, which sags in the back as if carrying a big load. One year, it broke down midparade and had to be pushed along the route.

The commander of the American Legion introduces Alice. She stands and smiles. Everyone applauds. At Christmas and Mother's Day, the American Legion sends Alice a nice basket of flowers.

Along the far side of the cemetery, Emma Hildenbrand and Ernestine Hepp sit on white plastic lawn chairs pulled right up to the iron fence separating the cemetery from Ernestine's backyard. They can't hear the speakers, but they can hear the Ringold Band playing "Stars and Stripes Forever," the guns being fired, and taps.

They did their part in the war, saving fat cooked off meats and bacon grease and putting them in a can in the refrigerator. Once the fat and grease hardened, they took it to the butcher who paid them a few cents a pound. Emma wasn't Catholic, but she would go to a neighbor's house and say the rosary for peace.

They are busy talking. Behind them Ernestine's children plant new flowers. They want to finish this afternoon because if they don't, they know Ernestine will be out tomorrow digging and planting. Ernestine has already given her children specific instructions not to buy a new dress to bury her in. Just pick one of the two blue lace dresses she wore to weddings. One has beads all along the neckline and the other doesn't. Emma hasn't given it a thought.

Emma's garden is in splendid bloom. She thinks it must have been that big bag of topsoil from the year earlier. Her next-door neighbor gave her the bag. All summer long Emma filled a little pan with the black soil and sprinkled it among the flowers. Emma was out earlier today pulling a few weeds. She is glad for the rest.

The friends balance each other. Both are strong, but in different ways. Ernestine hauls the lawn mower up the cellar steps and feeds the sick. Emma's strength is in accepting change and life's ups and downs.

Neither of them really engaged in self-absorbed pursuits of perfection or wealth. That left them with energy for generosity.

They were, and are, content to be mothers and grandmothers, and in their eighties.

Their own children are happy about their friendship. Knowing that you matter deeply to someone is sustaining. "I think everybody depends, in a sense, on somebody," says Emma's daughter Jeanne. "She depends on me for a lot of physical help, but I'm sure there are things she would rather talk about with people her own age. My mom and Ernestine are there for each other."

The chaplain of the American Legion Post steps up to the microphone for the closing prayer. People bow their heads.

"O Lord, our heavenly Father, lead us to do right by our departed comrades. Make all of us ready to become soldiers in your spirited army, whose footsteps cause no sound. Lead us onward to do right for our God and our country. Amen."

The crowd begins to scatter. A group of Boy and Girl Scout leaders walk back to the Texaco station to line up the drinks, hot dogs, and chips for anyone who marched in the parade. The ladies' auxiliary slice tender roast beef and plug in the coffeepot. The band members carry their instruments to their cars.

The temporary stage is empty. Mary remains at the cemetery with a photographer, pointing out different styles of tombstones. A few weeks ago she was asked to serve on a prestigious committee reviewing religious properties. She was the only one at the meeting who knew the background of one small chapel.

"Being old and staying in one place has its advantages. I'm eighty-one and they still want me," she says. "To be needed and to be asked to give whatever I have are very stimulating. I don't think there is enough time left to say no."

Margaret needs to get home and bake a cake tonight for the Golden Agers' meeting. She can't do it tomorrow because she is singing at a funeral and has invited fellow choir members over for lunch.

Joann has taken the grandkids back. Margaret begins walking home. She stops at the bridge over Rialto Street.

One year the Christian Mothers had a big fund-raising dinner with the theme "Remember When." Margaret made a replica of Pig Hill. Joe helped, building the bridge over Rialto Street. One woman stood by the table and reminisced about not only pigs but cows coming up the hill. She complimented Margaret and said it looked just the way she remembered it. Margaret was thrilled and ran home after the dinner to tell Joe. Whenever she had to make something for church or school, Joe was at her side. "We did everything together," she says. "That's what makes it so hard."

This year she went to a daylong retreat for widows with Rose Snyder. Rose says her husband gave her the greatest Valentine's Day gift one year. He simply came up to her and told her, "You know, we've got nine great kids and it's all your doing."

Another friend from the hill, who isn't a widow, offered to drive Margaret and Rose to the retreat because it's a long drive and it was raining. The woman sat and waited for them to be finished. While there Margaret told the priest about Joe and how they always sang together and how at times it was hard to sing solo. He urged her to continue. So she does. "I'm lucky," she says. "Some people lose their voices when they get older. I can still sing."

Just the other week Margaret was playing a song game with some of her children at a family gathering. Each team picked a subject, like animals or fruit. Then the sides took turns coming up with a song pertaining to that category. The category was fruit. Everybody thought they had exhausted the fruit repertoire, when Margaret remembered one little ditty she used to sing on Helen's back porch.

> *No matter how young the prune may be, it's always full of wrinkles.*
> *Baby prunes are like their dad, they are wrinkled but not as bad.*
> *No matter how young a prune may be, hot water makes it swell.*

Her kids insisted she made that one up. "I did not. I heard that over at Steinmetz's house," she told them.

Back home she puts a bunch of candy in a goody bag for her great-grandchildren.

Ernestine's children put the chairs back. Ernestine goes inside and packs a tin of pizzelles for Emma.

Ernestine will spend the day with her children at a picnic. Next week her daughter Annamae is going to take Ernestine and Emma shopping and to lunch. They do that every few weeks. Emma needed batteries for her hearing aid once, and Annamae drove them all over until she found the right one. "Imagine that," says Emma.

"You going to the Red Door Wednesday?" Emma asks.

"Yeah," Ernestine replies.

Emma goes back home to Jeanne. They work in the garden. Their neighbor grills hamburgers and hands two over the fence to Jeanne and Emma. Jeanne stopped at a farmers' market on Friday and brought home sugar peas and soft tiny apricots. She made a cranberry-and-sweet-potato salad. Emma told her it was so good she should serve it to company.

The Guehls have already been to mass. Their niece and grand-niece and two great-grandnephews will probably drop over this afternoon. If they decide to stay for dinner, Loretta will throw a few more cups of water into the soup.

Edna is spending the day with Anna and her grandsons. They're planning a trip to the ocean this summer, the first since Art died. The grandsons are threatening to buy Edna a whistle in case she goes exploring. One of the boys told her about a new computer he saw and said she would love it.

A few weeks ago Edna and Anna went on a boat ride with one of Anna's friends. All three were standing at the railing. The friend knew Edna was eighty and noticed that she wasn't wearing glasses. Edna only wears glasses for reading.

The friend asked Anna, "Are you sure she can see?"

"Don't you worry, she can see," Anna said.

Edna piped in, "And I can hear, too."

ACKNOWLEDGMENTS

I WOULD LIKE TO THANK all of the people of Troy Hill for welcoming me into their community, homes and churches, and their lives. Each person provided a singular insight into the community, its history and fabric. And though many of them are not specifically noted in this book, they are present, nonetheless, in spirit.

I would like to mention some people in particular. When I was writing a story on Troy Hill for the *Wall Street Journal*, which was the genesis of this project, Mary Wohleber took me by the hand and introduced me to her friends and neighbors, providing me an entry. Her daughter, Sarah, offered important views. Margaret Fichter and all of her children, especially Madeline (Molly), Cecilia, and Joann Ibinson, were generous with their journals, private letters, and family stories. For her flowers and her warmth, I'd like to thank Emma Hildenbrand as well as her daughters, Jeanne and Joan. I'd like to thank Ernestine Hepp, who made my children pizzelle fans. Thanks go to her daughters, Ernestine Boss, Ruth Grabb, and Annamae Ubinger, and her sister Bernadette Shurman.

For her friendship and courage, I'd like to thank Edna McKinney, whose spirit and strength could never be appreciated without knowing the backdrop of her life. Thanks go to her daughter-in-law, Anna, as well. Thanks to the Guehls—Loretta, Cecilia, John Jr., and his wife Fern—and the Sprengs—Lynne, Frank, and Ann Spreng Meyer—and Thelma Wurdock for their wealth of perspective. Florence Klingman spent hours talking about her beloved Presbyterian church on Bohemian Hill, which has since closed and reopened as the Hallelujah Community Church. Mildred Mares's wonderful memories and recollections provided so much color and insight. I'd like to thank Rose Ptacek and her brother, Chuck, Louise Lacher, Bob and Ruth Leder, the Rev. Heidrich and all the members of the Presbyterian Church, as well as Helen Lindenfelser and the ladies at the Grace Lutheran Church. Thanks to Helen Steinmetz, Cecilia and Selma Uhlig, Mildred (Pinky) McGlothlin, Eileen Schullek, Rose Snyder, Carole Brueckner, Anna Wehner, Norma Weir, the Troy Hill Citizens, the Christian Mothers, Fr. Schorr and Sr. Margaret Liam Glenane, Ethel Brendel, Audrey Martin, James Cichra, John Lyon, Chick Ambrass, Margaret Christopher, Ethel White, the Grindels, and Catherine Besterman. I'm indebted to Christine Nicodemus and Patty Koval for carefully and patiently transcribing dozens of tapes.

I'd like to thank the *Wall Street Journal* for the opportunity to pursue this project and my agent, Laurie Liss, who believed in it. Many, many thanks to my editor Jane Isay for her invaluable wisdom and guidance.

I'd like to thank my parents, Jay and Coletta, for their endless devotion and for instilling in their children an appreciation of that which is good. I'd like to thank my brothers and sisters, Jay, Brian, Chris, and Micki, for a lifetime of support.

I'd like to thank my darling children, Jessie and Peter, who cheered me through this process. Finally, I'd like to thank my husband, Matthew, who patiently read draft after draft, was gentle with suggestions, and strong with encouragement.

Reading Group Guide

1. Troy Hill is more than a setting or backdrop for this book. It represents a way of life. How did Troy Hill shape the lives of these women? How did the women shape Troy Hill? Would you like to live in a place like Troy Hill? What are its virtues? Its faults?

2. Community, a sense of belonging, and permanence are elemental themes of this book. What is the status of community, and all that it represents, today? Is it possible to exist in such a mobile society? What are the ramifications of moving around the way many Americans now do?

3. Mildred Mares summarizes their way of life in four words: "Men worked, women neighbored." Now women and men work. Who does the neighboring? Do women still see that as their job? Do they welcome or feel burdened by it? Has neighboring taken new forms today and does it have the same impact on the individuals and community? Do neighborhoods exist in any permanent or lasting way now?

4. What role does Mary Wohleber play in this book and also in the community? At one point, she says she has always been a little different than everyone else—almost, but not quite, like an outsider—and yet at the same time she is the public face of Troy Hill. How can you be so much a part of something, yet feel distant?

5. Emma's daughter Jeanne and Margaret's daughter Cecilia see their mothers as very strong, but for different reasons. Discuss those differences. How does our view of our parents change as we grow older? How are daughters shaped by a mother's self image?

6. As independent and competent as these women are, they are also deferent. Margaret drove her husband around until he got his license and then let him take over. Edna Mckinney ran the house but let her husband think he did. Cecilia Guehl says she didn't go to college because that is just the way things were. These women didn't expect much. Were they too accepting of what was dealt to them? Emma is an accepting and tolerant woman, yet content and happy. Is tolerance a factor in happiness?

7. The church was a significant force on Troy Hill, as it was in many communities that were literally built around their places of worship. Discuss how and why the role of the church has changed in communities. Is it still a major force?

8. Do you agree with the notion that faith begets habit and

habit begets faith? Or do you think one is more important than the other?

9. Tradition is a big part of these women's lives from festivals to Fastnaught Day and weekly novenas. It was also instrumental in keeping families together. Some people want to break away from tradition. Others cling to it. What are the merits and demerits of traditions? Do our attitudes about tradition change with time? What are some of the traditions your parents created for you? How do you feel about them?

10. All of these women had different relationships with their husbands. Margaret and Joe's relationship was very different than Edna and Lou's relationship. Discuss the differences and similarities in their relationships and in how they expressed devotion.

11. Emma kept the outline of her granddaughter's footprint, her daughters' report cards, and tiny articles in the newspaper about them. Edna kept all of her sons' yearbooks and many of their grade school papers. They can't keep every momento. What does their choice signify? Why is it important to keep such things? Do you think they are preserving it for themselves or their children? What keepsakes do you cherish? How do children feel when they discover that their parents have preserved an old letter, or a handmade gift?

12. Cecilia and Thelma were friends for seventy-five years. Emma and Ernestine were friends for about ten years. Does

longevity or the sheer expanse of shared experiences make a friendship stronger? In both cases, each woman is different from her best friend. Is accepting differences a critical part of friendship?

13. These women are comfortable with growing older. Do you think we as a society are comfortable with aging? How does growing up around older people shape attitudes? If you grew up close to an older relative, what did they add to your life? If you didn't, do you wish you did? Does everyone gain wisdom with age?

14. When Joe died, Margaret told a priest that she didn't think it was fair, that she thought they would grow old together. When the priest responded "Well, you are old," she replied that she was not, even though she was in her eighties. Is anyone ready to die? Is life, even a full life, ever enough? Why do you think Dolly told the priest she was ready to die?

15. Which of these women do you feel most connected to and why? Do any of these women make you think of someone in your own life in a different way?

16. None of these women are famous. Why are their lives instructive?